For reference

Not to be taken from the room.

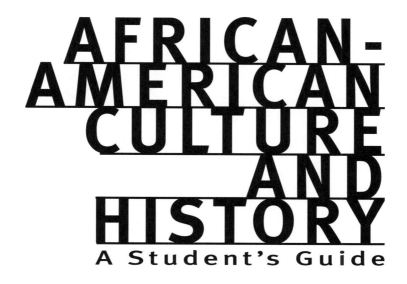

AFRICAN-AMERICAN CULTURE AND HISTORY
A Student's Guide

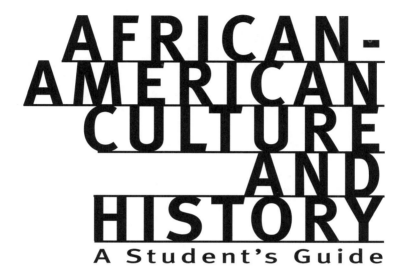

AFRICAN-AMERICAN CULTURE AND HISTORY
A Student's Guide

JACK SALZMAN
Editor-in-Chief

James S. Haskins
Consulting Editor

Evelyn Bender
Kathleen Lee
Advisors

volume **2**
D-I

Macmillan Reference USA
an imprint of the Gale Group
New York • Detroit • San Francisco • London • Boston • Woodbridge, CT

Macmillan Reference USA
1633 Broadway
New York, NY 10019

Gale Group
27500 Drake Rd.
Farmington Hills, MI 48331

Editorial and Production Staff

David Galens, *Project Editor*
Kelle Sisung, *Developmental Editor*
Kathy Droste, *Illustration Editor*
Shalice Shah, *Permissions Associate*
Mark Milne, Pam Revitzer, and Larry Trudeau, *Contributing Editors*
Tim Akers, Rebecca Blanchard, Elizabeth Bodenmiller, Anne Marie Hacht, and
    Tara Atterberry, *Proofreaders*
Robert Griffin, *Copyeditor*
Tracey Rowens, *Senior Art Director*
Randy Bassett, *Imaging Supervisor*
Pam A. Reed, *Imaging Coordinator*
Dan Newell, *Imaging Specialist*
Kay Banning, *Indexer*
Geraldine Azzata, *Further Resources Compiler*

Elly Dickason, *Publisher, Macmillan Reference USA*
Jill Lectka, *Associate Publisher*

Printing number
1 2 3 4 5 6 7 8 9 10

LIBRARY OF CONGRESS CATALOGING-IN-PUBLICATION DATA

African-American culture and history: a student's guide / Jack Salzman, editor-in-chief.
    p. cm.
    Adapted from the five-volume Encyclopedia of African American culture and history published by Macmillan in 1996; revised for a sixth- to seventh-grade, middle school audience.
    Includes bibliographical references and index.
    ISBN 0-02-865531-1 (set : hardcover : alk. paper) – ISBN 0-02865532-X (vol. 1 : alk. paper) – ISBN 0-02-865533-8 (vol. 2 : alk. paper) – ISBN 0-02-865534-6 (vol. 3 : alk. paper) – ISBN 0-02-865535-4 (vol. 4 : alk. paper)
Afro-Americans—Encyclopedias, Juvenile. 2.
Afro-Americans—History—Encyclopedias, Juvenile literature. [1.
Afro-Ameridans—Encyclopedias.] I. Salzman, Jack. II. Encyclopedia of African-American culture and history.

E185 .A2527 2000
973'.0496073—dc21

Table of Contents

VOLUME 1

Table of Contents
VOLUME 2

Table of Contents ▪▪▪

VOLUME 3

N

O–P

Table of Contents

VOLUME 4

Q–R

S

Preface

The history and culture of African Americans is to a great extent the history and culture of the United States. But as much as we may now accept this as a truism, it was not always so. It was not until the second half of the twentieth century that students and historians of the American experience began to document and carefully study the lives of people of African descent. Until then our knowledge of a people who comprise almost 15 percent of this country's population was shamefully inadequate. In 1989 Macmillan Publishing Co. decided to redress this situation by publishing a major reference work devoted to the history and culture of African Americans. I was asked to serve as editor of the new work, and in 1996 the five volume *Encyclopedia of African-American Culture and History* was published.

The encyclopedia contains close to two million words and covers all aspects of the African-American experience. In the few years since its publication it has come to be recognized as a mainstay in most high school, public, and academic libraries. *Rettig on Reference* (April 1996) found the set to be "scholarly yet accessible and immeasurably informative." *CHOICE* (1996) praised its "clear and succinct writing style" and its "breadth of coverage of general biographical and historical data." It received a Dartmouth Award Honorable Mention and appeared on every list of 1996 best reference sources. After spending six years compiling the encyclopedia it was gratifying to read, in *American Libraries* (May 1997), that the work "is of enduring value and destined to become a standard reference source."

The enthusiastic response to *Encyclopedia of African-American Culture and History* convinced us that students would benefit from a work with similar scope but one rewritten for a wider audience. *African-American Culture and History: A Student's Guide* is that work. It incorporates the same editorial criteria we used for the original encyclopedia : articles include biographies of notable African Americans, events, historical eras, legal cases, areas of cultural achievement, professions, sports, and places. Readers will find entries on all 50 states, 12 major cities, and 15 historically black colleges.

This comprehensive four-volume Student's Guide has 852 articles—arranged alphabetically—of which 597 are biographies and 255 are events, eras, genres, or colleges, states, or cities. Although for the most part articles in this set are based on entries from the original encyclopedia, our Advisory

Board recommended that we also cover several contemporary popular topics and figures. Entries were chosen to reflect the school curriculum and have been updated through Summer 2000.

African-American Culture and History: A Student's Guide has been carefully designed for younger readers, and professional writers have crafted the articles to make them accessible for the intended audience. In addition, readers will find that articles are enhanced with numerous photographs and sidebar materials. Lists, quotations, extracts from primary sources, interesting facts, and chronologies are to be found in the margins. A system of cross-references makes it easy to explore the Student's Guide. Within the text, terms and names set in boldface type indicate that there is a separate entry for this subject. Additional cross-references appear at the end of many entries. A comprehensive index for the entire set appears at the end of volume 4. A list of "Further Resources" in Volume Four includes books, articles, and web sites and will provide a starting point for students who are beginning to explore the extraordinary history and accomplishments of African Americans.

Many people have provided invaluable help with *African-American Culture and History: A Student's Guide.* In particular, I would like to single out Jill Lectka and David Galens of the Gale Group and Kelle Sisung. I would also like to thank our editorial advisors, Evelyn Bender, Librarian, Edison High School in Philadelphia; and Kathleen Lee, Librarian, John P. Turner Middle School in Philadelphia. Thanks, too, to Jim Haskins, Professor of Education, University of Florida and author of numerous books for young adults. These three professionals provided valuable guidance as I developed the article list and helped design the margin features. It was at their urging that we included curriculum-related web sites in the resources list. Finally, to Becca, Phoebe, Jonah, and Libby, who soon will be able to make use of these volumes: thank you for being as wonderful as you are and for bringing so much to me and Cec.

Jack Salzman
New York City

Contributors

The text of *African-American Culture and History: A Student's Guide* is based on the Macmillan *Encyclopedia of African-American Culture and History*, which was published in 1996. We have updated material where necessary and added new entries. Articles have been condensed and made more accessible for a student audience. Please refer to the Alphabetical List of Articles on page xi of the first volume of *Encyclopedia of African-American Culture and History* (also edited by Jack Salzman) for the names of the authors of the articles in the original set. Their academic affiliations are noted in the Directory of Contributors. This title also includes entries from the Supplement to *Encyclopedia of African-American Culture and History* published by Macmillan late in 2000. The Supplement has its own Alphabetical List of Articles and Directory of Contributors. Here we wish to acknowledge the writers who revised entries from those two publications and wrote new articles for this set:

Sheree Beaudry
Craig Collins
Stephanie Dionne
Rebecca Ferguson
David Galens
Robert Griffin
Cathy Dybiec Holm
Paul Kobel
Paula Pyzik-Scott
Ann Shurgin
Kelle Sisung
Larry Trudeau

Dance. *See* **Ballet; Breakdancing; Dance Theater of Harlem; Social Dance; Tap Dance; Zydeco**

Dance Theatre of Harlem

The world's first all-black ballet troupe, the Dance Theatre of Harlem (DTH) was founded August 15, 1969, by dancer and choreographer (someone who creates new dances) **Arthur Mitchell** (1934–) and his mentor (teacher), Karel Shook. Mitchell wanted to prove that black dancers have "the physique, temperament and stamina, and everything else it takes to produce what we call the 'born' ballet dancer." In 1971 the DTH dance company made its official debut in New York City and at Italy's Spoleto Festival; the performances were a great success.

In 1972 the DTH moved to its permanent home at 466 West 152nd Street in Harlem. It offered dance and choreography classes and organized outreach programs to take dance into the community, where it could be enjoyed by Harlem's senior citizens and children.

Over the next two decades, the troupe became known around the world, dancing at arts festivals and touring in the Caribbean, Europe, and Africa, where they often performed before sellout crowds. The DTH also expanded its boundaries to become a multicultural institution, and today it is a school and community arts center, boasting an internationally famous dance company.

DANCE THEATRE OF HARLEM: REPERTOIRE

The DTH program has included classical ballet works such as Russian-American choreographer George Balanchine's *The Four Temperaments* and Russian-American composer Igor Stravinsky's *Firebird,* as well as innovative contemporary works like DTH founder Arthur Mitchell's *Rhythmetron,* American choreographer **Alvin Ailey**'s *The River* (set to music by jazz great **Duke Ellington**), and American dancer Louis Johnson's *Forces of Rhythm.*

Dandridge, Dorothy

ACTOR, SINGER
c. 1923–September 8, 1965

Dorothy Dandridge was born in Cleveland, Ohio, and was groomed for a stage career by her mother, Ruby Dandridge, who was a performer herself. As a child, Dandridge performed in her mother's show. During the 1940s Dorothy and her sister Vivian joined with another young African-American woman, Etta Jones, to form a singing act called The Dandridge Sisters.

During this time Dandridge also managed to land a few minor Hollywood roles. Exceptionally beautiful, Dandridge worked actively at cultivating a sophisticated image. She also became increasingly well known as a nightclub singer. Her big break as a motion picture actress came in 1954, when she got the title role in the all-black production *Carmen Jones*. For that role, she became the first black woman to be nominated for a best-actress Oscar.

That she had achieved celebrity status was obvious by her appearances on the cover of *Life* magazine and by articles about her in other national and international magazines. However, three years were to pass before Dandridge made another film. Because of the racial discrimination of the period, she was never to achieve the stardom she longed for. Although Dandridge won praise in 1959 for her portrayal of Bess in the film *Porgy and Bess*, she received fewer and fewer **film** and nightclub offers as time passed. Eventually, she was forced to file for bankruptcy. Dandridge died when she was only forty-one years old, in 1965. Her **autobiography**, *Everything and Nothing*, was published in 1970. In 1977 she was inducted into the Black Filmmakers Hall of Fame. A 1999 HBO movie about Dandridge's life, *Introducing Dorothy Dandridge*, featured actress Halle Berry in the title role.

Dash, Julie

FILMMAKER
October 22, 1952–

Julie Dash is known for her films portraying the problems facing a diverse group of black women. Born and raised in New York City, Dash began studying **film** as a teenager at the Studio Museum of Harlem. After receiving a B.A. degree in film production from the City College of New York, Dash moved to Los Angeles, California, and became the youngest student ever to attend the Center for Advanced Film Studies at the American Film Institute. While at the institute, she directed several films, some of which received or were nominated for awards. Dash later did graduate work at the University of California.

Dash's films are sensitive and complex and capture the lives of black women. In 1986 Dash moved to Atlanta, Georgia, where she began work on

Julie Dash: Selected Films

Four Women
(1973)

Diary of an African Nun
(1977)

Illusions
(1983)

Daughters of the Dust
(1992)

Daughters of the Dust and formed Geechee Girls Productions—the company that produced *Daughters of the Dust.* According to Dash, the company "brings to bear the power and the voice of the African- American female's spirit into the area of media production." The film was the first full-length film by an African-American woman, and it opened in 1992 to overall praise. One critic remarked that Dash's approach to filmmaking is to "show black women at pivotal moments in their lives[to] focus on and depict experiences that have never been shown on screen before."

Dash later moved to London to collaborate on a screenplay. She also began work on a series of films depicting black women in the United States from the turn of the twentieth century to the year 2000. Dash once said of her work, "Our lives, our history, our present reality is no more limited to 'ghetto' stories, than Italian Americans are to the Mafia, or Jewish Americans to the Holocaust. We have so many stories to tell. It will greatly enrich American filmmaking and American culture if we tell them."

Angela Davis (AP/Wide World Photos. Reproduced by permission)

Davis, Angela Yvonne

POLITICAL ACTIVIST
January 26, 1944–

Angela Davis was one of the most outspoken political activists of the 1960s. Both of Davis's parents were educators and taught their children not to accept the socially segregated society that existed at the time. After graduating from Brandeis University in 1961, Davis spent two years in Europe, where she was exposed to student political radicals. Her own activism came into focus with the murder in 1963 of four young black Sunday school children in a Birmingham, Alabama, church bombing. In California, where she went to pursue graduate study, Davis began working with the **Student Nonviolent Coordinating Committee (SNCC),** the **Black Panther Party,** and the Communist Party.

Hired in 1969 by the University of California at Los Angeles (UCLA) to teach philosophy, Davis was eventually fired because of her Communist Party activities. Ultimately, her case went to the Supreme Court, which overturned the dismissal. By that time, however, Davis was in hiding as a result of an incident at the Soledad state prison. In August 1970, George Jackson, a prisoner and member of the Black Panthers, assisted by his brother Jonathan, supposedly attempted to escape using smuggled guns. Both brothers were killed, and some of the guns were traced to Davis. Fearful for her safety and distrustful of the judicial system, Davis disappeared for two months before being arrested. She was in jail for sixteen months before being tried for murder and conspiracy. In June 1972 she was acquitted of all charges against her. Davis resumed her teaching career at San Francisco State University and the University of California. She left the Communist Party in 1991 but remains politically active. She is the author of several books, including *If They Come in the Morning* (1971), *Women, Race, and Class* (1983), *Women, Culture, and Politics* (1989), and *Blues Legends and Black Feminism* (1998). Her **autobiography,** *Angela Davis: An Autobiography,* originally published in 1974, was reissued in 1988.

Davis, Anthony

COMPOSER, PIANIST
February 20, 1951–

Anthony Davis has been recognized around the world for his musical works and masterful performances. Davis was born in Paterson, New Jersey. His father, Charles T. Davis, was a pioneer in black studies and a university professor. Anthony Davis studied classical piano as a child and continued his studies at Yale University (Connecticut), earning his undergraduate degree in the early 1970s.

Davis played with various **jazz** ensembles before forming his own group, Episteme, in 1981 to play his original compositions. He believes improvisation (making up passages of music while playing) "is one compositional [writing] tool within the framework" of a jazz piece. In the early 1980s Davis began teaching piano and Afro-American studies at Yale, but he continued composing music, both classical and jazz. Among his works are a Pulitzer Prize-nominated piano concerto (*Wayang* No. 5) and the piano composition *Middle Passage*, about the **slave trade.**

Davis has also written several **opera**s, including *X: The Life and Times of Malcolm X* (1985), about the slain black nationalist leader **Malcolm X** (1925–1965), and *Amistad* (1998), which tells the story of the 1839 capture of a slave ship and the overthrow of the captors that followed.

Davis, Benjamin Jefferson Jr.

LAWYER, POLITICIAN
September 8, 1903–August 22, 1964

Benjamin Jefferson Davis Jr. was a prominent member of the U.S. Communist Party, whose goal is to protect and promote the rights of the working class. Born in Atlanta, Georgia, Davis earned a degree from Amherst College (Amherst, Massachusetts) in 1925 and a law degree from Harvard University (Cambridge, Massachusetts) in 1929.

In 1932 Davis chose to defend Angelo Herndon, an African-American Communist charged with causing a riot. (Communists believe in the elimination of private property, and believe that all material goods should be owned and shared by all of the people and distributed as needed; historically, they have advocated violence and revolution to achieve that goal.) By taking on this case, Davis put his life at risk, because the great majority of Americans despised Communism, which also discouraged **religion** and punished people who engaged in religious worship. After receiving death threats, Davis fled to New York City and joined the Communist Party.

In 1942 a friend, the Reverend **Adam Clayton Powell Jr.,** helped Davis gain a city council seat. Davis served on the council and gained popularity until 1948, when he was arrested for belonging to an organization (the Communist Party) that advocated "the violent overthrow of the government." After serving three years in jail, Davis went back to promoting his beliefs in 1955. He was chosen as national chairman of the Communist Party

in 1959. However, he was once again charged with a political crime in 1962. Davis died in 1964 before he could be tried.

Davis, Benjamin O. Sr.

GENERAL
May 28, 1880–November 26, 1970

Benjamin O. Davis, a general in the U.S. Army, fought for freedom and democracy, and for the right of blacks to serve in the **military** without discrimination. During his fifty years of military service, Davis served in the Spanish-American War (1898) and **World War II** (1939–45). He was the first black general in the U.S. Army.

Born in Washington, D.C., Davis started his long military career by volunteering to serve in the Spanish-American War. He spent the next twenty years in various teaching positions with the army—at **Wilberforce University** in Ohio, with the Ohio National Guard, and at Tuskegee Institute (now **Tuskegee University**) in Alabama. In 1917 President Franklin D. Roosevelt (1882–1945) made Davis a general.

While serving in the military, Davis worked on solving racial problems. At this time in American history, racial tensions were high and some whites objected to blacks serving in the military. At the peak of World War II, when American combat soldiers were scarce, Davis proposed that black service troops be trained to fight and be included in white combat units. Not only did Davis pave the way for blacks to serve in the military, he also helped to dissolve the military's policy of segregation.

After the war Davis served in a variety of positions before he retired in 1948. In the next decade he worked for the District of Columbia (Washington, D.C.) and the American Battle Monuments Commission. He died in 1970 in Chicago, Illinois.

Davis, Benjamin Oliver Jr.

GENERAL
December 18, 1912–

Benjamin Oliver Davis Jr. followed his father's lead to become the first African-American lieutenant general in the U.S. Air Force. (His father was Benjamin Davis Sr., the first African American in the U.S. Army to reach the rank of general.) He also continued the fight his father started against segregation and discrimination in the U.S. military. Davis devoted his entire life to serving his country and, in the process, opened the door for other black soldiers.

Born in Washington, D.C., Davis learned to respect his father and his line of work at an early age. He saw his father face down a **Ku Klux Klan** march, which left a lasting impression. Davis was an excellent student and enrolled at the University of Chicago. He soon discovered, however, that his true calling was the **military.** In 1932 he entered West Point, the nation's top military academy and graduated in the top 12 percent of his class. Davis's goal was to become a military pilot, however, racism in the military stood in his way.

Davis finally got the chance to fly in 1941 when the army decided to allow blacks into the Army Air Corps. By April 1943 Davis was flying **World War II** (1939-45) combat missions, had became a colonel of an all-black flying unit, and had won the Distinguished Flying Award. After the war Davis concentrated his efforts on ending segregation. In 1948 President Harry Truman issued an executive order to end discrimination in the military, and Davis put forth a plan to end segregation.

After retiring from the military in 1970, Davis served in a number of civilian government posts, such as the President's Commission on Campus Unrest and the Department of Transportation. In 1978 he once again followed in his father's footsteps by working for the Battle Monuments Commission. In 1998, when Davis was eighty-five, President Bill Clinton appointed him as the first African-American four-star general; Davis was the first black to receive the honor after retiring from the military.

Davis, Miles Dewey III

JAZZ TRUMPETER, COMPOSER
May 26, 1926–September 28, 1991

Miles Davis was one of the most influential and original musicians of the twentieth century. He defined or contributed to the development of several **jazz** styles, including cool, hard bop, modal, and fusion.

Born in Alton, Illinois, Davis grew up in nearby East St. Louis, across the Mississippi River from St. Louis, Missouri. His mother was a classically trained pianist and violinist. His father, a successful dentist, gave Davis his first trumpet at age thirteen. In high school he studied music and began performing with bands in St. Louis and Chicago. In 1944 the trumpeter moved to New York City to study at the Juilliard School. He began playing in the jazz clubs of Harlem and 52nd Street, where young musicians were making bebop (a new form of jazz) popular.

In 1945 Davis joined saxophonist **Charlie "Bird" Parker**'s (1920–1955) quintet (five-member group). The Parker ensemble made several groundbreaking recordings. Davis also worked with other jazz greats, including pianist **Thelonious Monk** (1917–1982) and saxophonist **Coleman Randolph Hawkins** (1904–1969).

In 1948 Davis left the Parker quintet. With arranger Gil Evans (1912–1988) he formed an experimental nine-piece group. Though the ensemble soon broke up, recordings made between 1949 and 1950 endured: The tracks on *The Birth of the Cool* spawned the cool jazz movement. (The movement was named "cool" to differentiate it from the "hot" sounds of bebop; in fact, cool jazz has a "laid-back" sound and gave rise to the word "cool," now part of everyday vocabulary.)

Davis continued to perform and record in the cool style, often teaming with saxophonist **Theodore "Sonny" Rollins** (1930–). It was not long

Jazz trumpeter and composer Miles Davis
(Courtesy of the Library of Congress)

before the great innovator developed a new style: hard bop, a more rugged and blues-inspired version of bebop jazz, made its debut with the 1954 recording *Walkin'*. The following year, Davis formed a quintet that included tenor saxophonist **John Coltrane** (1926–1967), releasing the landmark recording *Round About Midnight*.

In 1958 the Davis ensemble introduced modal jazz. In this style, modes (scales) determine a song's harmonies. The next year Davis recorded what is considered his greatest work and perhaps the greatest jazz album, *Kind of Blue*. Teaming again with arranger Gil Evans, Davis's ensemble spent the late 1950s producing three highly acclaimed orchestral works, including *Sketches of Spain* (1959–60).

In the late 1960s Davis produced an all-new sound with greater commercial appeal. Inspired by funk rhythms and new electronic music, Davis added electric piano and guitar to his ensemble. While he scored a best-seller in 1969, Davis's new direction left his jazz fans cold.

Ossie Davis with his wife, the actress Ruby Dee (AP/Wide World Photos. Reproduced by permission)

Ossie Davis with his wife, the actress Ruby Dee (AP/Wide World Photos. Reproduced by permission)

A car accident in 1972 combined with the musician's ongoing struggle with alcohol and drug abuse convinced him to retire. Davis returned to music at the end of the decade, again playing the electric form of jazz now known as fusion. He recorded often but never again reached the lofty heights he had during the 1950s. He died in 1991 from circulatory and respiratory ailments.

Davis, Ossie

ACTOR, PLAYWRIGHT
December 18, 1917–

In 1937 Ossie Davis began his long and varied acting career when he went to New York City, where he joined Harlem's Rose McClendon Players in 1939. In 1946 he successfully auditioned for the play *Jeb*, in which he starred opposite actress **Ruby Dee.** Davis and Dee were married in 1948.

In the 1960s Davis achieved broad success in the performing arts. In 1960 he appeared with Ruby Dee in the play *A Raisin in the Sun*. The following year, his play *Purlie Victorious*, a play about southern racism, opened on Broadway to an enthusiastic response. Davis also wrote and starred in the film version of *Purlie Victorious*, entitled *Gone Are the Days* (1963). He appeared in several other films and on several television shows. In 1969 Davis directed, cowrote, and acted in the film *Cotton Comes to Harlem*.

Davis was also politically active. He testified before the U.S. Congress on racial discrimination in the theater and joined the advisory board of the **Congress of Racial Equality (CORE)**. In 1965 Davis delivered a speech at the funeral of his friend **Malcolm X**.

Through the 1970s, 1980s, and early 1990s, Davis continued his performing career, in a **radio** series, the *Ossie Davis and Ruby Dee Hour* (1974–1976); in the public **television** series *With Ossie and Ruby* (1981); and in the **film**s *Do the Right Thing* (1989), *Jungle Fever* (1991), and *I'm Not Rappaport* (1996). In the early 1990s, he was a semiregular on the television series *Evening Shade*.

Davis also has written several children's books and a novel, *Just Like Martin* (1992), about a southern boy inspired by the life of the Reverend Dr. **Martin Luther King Jr.** In 1998 Davis celebrated his fiftieth wedding anniversary with Ruby Dee by publishing a joint memoir, *With Ossie and Ruby Dee: In This Life Together*.

Davis, Sammy Jr.

SINGER, DANCER, ACTOR
December 8, 1925–May 19, 1990

Sammy Davis Jr. is believed by many people to be one of the best entertainers of the twentieth century. Davis could do it all—sing, dance, act, clown—and he did it all with amazing energy and talent. He began performing with his father, a vaudeville entertainer ("vaudeville" refers to stage entertainment featuring a mix of songs, dances, acrobatic acts, magic acts, and skits) before his fourth birthday and made his first **film** when he was eight. By the time he was fifteen, he had traveled widely throughout the United States with the Will Mastin Trio, which consisted of Davis, his father, and Davis's adopted "uncle," Will Mastin. Although they often played to white audiences, the trio was forced to eat and sleep at Negro establishments.

After serving in **World War II** (1939-45), Davis returned to the Will Mastin Trio and received his first big break when entertainer Frank Sinatra asked the trio to open for his show.

In November 1954 Davis was involved in a near-fatal car accident, lost his left eye, and was hospitalized for several months. While in the hospital, he began to study Judaism (the Jewish religion). Davis felt that there was a deep connection between the historically oppressed black and Jewish cultures. He was so moved that he converted to Judaism.

Actor, singer, and dancer Sammy Davis, Jr.
(Courtesy of Library of Congress)

Davis is perhaps best known for the films he made during the 1960s, when he worked and socialized with the "Rat Pack," a group of Hollywood actors that included Sinatra, Dean Martin, Peter Lawford, and Joey Bishop, who were featured, along with Davis, in such films as *Oceans Eleven* (1960) and *Robin and the Seven Hoods* (1964). In addition, Davis continued to perform in clubs and on Broadway, where he was praised for his work in the play *Golden Boy*.

Davis also appeared on **television** in many comic and dramatic roles. He continued to record albums and produced such hit songs as "Candy Man" and "Mr. Bojangles." Throughout the 1960s Davis worked to promote civil rights and African-American and Jewish relations by giving benefit performances and substantial donations. His first **autobiography,** *Yes I Can,* was published in 1965.

Throughout the 1970s Davis performed regularly on the Las Vegas, Nevada, club circuit. From 1975 to 1977 he starred in the television show *Sammy and Company*. He became the first recipient of *Ebony* magazine's Lifetime Achievement Award in 1979.

Davis's second autobiography, *Hollywood in a Suitcase*, was published in 1980. Throughout the 1980s Davis continued to appear in films, on television, and on stage. He published a third autobiographical work, *Why Me?* (1989), before dying of throat cancer in 1990.

Day, Thomas

FURNITURE MAKER
c. 1800–1860

The origins of early American furniture maker Thomas Day are sketchy, as is the case with many other **free blacks** who lived in the South during the 1800s. He was born in either the West Indies or rural North Carolina. He did most of his work in Milton, North Carolina, where he became a wealthy and respected craftsman.

Day carved mahogany and walnut chairs, tables, and footstools. He began studying woodcarving in Boston and Washington, D.C. By 1818 he was selling furniture to the residents of Milton. A prominent local family, the Donohos, passed many pieces of Day's work through several generations. The pieces show his classic designs and exceptional skills as a carpenter and woodcarver. Other pieces of his furniture are located throughout North Carolina. At Day's death, just before the American Civil War (1861–65), his estate was estimated to be worth more than $100,000.

DeCarava, Roy

PHOTOGRAPHER, PAINTER
December 9, 1919–

One of the foremost photographers of the twentieth century, Roy DeCarava developed a black aesthetic (artistic sensibility) in photography. His images have immortalized such jazz greats as **Billie Holiday** and **John Coltrane**.

Born and raised by his mother in **Harlem (New York)**, DeCarava studied art at Straubenmuller Textile High School. In his teens he worked as a sign painter and display artist (one who designs and sets up store displays). Graduating in 1938, he supported himself as a commercial artist while continuing his studies at Cooper Union (New York) and other art schools. His first one-person show was staged by a New York City gallery in 1947.

DeCarava began using photographs to "sketch" ideas for his paintings. By the late 1940s he had turned his attention entirely to **photography** as an art form, saying it was "just another medium that an artist would use."

He developed a distinctive style: DeCarava's photos are candid (spontaneous) shots that are nonetheless carefully composed. His first subject was the people of Harlem. Feeling that African Americans were not viewed by most photographers as "worthy subject matter," he became determined to portray black people in a way that he describes as serious, artistic, and human.

Staging his first show of photographs in 1950, DeCarava soon sold prints to the Museum of Modern Art (MOMA, New York). In 1955 he collaborated with writer **Langston Hughes** (1902–1967) to produce the classic book *The Sweet Flypaper of Life*, a collection of 141 photos accompanying a narrative of the everyday lives of a fictional Harlem family.

DeCarava further refined his art into the 1960s, conducting workshops, displaying his photos in exhibitions, and supporting himself as a freelance photographer (he worked for *Sports Illustrated* from 1968 to 1975). DeCarava began teaching at New York City's Hunter College in 1975.

DeCarava's works have been exhibited in solo shows and acquired as part of the permanent collections of major museums around the world, including Washington, D.C.'s Corcoran Gallery of Art and the MOMA. An award-winning 1984 documentary film, *Conversations with Roy DeCarava*, interweaves more than a hundred of his photos with reflections on his past struggles and his efforts to encourage young black photographers.

Dee, Ruby

ACTRESS
October 27, 1924–

Ruby Dee is an award-winning actress who is as well known for her commitment to social causes as she is for her performing talents. After graduating from high school, Dee attended Hunter College in New York City and prepared for a stage career. She had her first starring role on Broadway alongside actor **Ossie Davis.** Two years later, she married Davis, who appeared with her in several productions. Dee's first **film** appearance was in *The Jackie Robinson Story* (1950). In 1965 she joined the American Shakespeare Festival and was the first black actress to play major roles in the company. Dee helped write the screenplay for *Uptight* in 1968 and wrote the musical *Twin-Bit Gardens* (1979).

Dee has long been a participant in civil rights efforts. She has served on national committees of the **National Association for the Advancement of Colored People (NAACP)** and the **Southern Christian Leadership Conference (SCLC),** and has performed in numerous fund-raising benefits. Her other activities include reading for the blind, raising money to fight drug addiction, and helping black women study **drama.**

A frequent reader of poetry and drama on national tours, Dee has also written several books of poetry and short stories and has contributed columns to the *New York Amsterdam News.* She was the assistant editor of the magazine *Freedomways* in the early 1960s. In 1990 Dee wrote the script and starred in *Zora Is My Name*, a one-woman show based on the life and work of **Zora Neale Hurston.** In 1998 Ruby Dee and Ossie Davis celebrated their fiftieth wedding anniversary by publishing a joint memoir, *With Ossie and Ruby Dee: In This Life Together.*

DeFrantz, Anita

ATHLETE, LAWYER
October 4, 1952–

Anita DeFrantz was an Olympic rower and the first female African American to serve on the International Olympic Committee (IOC). She has dedicated her life to athletics and has become a role model for women and blacks with her devotion to mental and physical development.

Born in Philadelphia, Pennsylvania, DeFrantz did not train to be an athlete when she was growing up. When she picked up rowing at Connecticut College, however, it seemed to come naturally to her. After graduating, she went to law school at the University of Pennsylvania in 1974. DeFrantz trained vigorously and entered rowing competitions in 1975. The following year, she became captain of the first Olympic women's eight-member rowing team. She helped the team win a bronze medal, and in 1978 she won a silver medal in the world championship games. Her Olympic rowing career came to an end in 1980 when the United States boycotted the games to protest the Soviet invasion of Afghanistan.

In 1980 DeFrantz was awarded the Olympic Order Medal by the International Olympic Committee, and she carried the torch for the 1984 Olympic Games, a tremendous honor. In 1988 DeFrantz began a long career with the International Olympic Committee, which resulted in her being elected to the prestigious eleven-member executive board. As a board member, DeFrantz has contributed to promoting and shaping Olympic policies. The IOC came under heavy criticism in early 2000 when a memo was released hinting that some committee members were taking bribes. DeFrantz was not accused of any improper behavior and worked to repair the damage done to the IOC's reputation.

Delaney, Beauford

PAINTER
c. 1902–March 26, 1979

Born in Knoxville, Tennesee, Artist Beauford Delaney was a well-known portrait artist who also created abstract art. His younger brother Joseph Delaney (1904–1991) was also a well-known painter. Beauford Delaney's talent was recognized early. Lloyd Branson, an elderly white artist, gave him lessons as well as the financial assistance to obtain further training. From 1924 to 1929 he studied in Boston, Massachusetts. Delaney moved to New York in 1929, "hopped bells" (worked as a bellhop, carrying guests' luggage) at night at the Grand Hotel, and by day painted the people near Billy Pierce's Dancing School on West 46th Street.

In 1930 twelve of Delaney's portraits were included in a group showing at the Whitney Studio Galleries. The Whitney's Juliana Force was an early patron (supporter of artists) and offered him a job with free studio and living space. He worked at the Whitney about three years as a guard, telephone operator, and gallery attendant. In an article at the time of the Whitney showing, Delaney said, "I never drew a decent thing until I felt the rhythm of New York as distinct as the human heart. And I'm trying to put it on canvas." His first one-man show took place in May 1932 at the 135th Street branch of the New York Public Library.

Delaney, because of his skill and special personality, was soon painting portraits of such musicians as **Louis Armstrong** (1901–1971), **Duke Ellington** (1899–1974), and **Ethel Waters** (c. 1896–1977). During the 1930s and 1940s Delaney continued to show his work. He spent the summers of 1951 and 1952 at the Yaddo Art Colony in Saratoga Springs, New York, and in 1953 he sailed for Paris, France, where he remained for the rest of his life.

Despite regular exhibitions of his work, good reviews, and important friends, Delaney was never free of money worries. He shared or gave away what he had with friends, including a $5,000 award from the National Council on the Arts in 1968. Earlier, on a trip to Greece in 1961, he suffered a nervous breakdown, which required lengthy hospitalization. When he recovered, he moved to a new studio, where he remained until 1975.

Besides portraits, Delaney painted street scenes using geometric shapes and bright colors. Filled with energy, they seem to be moving. Delaney also turned to abstractions (art representing the qualities of something by using shapes, lines, and color, not showing its outer appearance as it would be seen in a photograph) to capture different aspects of light. Delaney was confined to a mental hospital in Paris in 1975, and he remained there until his death in 1979.

Delany, Martin Robinson

ABOLITIONIST, WRITER
May 6, 1812–June 24, 1885

Writer and abolitionist Martin Delany was educated at the school of Rev. Louis Woodson in Pittsburgh, Pennsylvania. Between 1843 and 1847 Delany published the *Mystery*, the first African-American newspaper west of the Allegheny Mountains (a mountain range extending from Pennsylvania in the north to West Virginia in the south). In 1847 he joined **Frederick Douglass** as co-editor of the newly founded *Rochester North Star*.

Delany left the *North Star* in 1849 as his beliefs began to differ from those of Douglass: Delany thought that blacks should be more self-reliant in their fight to gain rights, whereas Douglass welcomed the support of white reformers. In 1852 Delany published the first book-length analysis of the economic and political situation of blacks in the United States, entitled *The Condition, Elevation, Emigration, and Destiny of the Colored People of the United States, Politically Considered* (Philadelphia, Pennsylvania, 1852). In 1859 the

Martin R. Delany in the Union Military during the Civil War (Archive Photos. Reproduced by permission)

Anglo-African Magazine published his only novel, *Blake*, in installments; the *Weekly Afro-American* also published the novel in 1861-62.

After the **Civil War** (1861–65) broke out and the War Department reversed its refusal to enroll black volunteers, Delany became a full-time recruiter of black troops for the state of Massachusetts. In early 1865 he was commissioned a major in the Union army, the first African American to be made a field officer. He was in the South Carolina Low Country at the end of the war and went to work for the Bureau of Refugees, Freedmen, and Abandoned Lands (Freedmen's Bureau).

Immediately after the war, Delany was a popular speaker among **free blacks** because he symbolized both freedom and African Americans. Delany eventually went into the real estate business and ran unsuccessfully for sev-

Science fiction author Samuel R. Delany (Corbis Corporation. Reproduced by permission)

Samuel R. Delany: Selected Publications

The Jewels of Aptor
(1962)

The Einstein Intersection
(1967)

Nova
(1969)

The Tides of Lust
(1973)

Dhalgren
(1975)

Triton
(1976)

Stars in My Pocket Like Grains of Sand
(1984)

The Motion of Light in Water
(1988)

Silent Interviews
(1994)

The Mad Man
(1994)

Atlantis: Three Tales
(1995)

Bread and Wine: An Erotic Tale of New York
(1999)

eral state offices. Before he died in 1885, he published *Principia of Ethnology: The Origin of Races with an Archaeological Compendium of Ethiopian and Egyptian Civilization* and sold the book on a lecture tour.

Delany, Samuel R.

SCIENCE FICTION WRITER
April 1, 1942–

Author Samuel Delany is the first African-American author to write in the **science fiction** genre (category). Born in New York's Harlem district into comfortable circumstances, he graduated from the Bronx High School of Science and briefly attended City College of New York. Despite serious dyslexia (a learning disorder), he started writing early in life, publishing his first novel in 1962.

Delany has been an extremely productive writer. By the time of his eighth novel, he had already achieved star status in science fiction. Delany won several of science fiction's most prestigious awards. He is considered to be one of the masters of the field, and he has also produced books of sword-and-sorcery fantasy.

Although Delany was the first significant black figure in the science fiction field, he was not the first writer to introduce black themes or characters into science fiction. Delany has written of how startled he was to discover that the hero of celebrated science fiction writer Robert Heinlein's classic *Starship Troopers* (1959) was non-Caucasian.

Delany's importance as a writer stems primarily from the way his work has focused on desire, differences between people, and the nature of freedom. In his four-volume *Neveryona* fantasy series (1983-87), these themes are played out in a mythical past. Delany's second major contribution to writing is his successful blending of critical thinking in the stories of science fiction and fantasy. He has brought to these often-scorned forms a depth and sophistication seldom before displayed.

In 1961 Delany married the poet Marilyn Hacker. The two separated in 1975. They have a daughter, Iva Alyxander, born in 1974. Delany has taught at the State University of New York at Buffalo, the University of Wisconsin in Milwaukee, and Cornell University in Ithaca, New York. Since 1988 he has been a professor of comparative literature at the University of Massachusetts at Amherst.

DeLavallade, Carmen

DANCER, CHOREOGRAPHER
March 6, 1931–

Carmen deLavallade was famous as a dancer before making a second career as a respected choreographer (someone who creates dances) and teacher. Born in New Orleans, Louisiana, in 1931, she was raised in Los

Angeles, California, by her aunt. She began studying with Lester Horton at sixteen and was a lead dancer for his dance company from 1950 to 1954. Horton gave deLavallade a broad-based training, including ballet, modern, and ethnic dance forms, as well as painting, music, acting, and set design.

Known for her physical beauty, elegance, and technical skill, deLavallade was soon dancing with famed dancer **Alvin Ailey** (1931–1989) and appearing in Hollywood films, including *Carmen Jones* (1955). She was cast in the Broadway musical *House of Flowers* (1954), which led to her meeting and marrying the dancer and actor **Geoffrey Holder** (1930–). He choreographed what would become DeLavallade's signature piece, *Come Sunday*, a solo danced to black spirituals.

DeLavallade was prima (leading) ballerina of the New York Metropolitan Opera from 1955 to 1956. Shortly after that, she became a principal dancer in John Butler's company and made her television debut in his ballet *Flight*. In 1966 she won the coveted *Dance Magazine* award for her contribution to the art of dance.

DeLavallade also pursued an acting career and appeared in several Off-Broadway productions before joining the Yale University (New Haven, Connecticut) School of Drama as a choreographer and performer-in-residence in 1970. She later became a full professor and a member of the Yale Repertory Theater. DeLavallade left Yale around 1980 to teach, lecture, and perform. In 1993 she appeared with the **Bill T. Jones**/Arnie Zane Dance Company in New York City. That same year, she choreographed dances for the opera *Rusalka* at the Metropolitan Opera.

Delaware

First African-American Settlers: A year after the first permanent European settlement in Delaware, a Swedish ship carrying a slave known as "Black Anthony" arrived from the West Indies. The first significant numbers of Africans arrived after the Dutch conquered the Swedish colony in 1655.

Slave Population: By the time of the English conquest of Delaware in 1664, 20–25 percent of Delaware's residents were enslaved blacks. The African population then declined, and by 1700 less than 5 percent of Delaware's population was African American. When **slavery** reached its height around 1763, enslaved blacks again made up almost 25 percent of Delaware's population. Most black slaves lived and labored in slave units that worked in the corn and wheat industries. Delaware became the first state of the union in 1787.

Free Black Population: From 1775 to 1810 a strong antislavery movement led by Quakers and Methodists swept through Delaware. By 1810 approximately 75 percent of the state's African Americans were free. Although only 8 percent of Delaware's blacks were still enslaved in 1860, it took the passage of the Thirteenth Amendment in 1865 to finally end slavery in the state.

Civil War: From the American **Civil War** (1861–65) to **World War I** (1914–18), most black Delawareans continued to live in the countryside, where the men were hired hands or tenant farmers (farmers of land owned by others) and some women worked as domestics.

Reconstruction: Because of dramatic growth in the white population, the percentage of blacks dropped from 25 percent in 1840 to 15 percent in 1914. At the beginning of World War I, however, Delaware experienced massive immigration of rural African Americans from Maryland, Virginia, and the Carolinas, drawn by the promise of blue-collar jobs.

The Great Depression: The migration of blacks to Delaware peaked after **World War II** (1939–45). The black population increased from 13 percent in 1940 to 44 percent in 1970.

Civil Rights Movement: After decades of challenge by Delaware's black leaders, all public schools and most other public facilities were integrated by 1967. The assassination of civil rights leader Rev. **Martin Luther King Jr.** in 1968 caused an eruption of arson and looting in Wilmington that hastened "white flight" to the city's suburbs.

Current African-American Population: According to U.S. Census Bureau estimates, the total black population in Delaware was 144,380 (almost 20 percent of the state population) as of July 1, 1998.

Key Figures: Peter Spencer (1782–1843), founder of the African Union Church; **Richard Allen** (1760–1831), former slave and founder of the **African Methodist Episcopal Church.**

(SEE ALSO **AFRICAN METHODIST EPISCOPAL CHURCH.**)

Dellums, Ronald V. "Ron"

CONGRESSMAN
November 24, 1935–

Ronald V. Dellums is considered to be one of the most extreme politicians to serve in Congress in modern times. One of his greatest achievements was pushing through a law to impose sanctions (economic or military penalties) against South Africa (1986) to try to pressure it to end its system of "apartheid," or strict separation of blacks and whites.

Born in Oakland, California, Dellums earned bachelor's degrees from Oakland City College and San Francisco State University and a master's degree from the University of California at Berkeley. He earned a seat in Congress by campaigning against the **Vietnam War** (1959-75).

Dellums has served as the chairman of the House Armed Services Committee (1993) and chairman of the Congressional Black Caucus (1989-91). He has consistently opposed U.S. involvement in any military conflicts throughout his lengthy career as a congressman (1970-98). Some of the bills Dellums has introduced include a law to remove restrictions on abortion and marijuana, create a national health care system, and to grant amnesty (legally pardon) those who refused to fight in Vietnam. Dellums left a lasting impression on Congress when he retired at the age of sixty-two.

"I'm just a guy. If you hit me I hurt, and if you cut me I bleed. And there were many times when you hit me, and there were times when I went to my office at night, and, sometimes with tears in my eyes, I prayed just to have the strength to march back to the floor with my pride and my dignity and to continue to try to fight back."

(Source: Ron Dellums. "Retirement Speech." *Washington Post,* February 7, 1998, p. B01.)

Demby, William E. Jr.

WRITER, EDUCATOR
December 25, 1922–

Born in Pittsburgh, Pennsylvania, William Demby was raised in Clarksburg, West Virginia, the coal-mining town that inspired his first novel, *Beetlecreek* (1950). Demby saw **military** service in both Italy and North Africa in **World War II** (1939–45) and wrote for the U.S. military magazine *Stars and Stripes*. He returned from the war to **Fisk University** in Nashville, Tennessee, received a bachelor's degree in 1947, and promptly returned to Italy, where he studied art history and worked as a **jazz** musician, translator, and writer for **film** and **television**. He returned to the United States in 1963 and worked for an advertising agency in New York City before becoming a professor of English at the College of Staten Island in 1969, where he taught until 1989.

Beetlecreek, written in Italy and published in 1950 (reprinted, 1998), is based on a short story Demby wrote while at Fisk, in which a bleak small town serves as the setting for a tale of spiritual poverty, isolation, and murder. In 1965 Demby published *The Catacombs (reprinted, 1991)*, a novel set in Rome. His novel *Love Story Black* (1978) is a portrait of the life of a black middle-aged professor in New York City.

Denmark Vesey Conspiracy

Denmark Vesey (c. 1767–1822), a former slave carpenter who had bought his freedom with lottery winnings in 1799, was committed to the African-American freedom struggle. He preached continually to his friends that blacks should be equal to whites. In the winter of 1821–22 he began organizing for an armed revolt. Vesey and his recruits met at the local African church, where they formed a plan for a mid-July revolt: the plan was to take over the arsenal and guardhouse in Charleston, South Carolina, start several fires, and kill white members of the community as they left their homes.

One of Vesey's recruits, however, informed his master. When white authorities were told the story, they at first could not believe it. But after they questioned suspects and hired a black spy in the African church, the details of the conspiracy came out. During the summer of 1822 authorities arrested and executed thirty-five blacks and deported forty-three more. Vesey was captured and after a trial was executed on July 2. One of Vesey's followers, Gullah Jack Pritchard, tried to continue the revolt and free the jailed rebels, but he, too, was captured and hanged.

In the year following the revolt, frightened South Carolina legislators passed a series of laws restricting the movement of African Americans, including a law ordering all free black sailors to be jailed while their ships were in port. Federal courts eventually ruled such laws unconstitutional, which fueled a debate over states' rights. Some Americans consider Vesey to be a patriot and martyr for African-American civil rights; others see him as a dangerous agitator. Not surprisingly, a proposal in modern-day Charleston to commemorate Denmark Vesey with a public portrait has led to heated debate.

Dent, Thomas

PLAYWRIGHT
March 20, 1932–June 15, 1998

Playwright Thomas Dent was born in 1932 into a New Orleans, Louisiana, family committed to social causes. He attended **Morehouse College** in Atlanta, Georgia, where he edited the *Maroon Tiger*, a literary journal, and earned a bachelor's degree in political science.

In 1959 Dent was a journalist for the African-American newspaper *New York Age*, and in 1960 he was copublisher of the political journal *On Guard for Freedom*. In 1962 he cofounded Umbra Workshop, a team of black artists, thinkers, and activists (people active in promoting a cause or an issue). The workshop published *Umbra*, a poetry magazine.

From 1966 to 1970 Dent was associate director of the Free Southern Theatre (FST) in New Orleans, an organization composed of artists and activists fighting racism and segregation. During this period his one-act plays *Ritual Murder* (1966), *Negro Study 34A* (1969), and *Snapshot* (1970) were produced. Dent's 1972 *Inner Black Blues: A Poem/Play for Black Brothers and Sisters*, was a bitter criticism of black oppression by whites. In 1974 he founded the Congo Square Writers Union of New Orleans, another team of writers and artists. Two years later, he published *Magnolia Street*, which was followed in 1982 by *Blue Lights and River Songs: Poems*. Dent continued to live and write in New Orleans until his death in 1998. (*See also* **Black Arts Movement.**)

DePreist, James Anderson

CONDUCTOR
November 21, 1936–

Hailed by the *Chicago Tribune* as "one of the finest conductors this nation has produced," James DePreist was born in Philadelphia, Pennsylvania. His family was musical (his aunt was the great singer **Marian Anderson** [1897–1993]), and as a child he studied piano and percussion instruments. DePreist attended the University of Pennsylvania, earning his undergraduate degree in 1958 and a master of arts degree in 1961. He later studied with the well-known composer Vincent Persichetti (1915–1987) at the Philadelphia Conservatory of Music.

DePreist made his conducting debut in 1962 with the Bangkok, Thailand, Symphony Orchestra during a U.S. State Department–sponsored tour of the Far East. While on tour he became sick with polio and returned to the United States, where he soon recovered. He has held positions with the New York Philharmonic, where he worked with famed American com-

poser and conductor Leonard Bernstein (1918–1990); the Symphony of the New World, New York; the National Symphony Orchestra, Washington, D.C.; and the Quebec Symphony, Canada. He has been music director and conductor of the Oregon Symphony since 1980. He has made more than thirty-five recordings.

James DePriest conducting the New York Philharmonic Orchestra (AP/Wide World Photos. Reproduced by permission)

Desdunes, Rodolphe Lucien

WRITER, ACTIVIST
November 15, 1849–August 14, 1928

Rodolphe Lucien Desdunes was an early advocate of civil rights and a writer. Born in New Orleans, Louisiana, his father was Haitian and his mother was Cuban. Educated in Catholic schools, he later became a school principal.

In 1882 Desdunes earned a degree in law. Since he was able to speak both English and French, he was hired to work at various jobs in a U.S. Customs House. During his thirty-two years there he remained involved in politics. Desdunes organized several groups to work for civil rights and black **suffrage** (voting rights). One of the organizations that he founded sponsored Homer Plessy's challenge to the Louisiana law segregating blacks from whites in public transportation. (Plessy, who was one-eighth black, was arrested for riding in the whites-only railroad car.) Desdunes later wrote about the *Plessy v. Ferguson* court case, which upheld the "separate but equal" rule.

Desdunes wrote articles for the *Daily Crusader* newspaper. He also published several pamphlets. Written in French, Desdunes's 1911 work titled *Our People and Our History* was a portrayal of the **Creoles** of New Orleans. The book stirred a controversy because Desdunes described Creoles as free people of color; many people of Creole dissent preferred to focus on their French heritage, disavowing African-American roots.

Detroit, Michigan

Throughout much of its history Detroit has been an important destination for African Americans seeking a better life. The final U.S. point on one branch of the **Underground Railroad,** Detroit later became the goal for many workers in the early twentieth century seeking jobs in the city's automobile factories and other industries. Today it is one of the largest cities in the nation with a majority African-American population.

Detroit Beginnings

Detroit was founded in 1701 by Antoine de la Mothe Cadillac, a French explorer. At the end of the French and Indian War in 1763, the city was turned over to the English, who controlled it until 1796, when a treaty gave it to the United States. It is not clear when the first blacks arrived in Detroit, but they began migrating to Michigan in the early 1800s. Some white Detroiters owned slaves, although slavery was officially banned. The 1810 census reported seventeen slaves in the city. In the 1820s there were sixty-seven blacks in town, 4.7 percent of the population.

In 1827 Michigan passed a Black Code that required all African Americans to have a certificate of freedom and to register with the county clerk. Blacks were also required to pay a $300 bond of good behavior, although most actually avoided paying. The law was supposed to protect blacks from slavehunters, but its real purpose was to discourage black migration. In 1833 the city had its first major racial disturbance, called the Blackburn riot. After police arrested a fugitive slave couple, Thornton and Ruth Blackburn, in order to return them to Kentucky, blacks attacked the sheriff, who later died from his injuries, and a riot ensued. The Blackburns escaped to Canada. Although more than thirty blacks were arrested (some who were not involved in the disturbance) none were convicted. In 1837, the year that Michigan became a state, its legislature abolished slavery. The same year the Detroit Anti-Slavery Society was founded. Detroit became a major stop on the Underground Railroad, and black abolitionists were active in the Colored Vigilance Committee, which was formed in 1840.

The Civil War Years

The **Civil War** (1861–65) was a turning point in Detroit's history. Many Michiganians opposed slavery, but many others were also openly racist. The most hostile forces toward blacks in the city were the group of white immigrants from Ireland and Germany, who resented black competition for jobs. In 1863 Detroit had a race riot, the only major racial disturbance in the western states during the war. A black man, William Faulkner, who was convicted of raping two nine-year-old girls, one white and one black, was sentenced to life in prison. A white mob, mostly Irish and German, attempted to lynch him. Militia officers who came to protect Faulkner fired at the mob in self-defense, and one man was killed. The mob, frustrated in its lynch attempt, moved to a black area, where they beat the residents, killing two and injuring over twenty, and burned down more than thirty of their houses. White Detroiters condemned the mob and paid blacks for their losses, but **Frederick Douglass** used the defenselessness of Detroit blacks as an example of the need for black soldiers. After 1863, 895 black Michiganians, many from Detroit, joined the Union Army.

Between 1860 and 1870 Detroit's black population soared, due largely to migrants from Canada, rural Michigan, and elsewhere. During this time blacks were confined to shabby tenements and run-down houses. Although people of mixed race could vote as early as 1866, black efforts to gain the right to vote were repeatedly voted down in Michigan until 1870, when the **Fifteenth Amendment** of the U.S. Constitution was passed. The public schools, despite orders of the state legislature, remained segregated until the following year. Once blacks could vote, they immediately organized a Colored Republican Club. In 1875 Samuel Watson became Detroit's first African-American elected official when he was elected to the Board of Estimate, the city legislature's upper house. In 1883 a group of blacks started the weekly newspaper *Plaindealer* as the voice of black protest, black business, and black Republicanism. It was one of the first publications to use the term "Afro-American" rather than "Negro."

The Early Twentieth Century

After the turn of the century blacks from the deep South began to migrate to Detroit. By 1915 increased manufacturing due to **World War I** (1914–18) led Henry Ford and other factory owners to employ blacks in large numbers, which caused a mass migration to Detroit. Black organizations like the Detroit Urban League were set up to find jobs and housing for the new arrivals. The city's black population, which was 5,000 in 1910, reached 120,000 in 1930. The collapse of the economy during the 1930s left many blacks unemployed and ill-housed. Since the flow of friends and relatives from the South looking for work continued, conditions for Detroit blacks worsened. As competition for housing increased, many blacks were forced into the Black Bottom neighborhood, also known as Paradise Alley. The automobile industry cut down its hiring of blacks. Nevertheless, the black community continued to develop. In 1936 John Sengstacke, who later put together a chain of black newspapers, created the *Michigan Chronicle*, which became the major source of news for black Detroit. Many black religious denominations thrived in Detroit. The Rev. James Francis Marion Jones (Prophet Jones), who arrived in the city in 1938, became a popular cult leader and radio evangelist. Of more lasting significance was the **Nation of Islam,** founded by **W. D. Fard** about 1930 and led after his death by **Elijah Muhammad.** However, by far the best-known black Detroit resident in the first half of the twentieth century was **Joe Louis,** who moved to Detroit at the age of twelve. The heavyweight boxing champion from 1935 through 1949, Louis began his career in local Detroit clubs, and his swift rise to boxing eminence was aided by John Roxborough, a black Detroit businessman.

The coming of **World War II** (1939–45) and the increased building of weapons by Detroit industries sparked massive renewed migration to Detroit. **Walter White** of the **National Association for the Advancement of Colored People (NAACP)** estimated that 350,000 people, including 50,000 blacks, entered the city between March 1942 and June 1943. Hate strikes by white workers against blacks, and the past refusal of many blacks to join unions in strikes, had left great bitterness. In February 1942 blacks turned to protests and violence when the **Sojourner Truth** Homes, a federal housing project built for blacks, was suddenly reassigned to whites. The change was eventually canceled, but racial tensions grew as job competition and the housing crisis grew worse. The tensions finally exploded into the Detroit Riot of 1943.

The Civil Rights Era

After the war the African-American population of Detroit climbed, doubling again between 1940 and 1950, and reaching 482,000 in 1960, 29 percent of the city's population. The black middle class expanded. Churches also expanded, and the Rev. C. L. Franklin and the Rev. Charles Hill became legends in their own time. The Rev. Albert Cleague also began the Black Messiah Movement in Detroit in 1952, turning his United Church of Christ into the Shrine of the Black Madonna. Detroit had the largest NAACP chapter in America.

However, large-scale discrimination persisted. Detroit's police, segregated and almost all white, were notorious for bigotry. Only 3 percent of the 300,000 units of new housing built in the 1950s in Detroit were given to blacks. While large numbers of blacks moved into the formerly Jewish neighborhood on 12th Street, those who tried to move into other all-white neighborhoods were met by mobs and brick-throwers. During the 1960s Detroit achieved a somewhat undeserved reputation as a "model city" in terms of race relations. Reform Mayor Jerome Cavanaugh, whose 1961 campaign had been supported in large numbers by blacks angered at the previous mayor's policy of random police searches, put a liberal police commissioner in office. In five years Cavanaugh brought in an estimated $230 million in federal money for programs, some designed by city officials, for black Detroiters. In June 1963, after black militants planned a civil rights protest march, Mayor Cavanaugh persuaded more moderate groups to participate, and invited the Rev. Dr. **Martin Luther King, Jr.,** to speak. About 125,000 people participated in the Walk to Freedom, making it the largest civil rights protest up to that time. In 1964 a militant black lawyer, **John Conyers,** was elected to Congress.

Nevertheless, discrimination continued. Whites fought housing integration, and year after year little money was spent on schools. Police bigotry proved resistant to change. Poor, unemployed inner-city blacks resented the high prices they faced in stores owned both by whites and by the black middle class, whom they felt were "collaborators" with the whites in power. The

THE HOME OF MOTOWN

In 1959 Berry Gordy founded the Motown Record Corporation, which would become a cultural force, and the Detroit's first black-owned multimillion dollar corporation. It created the "Motown sound," tuneful pop-oriented rhythm and blues, and features such groups as the Supremes, the Temptations, the Four Tops, and the Jackson Five. Black performers such as Diana Ross, Smokey Robinson, and Aretha Franklin became superstars in the music industry.

Detroit Riot of 1967, a gigantic urban rebellion, scarred Detroit physically and destroyed its "model city" image. With the cooperation between African Americans and white liberals ended, the black community concentrated on electing African-American officials. In 1973 **Coleman Young** was elected to the first of five terms as mayor. Mayor Young reshaped the police force and brought blacks into city government.

Around 1975 Detroit became a black majority city. By 1990 the city had the largest percentage of African Americans of any big city in the United States, but it had lost one-third of its population in the previous twenty years as the auto industry and manufacturing companies declined and more affluent whites and blacks moved to nearby suburbs. Despite the mayor's efforts to stimulate development, symbolized by the Renaissance Center, and revive the local economy through job-creating projects, 34 percent of Detroit's residents were receiving public assistance in 1987. Detroit's large black middle class gave it the highest black average household income in America in the 1980s. Nevertheless, the city experienced chronic high unemployment through the early 1990s as crime rose and neighborhoods decayed.

Detroit Today

In 1994 Dennis Archer became Detroit's second black mayor. In the time since his election Mayor Archer has worked to revive the city. He has encouraged large companies to move to Detroit, thus providing jobs to residents. He has also promoted the rebuilding of Detroit's old Theater District and the construction of a new baseball stadium for the Detroit Tigers. These projects are part of an effort to make Detroit a major entertainment and cultural center once again.

(SEE ALSO MOTOWN; THE UNDERGROUND RAILROAD; JOE LOUIS.)

Dett, Robert Nathaniel

COMPOSER, PIANIST
October 11, 1882–October 2, 1943

Robert Nathaniel Dett is known for translating spirituals (African-American religious songs) into works for the concert stage. He began studying piano as a child, performing in churches and hotels in his hometown of

Niagara Falls, New York. Dett published his first composition, titled "After the Cake Walk," in 1900.

After studying music in a New York conservatory, Dett continued his education at Oberlin College (Ohio). There, he directed a church choir and continued writing music. Graduating in 1908, Dett held teaching posts at colleges in Tennessee and Missouri. In 1913 he accepted the job of music director at the **Hampton Institute** (Virginia). Remaining there until 1932, Dett worked with the choir to revive the tradition of singing spirituals. He also wrote his best-known work, *In the Bottoms* (1913), performed piano concerts, and founded (in 1919) the National Association of Negro Musicians.

In 1932 Dett returned to upstate New York, settling in Rochester, where he taught and continued arranging spirituals and writing original works. He held teaching positions in Texas and North Carolina before joining the United Service Organizations (USO; a group that entertains U.S. military personnel), in Michigan. He died there in 1943.

Diaspora

"Diaspora" comes from the Greek word for "dispersion," or scattering. It usually refers to the scattering of Jews from their homeland in Israel beginning in 586 B.C. The Jews were first conquered by the Babylonians and over the centuries by other invaders, including the Romans. With each invasion, the Jewish people were forced from their homeland to live in communities around the world. These communities form the Jewish Diaspora.

In the late twentieth century the term "diaspora" was applied to people of African origin who lived outside **Africa**. Like the Jews, many Africans were taken from or forced to leave their homeland. Most were captured between the 1500s and the 1800s to become slaves in North America, the Caribbean, and the West Indies. By the second half of the twentieth century, Africans were leaving their home countries because of war and for educational or economic opportunities.

The term "African Diaspora" was particularly popular during the 1960s and 1970s in the United States. It was especially used by African-American political leaders, such as members of the **black nationalism** movement, who stressed that it was important for peoples of African ancestry living all over the world to unite. In the 1980s and 1990s the term continued to be used, and the African Diaspora continues to be studied. Students of the African Diaspora compare the experiences of peoples of African ancestry living throughout the world and try to understand the relation these people have to Africa and their African heritage.

According to the 1990 census, the last time an official count was taken, the number of people considered part of the diaspora, meaning the number of Africans not living in Africa, was approximately 150 million. The number of African Americans living in the United States was approximately 30 million. Black populations also exist in the Caribbean (34 million); Central and South American countries, such as Guyana, Panama, Belize, and Brazil; and in European cities, in particular in London and Paris. Smaller concentra-

tions of African peoples can also be found in the Persian Gulf, India, and China. (*See also* **Afrocentricity; Slave Trade**.)

Dickens, Helen Octavia

PHYSICIAN, MEDICAL EDUCATOR
February 21, 1909–

Helen Octavia Dickens, the first black woman admitted to the American College of Surgeons, was born in Dayton, Ohio. After attending public schools in Dayton, Dickens enrolled at Crane Junior College in Chicago and later at the University of Illinois, where she earned an M.D. degree in 1934. She was the only black woman in her graduating class of 175. In 1935, after completing her internship and residency at Chicago's Provident Hospital, she moved to Philadelphia, Pennsylvania, to share the family practice (a practice providing ongoing medical care for the individual and family) established by another African-American female physician, Virginia Alexander. Dickens left the practice seven years later to obtain additional medical training. She received a master's of medical science in 1945.

Dickens married Purvis S. Henderson, a doctor, in 1943. The couple remained together until Henderson's death in 1961, and they raised two children. Marriage and children did not slow Dickens's career. She became certified by the American Board of Obstetrics and Gynecology in 1946, and she was admitted to the American College of Surgeons four years later. She served as director of obstetrics and gynecology at Mercy-Douglass Hospital in Philadelphia from 1948 to 1967.

In 1965 Dickens joined the faculty of the University of Pennsylvania School of Medicine. She established one of the nation's first teen-pregnancy clinics and successfully recruited minority students. Dickens remained an active member of the university faculty. In 1993, at the age of 84, she still continued to practice medicine and counsel minority students.

Dickerson, Earl Burris

LAWYER, POLITICIAN
1891–September 3, 1986

Lawyer Earl Dickerson was a leader in the **Civil Rights movement.** Born in Mississippi, Dickerson moved with his family to Chicago, Illinois, when he was fifteen years old. He earned his undergraduate degree from the University of Illinois in 1914. He served in the army during **World War I** (1914–18), and upon his return he enrolled at the University of Chicago Law School. In 1920 he became the school's first black graduate.

After working in the Chicago mayor's office, Dickerson became the first black assistant attorney general for Illinois (1933–39). In 1941 he was one of two black members appointed by President Franklin Roosevelt (1882–1945) to the Fair Employment Practices Committee (FEPC), where he took a firm stand against job discrimination (inequality).

In 1938 Dickerson was elected to the Chicago City Council. In his six years as councilman, he led investigations into housing discrimination and succeeded in adding an anti-discrimination clause to a public transportation bill. Though he tried to advance his career in politics, Dickerson's strong defense of civil rights and his involvement in the Progressive Party stood in the way.

Dickerson found another avenue for his activism. In the 1920s he got involved in civil rights organizations. He served on the board of directors of the Chicago Urban League (1929–70) and as its president (1939–47, 1950–55). Joining the **National Association for the Advancement of Colored People (NAACP),** he soon took a leadership role. In 1939 he helped found its Legal and Educational Defense Fund. He served on the NAACP's national board for forty years (1941–80). A supporter of Dr. **Martin Luther King Jr.** (1929–1968), Dickerson was a lifelong participant in the civil rights struggle.

Diddley, Bo

RHYTHM-AND-BLUES SINGER AND GUITARIST
December 30, 1928–

Bo Diddley was born Otha Ellas (or Elias) Bates in McComb, Mississippi, and shortly thereafter was sent to **Chicago, Illinois,** to live with his cousins, whose last name, McDaniel, he adopted. He studied violin while still a child, taught himself guitar, and played trombone in Chicago's Baptist Congress Band. He attended Foster Vocational High School, and after graduating was a boxer and construction worker. In 1946 he married Ethel Mae Smith.

In the 1950s McDaniel adopted the name Bo Diddley, apparently in reference to the diddley bow, a one-stringed guitar. In 1955 he recorded "Bo Diddley" and "I'm a Man" and appeared on Ed Sullivan's television show. He soon became a significant figure in Chicago's **blues** scene, and in the 1960s he gained an international reputation for his electrifying live performances.

Bo Diddley was widely known for the customary rhythm used in most of his songs. He built a reputation as a powerful and outrageous singer, famous for shouting, growling, and howling boastful lyrics filled with physical suggestiveness. His guitar playing, combining blues and Afro-Cuban influences, was a prime influence on British rock bands in the 1960s. He appeared in three **film**s during this time, including *The Legend of Bo Diddley* (1966).

From the 1960s through the 1980s, Bo Diddley maintained a busy schedule. He performed all over the world, hailed as one of the pioneers of rock and roll. His connection with British rockers continued, with tours alongside The Clash in 1979 and with Rolling Stones guitarist Ron Wood in 1988. In 1987 Bo Diddley was inducted into the Rock and Roll Hall of Fame, and in 1989 he was a featured performer at President George Bush's induction into office in Washington, D.C. In 1996, the year in which he was honored with a Lifetime Achievement award by the Rhythm & Blues

Foundation, Bo Diddley released "A Man Amongst Men," a commemoration of his forty years in music.

Diggs, Charles Coles Jr.

CONGRESSMAN, MORTICIAN
December 2, 1922–August 24, 1998

Charles Coles Diggs Jr. was the first African American to represent Michigan in Congress. Throughout his twenty-six-year career in Congress, he helped draft several important laws that changed American society. Diggs's political career, however, was tainted by a conviction for mail fraud in 1978.

Diggs was born in Detroit, Michigan, where his father was involved in local politics and owned the state's largest funeral home. He began his college education at the University of Michigan, but it was interrupted when he fought in **World War II** (1939–45). After the war he earned a mortuary science degree from Wayne State University in Detroit. In 1950 Diggs's father, who had been imprisoned for taking bribes, won reelection to his Michigan state senate post in a special election, but the legislature refused to seat him. Diggs Jr. ran for the seat in a special election, defending his father's record, and won by a wide margin. He earned a law degree while serving in the senate.

Diggs was elected to the House of Representatives in 1954. During his lengthy career in public service, Diggs worked for civil rights laws, helped found the **Congressional Black Caucus**, helped to reduce the legal voting age to eighteen, and sponsored laws designed to help minority business owners. He also became the first black to serve on the House Foreign Affairs Committee.

In 1978, however, Diggs was accused of mail fraud and of improperly using funds. After an investigation by the House in 1979, he was forced to serve seven months in jail for the crime. Diggs claimed he was innocent and tried to clear his name by having the charges dropped. When his appeal failed, he went back to being a mortician. He died in 1998 at the age of seventy-five, insisting to the end that he was the victim of an unjust investigation.

Dillard University

Founded: Dillard University was established in 1930 when New Orleans University and Straight College merged.

Location: New Orleans, Louisiana

Known For: Dillard's campus is especially beautiful and is situated in a residential area of New Orleans. It is dotted with ancient oak trees and is known for its fine examples of historic architecture.

Religious Affiliation: United Church of Christ and United Methodist Church

Number of Students (1999–2000): 1,563

Grade Average of Incoming Freshman: 3.0

Admission Requirements: Four years of English, four years of math, three years of science (including a lab science), two years of social studies; ACT or SAT scores; personal essay; two letters of recommendation, one from a counselor or principal and one from a teacher.

Mailing Address:
Dillard University
Office of Admission
2601 Gentilly Blvd.
New Orleans, LA 70122

Telephone: (800) 216-6637

E-mail: admissions@dillard.edu

URL: http://www.dillard.edu

Campus: Dillard's 48-acre campus consists of 21 buildings, including laboratories, the Dillard University Art Gallery, and the Dillard University Theater. The library contains over 140,000 documents.

Extracurricular Activities: Student government; student newspaper, the *Courtboullion*; radio station; eight fraternities and eight sororities; over twenty organizations, including honor societies, religious groups, and a gospel choir; athletics (men's and women's basketball, cross-country, and tennis).

Dillard Alumni: Rheta Dumas, dean of nursing, University of Michigan; D. Mitchell Spelman, dean, Harvard Medical School.

Dinkins, David Norman

POLITICIAN
July 10, 1927–

As mayor of New York City, David Dinkins has earned a place of honor in African-American political history. In 1950 he graduated from **Howard University** (Washington, D.C.) and later entered Brooklyn Law School in New York, where he received a degree in 1956. From 1956 through 1975 Dinkins worked as an associate and partner in a law firm. He soon took an active interest in local politics and was elected to the New York state legislature in 1965 and as a state Democratic Party district leader in 1967. In 1975 he was named New York City's city clerk, a position he would hold for ten years. He ran for Manhattan borough (a political district) president and won the office in 1985.

In 1989 Dinkins ran for mayor of New York, presenting himself as someone who could handle the city's racial problems. He defeated Republican Rudolph Giuliani by a slim margin, becoming the first African-American mayor in New York's history.

Dinkins's turn as mayor had its share of financial and political problems. Dinkins earned a reputation for being a cautious and careful administrator. However, he was widely criticized as ineffective and biased in his handling of black boycotts of Korean-American shop owners in 1992 and in his response to riots in 1993. Following his narrow defeat for reelection by Rudolph Giuliani in 1993, Dinkins hosted a radio show and taught at Columbia University in New York.

Diseases and Epidemics

Diseases and epidemics have caused more suffering among African Americans than any other group in the United States. Blacks have a higher

Since the 1950s the difference in disease rates between black Americans and white Americans has remained. During the 1980s African Americans developed tuberculosis at more than six times the rate of white Americans

incidence of disease mostly because they have tended to be poorer than whites and, as a result, have not always had access to adequate medical care. Many blacks were also discriminated against by doctors and hospitals because of their race.

Before the **Civil War** (1861–1865), African-American slaves suffered from diseases they had brought from **Africa**, such as malaria, sleeping sickness, and hookworm. Once in America, they also suffered diseases they caught from whites, such as smallpox, measles, diphtheria, and syphilis. Because of the poor living conditions that slaves endured, these diseases often turned into epidemics, which means they spread to a large number of people before dying out. In 1793, for example, an epidemic of yellow fever crippled the entire city of Philadelphia, Pennsylvania.

In the years before the Civil War, U.S. slave owners were so financially dependent on their slaves that many of them worried about the health of the slaves as much as they did about that of their own families. Although diseases and epidemics took a higher toll on slaves than on whites, the death rate in both groups was extremely high. In 1850 the U.S. Census Bureau reported that the average age of death for blacks was 21.4 years, while for whites it was 25.5 years.

After the Civil War modern medicine made great progress in eliminating the threat of many diseases and epidemics. However, black Americans did not benefit from these discoveries to the degree that white Americans did. Since black Americans were no longer slaves, white American society no longer had an economic reason to make sure blacks were healthy. In general, white doctors and health care organizations paid attention to health problems in black communities only when those problems threatened whites. As a result, black professional associations and black doctors took on the responsibilities of black health care. Black physicians worked with black groups, churches, and schools to distribute information on disease control and health maintenance.

Since the 1950s the difference in disease rates between black Americans and white Americans has remained. During the 1980s African Americans developed tuberculosis at more than six times the rate of white Americans. In 1989 whites had a 50 percent chance of surviving five years after being diagnosed with cancer, while blacks had a 37 percent chance. This difference in survival rates exists in large part because African Americans still have less access to the kinds of medical treatment that would help them survive longer.

However, some dramatic improvements have been made. One example is sickle-cell anemia, a disorder that causes physical deformity of red blood cells and can produce pain, tissue damage, and a low blood count (anemia) in the patient. Sickle-cell anemia is genetic (inherited from parents) and strikes mostly African Americans (150 of 100,000 black children are born with the disease). In 1993 researchers discovered what causes the disease and how to treat it. That same year, Dr. David Satcher, an expert on minority and community health care, became the first African American to head the federal Centers for Disease Control and Prevention.

District of Columbia

First African-American Settlers: The ten-mile-square District of Columbia was created in 1791. Blacks were the largest population group in the area when the site was selected for a federal district, and their labor supported the region's plantation economy.

Slave Population: As the district's population grew, **slavery** remained common. Most slaves worked as skilled and unskilled laborers (domestics, coachmen, carpenters, barbers) in the capital city.

Free Black Population: In 1800, when Washington became the nation's capital, more than a quarter of its population was black, and about a quarter of those were free. In 1814, when Washington was attacked by British troops, **free blacks** helped build barricades, and several volunteered as soldiers to defend the city. Free blacks, however, had a curfew, were required to post "good behavior" bonds, were forbidden to operate businesses, and were banned from preaching.

Civil War: Slavery was abolished in the District of Columbia with compensation to slaveholders loyal to the Union (the North) in the spring of 1862. With the freeing of the district's slaves and the **Emancipation** Proclamation, a presidential decree declaring the freedom of slaves in the Confederacy (the South), blacks volunteered for the Union army, and three thousand black D.C. troops saw action in the **Civil War** (1861–65).

Reconstruction: By the end of the Civil War, forty thousand blacks had settled in the nation's capital. By 1870 the black population represented one-third of the total Washington population. As in other cities in the South, however, most of the gains Washington blacks made during **Reconstruction** were quickly lost; for example, although **suffrage** (voting rights) had been extended to black males in 1866, by 1874 Congress had abolished all local suffrage with the support of the majority white population. A two-day riot during the **Red Summer** of 1919 catalyzed black civil rights efforts and set in motion protests and the organization of race-relations groups. By 1920 Washington had the third-largest urban black population (110,000) in the country and was one-fourth black.

The Great Depression: During the **Great Depression** black community sources were mobilized to aid the needy. Civil rights efforts increased during the era, reducing employment discrimination and the segregation of public places. **World War II** (1939–45) led to an influx of black workers that strained the city's limited black housing resources. By the late 1950s Washington was a black-majority city—the first such large city in the nation.

Civil Rights Movement: The **Civil Rights movement** focused attention on the nation's capital with the great March on Washington in 1963 and the Poor People's Washington Campaign of 1968. In 1968, after the assassination of the Reverend Dr. **Martin Luther King Jr.,** the city was shaken by rioting.

Current African-American Population: According to U.S. Census Bureau estimates, the total black population in the District of Columbia was 325,840 (62 percent of the state population) as of July 1, 1998.

Key Figures: Benjamin Banneker (1731–1836), mathematician and astronomer; **Kelly Miller** (1863–1939), longtime dean of Howard University; **Carter Woodson** (1875–1950), founder of the Association for the Study of Negro Life and History; composer and bandleader **Duke Ellington** (1899–1974); musician **Marvin Gaye** (1939–1984); Nobel laureate **Ralph Johnson Bunche** (1904–1971); **Marion Barry** (1936–), politician.

(SEE ALSO HOWARD UNIVERSITY; NEW NEGRO.)

Dixon, Dean Charles

CONDUCTOR
January 10, 1915–November 4, 1976

Dean Dixon was the first African-American conductor to gain recognition around the world. He began studying violin at age four and as a teenager organized a symphony orchestra and chorus. In 1936 he earned his undergraduate degree from the Juilliard School of Music (New York) and continued his studies at Columbia University Teachers College (New York), earning his master's degree in 1939.

In 1938 Dixon made his conducting debut in New York City and founded the New York Chamber Orchestra. Three years later he became the first African American to appear as a guest conductor with the dynamic Arturo Toscanini's (1867–1957) NBC Symphony Orchestra. Dixon also worked with such major orchestras as the New York Philharmonic (1942) and the Philadelphia Orchestra (1943). But in spite of his education, training, and experience, he could not secure a permanent position in the United States.

From 1949 to 1970 Dixon pursued his career abroad. He worked with major orchestras in Israel (1950–51), Sweden (1953–60), Germany (1961–64), and Australia (1964–67). In 1971 he tasted success in his homeland when he conducted the New York Philharmonic on an extended tour. Dixon issued several recordings during his distinguished career, conducting European classics as well as works by twentieth-century American composers.

Dixon, Melvin

NOVELIST, POET, EDUCATOR
May 29, 1950–October 26, 1992

Born in Stamford, Connecticut, Melvin Dixon graduated from Wesleyan University (Middletown, Connecticut) in 1971 and received a Ph.D. degree from Brown University (Providence, Rhode Island) in 1975. He taught at various colleges and universities, including the City University of New York Graduate Center, where he was professor of English from 1986 to 1992. As a critic, Dixon helped to shape the emerging field of comparative African-American literary studies, but he was also an award-winning creative writer.

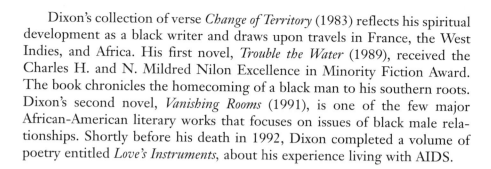

Dixon's collection of verse *Change of Territory* (1983) reflects his spiritual development as a black writer and draws upon travels in France, the West Indies, and Africa. His first novel, *Trouble the Water* (1989), received the Charles H. and N. Mildred Nilon Excellence in Minority Fiction Award. The book chronicles the homecoming of a black man to his southern roots. Dixon's second novel, *Vanishing Rooms* (1991), is one of the few major African-American literary works that focuses on issues of black male relationships. Shortly before his death in 1992, Dixon completed a volume of poetry entitled *Love's Instruments*, about his experience living with AIDS.

Dobbs, Mattiwilda

OPERA SINGER (SOPRANO)
July 11, 1925–

Hailed by *Gramophone* magazine for her poised singing and dramatic strength, Mattiwilda Dobbs is known around the world as a gifted soprano. Raised in Atlanta, Georgia, Dobbs began studying piano at age seven and later sang with her church choir. She studied voice at Spelman College (Atlanta), graduating in 1946. Not sure she could get work as a singer, she devoted the next two years to earning a master's degree in Spanish language and literature from Teachers College at Columbia University (New York).

In 1950 Dobbs entered the International Music Competition in Geneva, Switzerland. Winning first prize, she went on to study voice in Paris, France (1950–52) and perform with orchestras across Europe. Returning to the United States, she was among the first African Americans to perform at the San Francisco Opera House (1955) and made her debut at the Metropolitan Opera, New York (1956). In the late 1950s she performed in the United States, Europe, Australia, and Israel, securing an international reputation.

Settling in Europe in 1973, Dobbs returned to the United States to sing at nephew Maynard Jackson's (1938–) inauguration as mayor of Atlanta in 1974 (he was the first African-American mayor of a major southern city). Dobbs also returned to teach and serve as artist-in-residence at various American colleges and universities. From 1976 to 1991 she was professor of voice at **Howard University** (Washington, D.C.). In 1999 she released *Testament*, a collection of her arias (opera songs sung by a single voice) and songs.

Doby, Lawrence Eugene "Larry"

BASEBALL PLAYER
December 13, 1923–

Lawrence Eugene Doby was the first African American to play in **baseball**'s American League. He followed **Jackie Robinson,** who was the first African American to play in the National League. Both players are known for breaking into a sport that was dominated by white players; both suffered the same racist treatment from fans and their fellow teammates. Like Robinson, Doby ignored the critics and played the game he loved, paving the way for other blacks to play professional baseball.

Born in Camden, South Carolina, Doby moved to New Jersey in 1938, where he began his outstanding baseball career. In 1942 he played in the Negro National League. After taking time out to serve in **World War II** (1939–45), he returned to the league to help his team win a pennant. Doby then played in Puerto Rico and in 1947 was picked up by the Cleveland Indians. Although far less celebrated than Robinson, Doby had a remarkable career in the majors, making seven All-Star teams, achieving a .283 batting average, and twice leading the league in home runs. After retiring from the majors in 1962, Doby became the second black to play in a Japanese league.

Doby moved on to coaching with the Cleveland Indians and earned a head coach position with the Montreal Expos. Doby's coaching career was short-lived, however, and he pursued other activities. He served as director of bicycle safety in Essex County, New Jersey, and was later named the director of community relations for the National Basketball League's New Jersey Nets. In 1998 Doby was elected to the National Baseball Hall of Fame. In November 1999 Doby joined the Goldklang Group, which owns five minor league baseball teams.

Domino, Antoine Jr. "Fats"

SINGER, PIANIST, SONGWRITER
February 26, 1928–

Rock-and-roll singer, pianist, and songwriter Fats Domino taught himself to play piano by the age of nine. In his teens he had already mastered various popular styles of the period, including boogie-woogie, **the blues,** and **ragtime,** which provided the basic materials for his work in **rhythm-and-blues (R&B)** and rock. By age fourteen, Domino had quit school to pursue a career in music. He worked in a factory by day and performed at night in bars, developing the stride-like piano playing that became his trademark. At twenty-one he had become house pianist at the Hideaway Club, where he acquired the nickname "Fats" and met the trumpeter and bandleader Dave Bartholomew. He recorded *The Fat Man* (1950) with Bartholomew, a "jump" blues hit that launched Domino's career and introduced many parts of the country to the New Orleans rhythm sound.

Domino's singing and piano playing, backed by Bartholomew's band, established an R&B sound that appealed to both black and white audiences. In twelve years they turned out more than a dozen top ten hits on the Imperial label, including "Ain't That a Shame" and "Blue Monday." For a time Domino and Bartholomew were the most successful songwriting team in pop history. By the mid-1960s, however, their success in creating new music, along with their popularity on the charts, faded. Domino worked for a time in Las Vegas and Reno, Nevada, in casinos and hotels. He briefly recorded in the late 1960s and early 1970s, but with little success. Domino returned to New Orleans and became semiretired, although he successfully performed in Europe in the 1970s and 1980s. In the late 1990s Domino toured England, and in 1998 he was working on a new album. Fats Domino's recordings, which sold over 65 million copies, were an important early example of the "crossover" appeal of R&B, its ability to cross over

Fats Domino: Selected Discography

Fats Domino–Rock and Rollin'
(1956)

This Is Fats Domino
(1956)

Here Stands Fats Domino
(1957)

Fabulous Mr. D
(1958)

Let's Play Fats Domino
(1959)

I Miss You So
(1961)

Twistin' the Stomp
(1962)

Fats Is Back, Reprise
(1968)

Legendary Masters Series
(1972)

They Call Me the Fat Man
(1990)

Christmas Is a Special Day
(1993)

from being popular mainly with blacks to being popular with white audiences as well.

Dorsey, Thomas Andrew "Georgia Tom"

GOSPEL COMPOSER
July 1, 1899–January 23, 1993

Known as "the father of gospel," composer Thomas Dorsey was born in Villa Rica, Georgia. His mother taught him to play the pump organ, and he began piano lessons in his early teens. He learned technique, how to read music, and enough theory to be able to jot down musical ideas. He received a different kind of musical education while selling soda pop at the 81 Theater in Atlanta, Georgia, where he met the legendary **blues** singer **"Ma" Rainey** (1886–1939) and other performers.

Dorsey moved to Chicago, Illinois, in 1919 and studied for a while at the Chicago Musical College. Around 1924 he organized the Wildcats Jazz

THOMAS DORSEY'S "PRECIOUS LORD"

In 1932 gospel singer Thomas Dorsey was on the road when a telegram informed him that his wife had given birth to a child, but she had not survived the child's birth. Dorsey returned to Chicago, only to find that his newly born daughter had died as well. In his grief, he sat alone in a dark room for three days, emerging to write "Precious Lord," which is the second-most popular song in African-American Christian churches, after "Amazing Grace." The following lyrics have since been translated into more than fifty languages:

Precious Lord, take my hand, lead me on, let me stand.
I am tired, I am weak, I am worn;
Through the storm, through the night, lead me on to the light.
Take my hand, precious Lord, lead me on.

Band, a group that sometimes accompanied Ma Rainey. Dorsey produced a 1928 hit, "Tight Like That," with "Tampa Red" (born Hudson Whittaker). During this time Dorsey became known as "Georgia Tom" and "Barrelhouse Tom."

Although he worked with **jazz** and blues bands throughout the 1920s, Dorsey's interest in the new form of **gospel music** was steadily growing. His first gospel song was "If I Don't Get There," published by the **National Baptist Convention.**

In 1928 Dorsey suffered a nervous breakdown, after which he converted to Christianity. He gave up all secular (nonreligious) music and began composing gospel pieces. Dorsey organized one of the first gospel choirs at Chicago's Pilgrim Baptist Church in 1931. The next year, he opened the first publishing house in the country that sold only gospel music by African-American composers. Along with others, he also organized the National Convention of Gospel Choirs and Choruses.

Dorsey's compositions are known for their simple melodies and catchy phrases, such as "I'm Going to Live the Life I Sing About in My Song," "If We Ever Needed the Lord Before, We Sure Do Need Him Now," and "There Will Be Peace in the Valley for Me." Dorsey was so instrumental in the development of gospel music that, during the 1930s and 1940s, gospel songs were referred to as "Dorseys." Remembered as the most important person in gospel music to that date, in 1982 Dorsey was celebrated in the documentary *Say Amen, Somebody.*

Douglas, Aaron

PAINTER, EDUCATOR
May 26, 1899–February 24, 1979

Painter Aaron Douglas's work portrays African-American life using a bold, art deco style. Born in Topeka, Kansas, he earned a bachelor of fine

arts degree from the University of Nebraska in 1922. He then taught art at a high school in Missouri where his social circle included future civil rights leader **Roy Wilkins** (1901–1981) and future classical music composer William Levi Dawson (1899–1990). Wilkins and Dawson persuaded Douglas to work in New York. There, Douglas soon became one of the leading artists of the New Negro movement (a 1920s movement dedicated to racial progress) and developed a geometric style of depicting African Americans in dynamic silhouettes (outlines). He blended elements of West African sculpture and traditional European-American and modern design to create works with a hard-edged style (marked by geometric forms with clearly defined boundaries, or edges).

In 1925 Douglas earned three distinctions that launched his career, including first prize for a magazine cover illustration, first prize for a drawing from *Crisis* magazine, and a commission to illustrate **Alain Locke**'s (1885–1954) anthology *The New Negro*. The following year, Douglas married his high school classmate. He continued to illustrate numerous books and magazines throughout the 1920s and 1930s.

In the late 1920s Douglas studied with Fritz Winold Reiss, a German-American artist whose modern work Douglas admired. Locke and a peer encouraged Douglas to look to African art for inspiration and develop his own racially representative work. Through their influence Douglas received a one-year scholarship (1928-1929) to the Barnes Foundation in Merion, Pennsylvania, where he studied both African and modern European art.

In 1930 Douglas painted heroic murals of African-American culture and history in the library at **Fisk University** in Nashville, Tennessee; the Sherman Hotel in Chicago, Illinois; and Bennett College in Greensboro, North Carolina. In 1931 he went to Paris, France, for one year to study at the Académie Scandinave. Only one piece from his time abroad is known—*Forge Foundry*, a black-and-white illustration published in a French journal.

In the 1930s Douglas returned to New York as an arts leader and **muralist.** In 1938 he received a travel fellowship to the American South and the Caribbean nation of Haiti. He exhibited his paintings of Haitian life in New York the following year.

In 1939 Douglas began teaching art at Fisk University. He divided his time between Nashville and New York, where he completed a master's in art education in 1944. From the 1930s until the 1950s the Douglases frequently entertained artists and writers at their home, known as "the White House of Harlem," because the building's residents included prominent intellectuals and civil rights leaders. Douglas painted many of their portraits, in addition to landscapes.

Douglas brought numerous artists to the university for lectures and exhibitions. He was honored by President John F. Kennedy at a White House reception commemorating the abolition of slavery. After retiring as professor emeritus in 1966, Douglas lectured widely and continued to paint until his death in 1979. Douglas's work has appeared in many major American museums and galleries and in university and community center exhibitions.

Douglass, Anna Murray

ABOLITIONIST
c. 1813–August 4, 1882

Anna Murray Douglass was the first person in her family to be born free. At the age of seventeen she made her way to Baltimore, Maryland, where at some point in the mid-1830s she met her husband, the future abolitionist (opponent of **slavery**) **Frederick Douglass.**

Anna Murray Douglass was an activist in her own right. Although she could read and write only a little, she participated fully in the circle of Massachusetts reformers. She met weekly with the antislavery women who mounted the annual Anti-Slavery Fair in Boston. In 1847 the Douglass family moved to Rochester, New York, where she continued her abolitionist activities.

Douglass's work as an antislavery activist was in addition to the labor necessary to support herself and her five children, especially when her husband traveled to Europe. She worked as a laundress and shoe binder and managed to set aside part of her earnings for the antislavery cause. In 1872 Anna Douglass, her husband, and her family moved to Washington, D.C., where she lived until her death.

Douglass, Frederick

ABOLITIONIST, JOURNALIST, ORATOR, SOCIAL REFORMER
February 1818–February 20, 1895

Born a slave, Frederick Douglass soon became the most famous African American of the nineteenth century. In his youth he was a personal slave to several whites. Consequently, he learned self-reliance and found a sense of belonging through his relationships with various families and individuals, white and black, who liked and encouraged him.

Taken in 1826 to Baltimore, Maryland, he taught himself to read and write. Baltimore, with its open environment and its large free African-American population, increased Douglass's desire to learn as much as possible about freedom, runaway slaves, and the abolitionist (antislavery) movement. Around the age of thirteen, Douglass purchased his first book, *The Columbian Orator,* which not only deepened his understanding of liberty and equality but also revealed to him the enormous power of oratory (public speaking) in swaying people to action. In 1836 Douglass escaped to freedom.

In the North, Douglass's speeches given to local black communities brought him to the attention of abolitionists, most of whom were white, and they asked him to join them as a lecturer. Douglass became an increasingly powerful lecturer for the Massachusetts Anti-Slavery Society. He also began to come into his own as an activist and a thinker. In 1845 his *Narrative of the Life of Frederick Douglass, an American Slave* was published, and its huge success, followed by a successful speaking tour of Great Britain, increased his celebrity. Douglass later wrote two more autobiographies, *Bondage and My Freedom* (1855) and *Life and Times of Frederick Douglass* (1881; revised 1892).

Douglass's deep involvement with the national Negro freedom movement, as well as with various state and local black conferences, furthered his impact. By 1850 he was the principal spokesman for African Americans. His fierce commitment to freedom and justice also led him to support the women's-rights movement, and he became one of the most important male supporters of women's rights in the nineteenth century. He attended the first Women's Rights Convention, in Seneca Falls, New York, in 1848.

Douglass also achieved a distinguished career in journalism. He edited the *North Star* (1847-51), *Frederick Douglass' Paper* (1851-60), *Douglass' Monthly* (1859-63), and the *New National Era* (1870-74). Stressing self-reliance, hard work, persistence, education, and morality (good character), Douglass echoed African-American values.

Douglass became involved in politics during the 1860s and was appointed to serve as the U.S. marshal for the District of Columbia (1877-81), recorder of deeds for the District of Columbia (1881-86), and minister to the West Indies island of Haiti (1889-91).

Douglass's status as a comfortable, middle-class statesman sometimes made it difficult for him to understand the harsh conditions confronting rural, poor, and migrant blacks. Still, it was clear that his commitment to justice never wavered. Douglass fully understood his people's struggle from **slavery** to freedom, from obscurity and poverty to recognition and respectability. (*See also* **Abolition; Douglass, Anna Murray.**)

Frederick Douglass (Courtesy of Library of Congress)

Dove, Rita

POET

August 28, 1952–

Award-winning poet Rita Dove was born in Akron, Ohio. She graduated from Miami University in Oxford, Ohio, in 1973 and spent the following year studying in Germany. In 1975 she enrolled in the Writers' Workshop at the University of Iowa, where she received her master of fine arts degree two years later. She taught creative writing at Arizona State University from 1981 to 1989 and later accepted a position at the University of Virginia, which named her Commonwealth Professor of English in 1992.

Dove's first volume of poems, *Yellow House on the Corner,* was published in 1980. It was followed by *Museum* (1983) and *Thomas and Beulah* (1986), which loosely narrates the lives of Dove's grandparents and was awarded the Pulitzer Prize for excellence in poetry in 1987. The poems of *Grace Notes* (1989) were praised for technical perfection and carefully crafted metaphor (symbolism). Other highly praised collections include *Mother Love* (1997), poems examining the mother-daughter bond, and *On the Bus with* **Rosa Parks** (1999).

The narrative style of *Thomas and Beulah* resembled Dove's first published fiction, *First Sunday* (1985), a collection of stories. Dove also published the novel *Through the Ivory Gate* in 1992, but her fiction has not been as critically popular as her poetry.

An African-American **F I R S T**

Rita Dove's gifts as a poet were most fully acknowledged in 1993 when she was appointed poet laureate of the United States. The U.S. poet laureate is the poet regarded as the leading or most representative poet in the country and is selected for this honorary position by the Library of Congress. "Laureate" comes from the ancient Greek custom of placing a wreath made from the leaves of the evergreen laurel tree on the heads of winners of sporting events. Dove was the first black writer and the youngest poet ever to be so honored.

Dove's career has received more public attention than that of any other contemporary African-American poet. She represents a generation of poets who have been trained in university writers' workshops and are sometimes criticized for their technical skill at the expense of emotional depth. Dove, however, has distinguished herself in her ability to filter complex historical and personal information through precise selections of poetic form.

Dove, Ulysses

MODERN DANCER, CHOREOGRAPHER
c. January 17, 1947–June 11, 1996

Ulysses Dove was a modern ballet dancer who became a well-known choreographer (creator of new dances). His ballets were marked by their speed, violent force, and physical energy.

Dove began to study dance while a premedical student at **Howard University** (Washington, D.C.) and graduated from Bennington College in Vermont in 1970 with a degree in dance. He then joined the famous Merce Cunningham Dance Company in New York City. In 1973 he joined the **Alvin Ailey** American Dance Theater, where he quickly rose to the rank of principal dancer.

Dove tried his hand at choreography at Ailey's suggestion and created the 1980 solo "Inside" for dancer Judith Jamison. He left the Alvin Ailey company to begin a freelance career that included choreographing for American and European dance companies. He spent three years as assistant director of a choreography study group at the Opera of Paris in France.

Several of Dove's ballets have been performed by the Alvin Ailey company, including "Night Shade" (1982), "Episodes" (1987), and "Vespers" (1994). His final project, "Red Angels," was premiered by the New York City Ballet in 1994. Dove died in 1996.

Dozens, The

"The dozens," or "playing the dozens," is a game that involves at least two players and an audience. The players trade insults and boasts, while the audience coaxes them on and eventually determines the winner. Playing the dozens, also called "sounding," "Joning," or "woofing," is popular among African Americans and is played by adults and children. Some of the insults are said in rhymes, and they generally poke fun at intelligence, achievements, or appearance.

The origins of the game are uncertain, but it may have come from the "joking" verbal duels between various African tribes. It may also have been used as a verbal, or nonviolent, way to resolve arguments. Over time, it has come to reflect the important value placed on verbal skills by people of African heritage. A modern version of "playing the dozens" can be heard in some rap music.

Drama

Long before blacks were allowed on American stages, white dramatists created stereotyped black characters like James Murdoch's foolish "Sambo" in *The Triumph of Love* (1795). The stereotype of an uneducated, clown-like black was hard to overcome when African Americans tried to establish themselves in serious theater, but they had done so by the mid-1800s.

In addition to performing classics like Shakespeare's tragedies, black theater has always portrayed black life and the struggle for freedom and equality in American society. One of the most well known examples is **Lorraine Hansberry**'s (1930–1965) *A Raisin in the Sun* (1959). At the beginning of the twenty-first century, black actors and dramatists have made their mark in theater in diverse ways as they continue to address the important issues of the day.

Early African-American Theater

The first professional black theater company was the African Grove Theatre, in New York City, which opened in 1821. Black actors performed Shakespearean plays and wrote and performed what is thought to be the first play by African Americans, *King Shotaway* (1823), about a slave uprising in the Caribbean. Because the play was produced within a year of an actual slave revolt in Virginia, white citizens, feeling threatened, destroyed the theater building, forcing the company to close. One of the black actors, **Ira Aldridge** (1807–1867), left for Europe, where he won gold medals from the Prussian and Austrian governments for his fine Shakespearean performances. Aldridge became known as one of the greatest actors of his time.

William Wells Brown (1815–1884), a former slave, is considered the first African American to have a play published, *The Escape; or a Leap for Freedom* (1857), which he read at abolitionist gatherings in northern states.

Angelina Weld Grimké's play *Rachel* (1916) was the first twentieth-century full-length play written, performed, and produced by blacks. The controversial play is about a young African-American woman who does not want to marry and become a mother because she fears her children will experience racism as she has.

In 1925 black leader **W. E. B. Du Bois** (1868–1963) founded an amateur theater company whose philosophy that black theater should be "about us . . . by us . . . for us . . . and near us" was carried over into the civil rights period of the mid-1960s.

The Federal Theatre Project

The U.S. government started the Works Progress Administration (WPA) during the **Great Depression** to create more jobs for Americans. One branch of the WPA was the Federal Theatre Project (FTP). Black theater groups created by the FTP gave many blacks their first formal training in acting, directing, and writing. One of the most popular musical plays during this period was a "voodoo" version of Shakespeare's *Macbeth*.

The FTP also produced serious black drama that questioned the makeup of American life, such as **Theodore Ward**'s (1902–1983) *Big White*

A Selection of African-American Tony Awards

Pearl Bailey,
Special Achievement in Theatre, 1968

James Earl Jones,
Best Actor for *The Great White Hope*, 1968

August Wilson,
Best Play for *Fences*, 1985

Gregory Hines,
Best Actor for *Jelly's Last Jam*, 1992

George C. Wolfe,
Best Direction for *Angels in America*, 1993

Fog (1938). A form of experimental theater performed by blacks and whites was the Living Newspaper, through which actors re-created historical and current events.

Playwrights Work for Social Change

Black poet and playwright **Langston Hughes** (1902–1967) used poetry, gospel and blues songs, dance, and short scenes to create a play called *Don't You Want to Be Free?* (1937). Actors spoke directly to the audience, encouraging them join together for workers' rights.

Amiri Baraka (LeRoi Jones) (1934–) was important in the Black Arts movement (1964–74). Associated with the **Nation of Islam** and **Malcolm X,** Baraka became a role model for younger blacks who wanted to show pride in their black identity. During the **Civil Rights movement** of the 1960s, the Vietnam War (1959–75) protest of the 1970s, and new women's rights movements, African-American playwrights gained popularity by criticizing society. Among them were **Ed Bullins** (1935–), **Richard Wesley** (1945–), and **Sonia Sanchez** (1934–). New African-American theater companies like the Richard Allen Cultural Center in New York City and the Inner City Cultural Center in Los Angeles, California, gained government funding and drew supportive audiences.

Adrienne Kennedy (1931–) offers a black woman's perspective on cultural issues and racism in plays like *Funnyhouse of a Negro* (1963). In 1976 black female playwright **Ntozake Shange** (1948–) introduced a new form of play that she calls a "choreopoem." Her play *for colored girls who have considered suicide/when the rainbow is enuf* uses music and dance along with poetry as the women characters talk about their experiences with men. By bringing out black women's negative experiences and their struggle for self-respect, Shange caused heated debate in the black community about women's rights. Two of Shange's more recent plays are *Three Views of Mt. Fuji* (1987) and *Fire's Daughters* (1993).

African-American playwright **Charles Henry Fuller** (1939–) won a Pulitzer Prize in 1982 for his drama *A Soldier's Play* (1981), about the murder of a black sergeant in charge of a unit of black soldiers during World War II (1939–45). Fuller's plays usually address the subjects of racism and discrimination.

LORRAINE HANSBERRY'S *A RAISIN IN THE SUN*

One of the most famous plays by a black dramatist is Lorraine Hansberry's *A Raisin in the Sun* (1959). It is about a poor black Chicago family that is waiting for a $10,000 insurance check paid on the death of the father. Each family member has plans for spending the money. The play makes a statement about the changing values of African Americans as they moved from the rural South to the industrialized North. It includes a Nigerian student who discusses that African nation's struggle to be free of colonial rule, and it brings to light the common belief in what people can accomplish as they try to better themselves.

The play represented several African-American landmarks in theater. It was the first time that an African-American woman's work had been produced at the Ethel Barrymore Theatre on Broadway, and it was the first time African-American director Lloyd Richards had directed a play in such a prestigious theater. *A Raisin in the Sun* brought widespread recognition for actors **Claudia McNeil, Ruby Dee, Sidney Poitier,** and Diana Sands, and it encouraged other black artists to express their visions of black America. The play won the New York Drama Critics Circle Award, beating out plays by famous white playwrights such as Tennessee Williams, Eugene O'Neill, and Archibald MacLeish. This put black playwrights on an equal footing with whites for the first time.

A Raisin in the Sun was made into a movie in 1961 starring McNeil, Dee, Poitier, Sands, and others. It was adapted for television in 1989 and starred **Danny Glover,** Esther Rolle, Starletta DuPois, and Kim Yancey.

African-American Drama in the Late Twentieth Century

Black dramatist **August Wilson** (1945–) set a goal to write a play for each decade of the twentieth century. One is *Two Trains Running* (1990), about a 1960s family trying to get rich by betting on horse races or consulting a fortune-teller. Wilson's characters often fight with ghosts, make a pact with the devil, or talk to Death in their search for spirituality.

Two new African-American playwrights of the 1990s are Suzan-Lori Parks (*The Death of the Last Black Man in the Whole Entire World*, 1990; *In the Blood*, 1999) and Bernard Branner (*Fierce Love: Stories from Black Gay Life*, 1991).

Dred Scott v. Sandford

In the Dred Scott decision of 1857, the Supreme Court ruled, in a seven-to-two vote, that **free blacks** were not citizens of the United States and that Congress lacked the power to stop **slavery** in the western territories.

Scott was a Virginia slave, born around 1802, who moved with his master, Peter Blow, to St. Louis, Missouri, in 1830. Blow sold Scott to Dr. John

OPENING PARAGRAPHS OF THE DRED SCOTT DECISION

The question is simply this: Can a negro, whose ancestors were imported into this country, and sold as slaves, become a member of the political community formed and brought into existence by the Constitution of the United States, and as such become entitled to all the rights, and privileges, and immunities, guarantied by that instrument to the citizen? One of which rights is the privilege of suing in a court of the United States in the cases specified in the constitution....

The words "people of the United States" and "citizens" are synonymous terms, and mean the same thing. They both describe the political body who, according to our republican institutions, form the sovereignty, and who hold the power and conduct the government through their representatives. They are what we familiarly call the "sovereign people," and every citizen is one of this people, and a constituent member of this sovereignty. The question before us is, whether the class of persons described in the plea in abatement compose a portion of this people, and are constituent members of this sovereignty? We think they are not, and that they are not included, and were not intended to be included, under the word "citizens" in the constitution, and can therefore claim none of the rights and privileges which that instrument provides for and secures to citizens of the United States. On the contrary, they were at that time considered as a subordinate and inferior class of beings, who had been subjugated by the dominant race, and, whether emancipated or not, yet remained subject to their authority, and had no rights or privileges but such as those who held the power and the government might choose to grant them....

Emerson, who took Scott to Illinois, a free state, and the Wisconsin Territory, where slavery was not allowed. In 1846, after Emerson's death, Scott sued for his freedom. In 1850 a St. Louis court ruled that because Scott was living in Illinois, a state that did not allow slavery, he was free. In 1852, however, the Missouri Supreme Court reversed the decision.

In 1854 Scott began a new lawsuit in United States District Court. Again a judge ruled that Scott was still a slave. Scott then appealed to the U.S. Supreme Court, the highest court in the country. The central political issue of the 1850s—the power of the federal government to prohibit slavery in the territories—was now before the Supreme Court.

The case was presided over by Chief Justice Taney, who was proslavery. According to Taney: (1) the Missouri Compromise was unconstitutional because Congress could not make laws for the individual territories; (2) freeing slaves in the territories violated the Fifth Amendment to the U.S. Constitution, which makes it illegal to take property without due process (slaves were considered property); and (3) blacks, even those in the North with full state citizenship, could never be U.S. citizens. Taney thought his decision would open all the territories to slavery. In essence, he ruled that racism and slavery were legal.

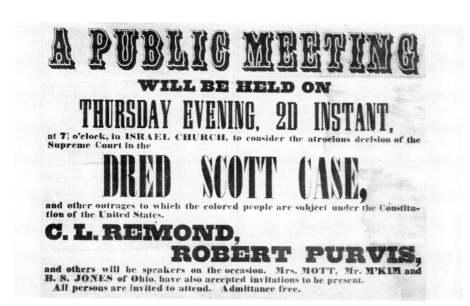

Northern Republicans and abolitionists (people who fought to end slavery) were stunned and horrified. Northern Democrats, on the other hand, hoped the decision would destroy the Republican Party by finally ending the national debate over slavery in the territories. Republicans made Taney and the decision the focus of their 1858 and 1860 campaigns, which helped lead to a Republican presidential victory in 1860. During the **Civil War** (1861–65), the Lincoln administration gradually reversed many of Taney's rulings about the status of blacks. This Republican policy resulted in the adoption of the Fourteenth Amendment (1868), which clearly overruled Dred Scott, declaring, "All persons born or naturalized in the United States . . . are citizens of the United States and of the State wherein they reside."

Drew, Charles Richard

PHYSICIAN
December 6, 1904–April 1, 1950

Charles Richard Drew was known for his work in improving the storage of blood. Born in Washington, D.C., he graduated from Amherst College (Massachusetts) and taught biology and chemistry at Morgan College, where he also served as football coach and athletics director.

In 1928 Drew began medical studies, eventually earning an M.D. degree and a master in surgery degree. He spent two years as an intern and as a resident in medicine at Royal Victoria and Montreal General Hospitals.

Drew was introduced to research on the chemical composition of blood and blood groups. A major problem facing medical science at the time was that quantities of fresh whole blood (unmodified) large enough to match blood group types between blood donor and blood receiver were not readily available. Drew was bothered by the deaths of seriously ill or injured patients because of blood loss. Learning more about blood and how to preserve it over long periods of time became a research interest that Drew carried with him when he began teaching at **Howard University** (Washington, D.C.) in 1935.

In 1938 Drew's research revealed that it was blood plasma (the fluid portion of blood as distinguished from suspended material) rather than whole blood that needed to be preserved for transfusions. Drew established an experimental blood bank at Columbia-Presbyterian Hospital. In 1940 Drew was awarded a doctorate at Columbia University with his thesis "Banked Blood."

Returning to Howard University in 1940, Drew devoted himself to training its medical students in surgery. His teaching was abruptly interrupted, however, by a call for blood plasma during **World War II**. He accepted an assignment to supply blood for the British Red Cross and, later, for the U.S. armed forces.

In 1941 the military established a system of refusing to use blood donations from nonwhites for transfusions to whites. Blood donated by blacks was stored separately and given only to blacks. As director of the Red Cross Blood Bank Program, Drew took a strong stand against the racial separation of banked blood. As a result, he was asked to resign his directorship position. He again returned to Howard University, where he became a professor and head of the department of surgery, and he also became surgeon-in-chief at Freedmen's Hospital.

While driving to a conference in 1950, Drew dozed at the wheel and the car went off the road near Burlington, North Carolina, and overturned. Although stories abound that his medical emergency was ignored because of his race, he received prompt medical attention. He died on April 1, 1950, from injuries resulting from the accident. Drew gained much recognition during his lifetime and received many awards for his work in the medical field.

Du Bois, Shirley Graham (Lola Bell Graham)

WRITER, POLITICAL ACTIVIST
November 11, 1896–March 27, 1977

Writer Shirley Graham Du Bois was as heavily involved in politics as she was in the arts. Born Lola Bell Graham near Indianapolis, Indiana, she was the daughter of an **African Methodist Episcopal** (AME) minister. After studying music at the Sorbonne (Paris, France) and Harvard University (Cambridge, Massachusetts), she enrolled at Oberlin College (Ohio), where she earned her bachelor's and master's degrees. After graduating, she became involved in writing and the theater.

Awarded fellowships and other honors for her creative writing, Graham became acquainted with influential people, including educator and writer **W. E. B. Du Bois** (1868–1963). On February 14, 1951, they were married. Shirley Du Bois joined her husband as a champion of reform. She was a founding editor of *Freedomways*, a quarterly publication about the black freedom movement.

In 1961 the Du Boises were invited by Ghana's president to move to that African nation. W. E. B. Du Bois died there in August 1963, but Shirley Du Bois stayed until 1966, working to organize Ghana's television. Later returning home, she was denied reentry into the United States, where her political activities were described as subversive (secretive and destructive to the government). She remained abroad the rest of her life.

Du Bois, William Edward Burghardt "W. E. B."

HISTORIAN, EDUCATOR, WRITER
February 23, 1868–August 27, 1963

Today W. E. B. Du Bois is considered one of the great black American intellects, but in his time he was both a leader and a controversial figure. Born in Great Barrington, Massachusetts, his mother was Mary Burghardt Du Bois, a member of a small African-American community that settled in the area before the **American Revolution** (1775–83). His father, Alfred Du Bois, abandoned the family when his son was a baby. Young William Edward Burghardt (W. E. B.) Du Bois was educated in the mostly white public schools and attended the Congregational church.

In 1885 Du Bois went to Nashville, Tennessee, where he attended **Fisk University**. In the South he first met with racism's more severe forms. Earning his bachelor's in 1888, Du Bois went on to Harvard University (Cambridge, Massachusetts), where he received another bachelor's degree in 1890 and his doctorate (Ph.D.) in history in 1895. As part of his graduate studies, he attended the University of Berlin (1892–94) in Germany.

In 1896 Du Bois married Nina Gomer, one of his students at Ohio's **Wilberforce University**, where he had been teaching since 1894. (The couple later had two children, Burghardt and Yolande.) In 1897 he joined the faculty at **Atlanta University** (now Clark Atlanta University) in Georgia. There, he oversaw the school's yearly Conference for the Study of the Negro and published eighteen studies of black life, each focused on a different topic, such as education or the church.

Segregation, discrimination, and violence toward blacks prompted Du Bois to accurately predict in 1900 that "the problem of the twentieth century is the problem of the color line." Continuing to teach, his ideas reached beyond the classroom. The man who had emerged as one of America's leading black thinkers was gaining a wide audience through the books he published, including the influential *The Souls of Black Folk* (1903).

In 1905 Du Bois and his associates founded the **Niagara movement**. The group worked to promote "manhood rights" (equal rights) for African Americans. Although the movement soon broke up, the **National Association for the Advancement of Colored People (NAACP)**, founded 1909, was heir to many of the ideas of the Niagara Movement.

Du Bois was a leader in the NAACP from the group's beginning. He founded its monthly magazine, *The Crisis*, which he edited until 1934. The publication became a forum for his views on race and politics.

Selected Writings of W. E. B. Du Bois

The Souls of Black Folk
(1903), essays

The Negro
(1915), study of African peoples around the world

Darkwater: Voices from Within the Veil
(1920), essays

Dark Princess
(1928), novel about overthrowing European colonialism

Black Reconstruction in America
(1934), reevaluation of the role of freedmen in the South following the Civil War (1861–65)

Africa with Black Folk: Then and Now
(1939), expansion and revision of *The Negro* (1915)

After **World War I** (1914–18) Du Bois wanted to change the course of African colonialism, to undo the settlement and domination of Africa by European countries. But his views (called Pan-Africanism) ran against those of leader **Marcus Garvey** (1887–1940), who was hailed by his many followers as "the black Moses," a redeemer. Such high-profile conflicts followed Du Bois the rest of his life.

In 1926 he visited the Soviet Union. Du Bois proudly declared his agreement with the country's socialism—the government there was working to own all industry and agriculture. The effort was viewed by those who supported it as a benefit to all people in the nation. In the United States, Du Bois's socialist outlook stirred controversy. In conflict with the NAACPs leaders, in 1934 he resigned as editor of *The Crisis* and returned to Atlanta University. After teaching and writing for the next ten years, in 1944 Du Bois was asked by the university to leave. He had clashed with the school's administrators.

The NAACP again hired Du Bois, who coordinated research projects for the group. But Du Bois's politics continued to become more radical—too radical for the organization. He was fired in 1948. Joining various left-wing political organizations, over the next ten years Du Bois continued to publish his ideas. But he had lost the attention of most of the black community. He wrote that "the colored children ceased to hear my name." His views also made him the target of the U.S. government, which labeled one of his organizations "subversive" (secretive and destructive).

Beginning in 1958 Du Bois traveled extensively outside the United States, visiting the Soviet Union and China (both countries where socialism was at work). In 1961, now a member of the U.S. Communist Party (a political party that promotes socialist ideas), he settled in the African country of Ghana. He lived there with his second wife, **Shirley Graham Du Bois** (a writer and political activist) until his death in 1963. He had denounced his U.S. citizenship earlier that year.

Dumas, Henry Lee

WRITER
July 20, 1934–May 23, 1968

Born in Sweet Home, Arkansas, writer Henry Dumas moved to New York City at the age of ten. He served in the U.S. Air Force from 1953 until 1957 and attended Rutgers University (New Brunswick, New Jersey) from 1958 to 1965, during which time he became increasingly active in the **Civil Rights movement.** For the next few years he worked in New York as a social worker (1965-66); in Ohio as an educational administrator (1967); and in Illinois as a teacher and counselor (1967-68).

From 1953 to 1968 Dumas was active in the editing, publishing, and distribution of several small magazines. Although he contributed poetry and short stories to these publications and others, Dumas did not live to see his work published in book form. While standing on the 125th Street station railroad platform in Harlem, New York, on May 23, 1968, Dumas was shot and killed under suspicious circumstances by a transit police officer.

Dumas's works were collected and edited by Eugene B. Redmond, a former colleague at Southern Illinois University. They include *Poetry for My People* (1970; reprinted as *Play Ebony, Play Ivory*, 1974); *Ark of Bones, and Other Stories* (1970); *Rope of Wind and Other Stories* (1979); a collection of short fiction, *Goodbye Sweetwater* (1988); and a volume of poetry, *Knees of a Natural Man* (1988). Many of Dumas's poems and stories focus on contemporary black experience in the South during the Civil Rights movement.

Dunbar, Paul Laurence

WRITER
June 27, 1872–February 9, 1906

Paul Laurence Dunbar, the child of former slaves, was the first African-American writer to attain widespread fame. Born and raised in Dayton, Ohio, he showed early signs of literary ambition, editing his high school newspaper and launching a small newspaper of his own. After graduation he worked as an elevator operator; but he also became increasingly dedicated to literature, especially to poetry. He published his first book of poetry, *Oak and Ivy*, in 1892. But Dunbar achieved real fame in 1896, when an expanded and revised collection, *Majors and Minors*, came to the attention of the prominent American writer William Dean Howells (1837–1920). Howells saw to

DUNBAR'S "THE POET AND HIS SONG"

A SONG is but a little thing,
And yet what joy it is to sing!
In hours of toil it gives me zest,
And when at eve I long for rest;
When cows come home along the bars,
And in the fold I hear the bell,
As Night, the shepherd, herds
his stars, I sing my song, and
all is well.

There are no ears to hear my lays,
No lips to lift a word of praise;
But still, with faith unfaltering,
I live and laugh and love and sing.
What matters yon unheeding
throng? They cannot feel my
spirit's spell, Since life is
sweet and love is long, I sing
my song, and all is well.

My days are never days of ease;
I till my ground and prune my
trees. When ripened gold is
all the plain,
I put my sickle to the grain.
I labor hard, and toil and
sweat, While others dream
within the dell; But even
while my brow is wet,
I sing my song, and all is
well.

Sometimes the sun, unkindly hot,
My garden makes a desert
spot; Sometimes a blight upon the tree
Takes all my fruit away from me;
And then with throes of
bitter pain Rebellious
passions rise and swell;
But—life is more than fruit or
grain, And so I sing, and all is
well.

Paul Laurence Dunbar, *Lyrics of Lowly Life*, (Dodd, Mead, & Co, 1896).

it that a larger volume, *Lyrics of Lowly Life*, was published that same year. It was the first of five major collections to be published during Dunbar's lifetime.

Poet Paul Laurence Dunbar (Courtesy of the Library of Congress)

What brought Dunbar fame was that much of his verse was written in black dialect (language) and created a sentimental portrait of African-American folklife in the pre–**Civil War** South. The publication of his work, together with public readings of it throughout the United States and abroad, made Dunbar among the most popular poets in the United States at the turn of the twentieth century. As his fame grew, dialect poetry began to appear frequently in black newspapers and magazines, and few collections of African-American poetry over the next two decades lacked at least some examples of dialect verse. Many were dominated by it.

Dunbar was never entirely comfortable with his fame. Much of his poetry was in standard English, and he believed this was his most important work. Much of this verse is in fact significant, addressing such issues as southern racial injustice and violence, and breaking from the traditional politeness that dominated African-American poetry.

Dunbar's other literary work included several novels, collections of stories, and even some writing for the theater. Although much of it influenced later African-American writers, it never received much public notice. It was only his dialect poetry that critics praised during Dunbar's lifetime. Dunbar's frustration with this fact spilled over into a personal life marked by difficulties, including problems in his marriage to the talented writer **Alice Dunbar-Nelson** (1875–1935) and the alcoholism and chronic ill health, culminating in tuberculosis, that led to his early death.

Dunbar-Nelson, Alice

WRITER, TEACHER, ACTIVIST
July 19, 1875–September 18, 1935

Writer and activist Alice Dunbar-Nelson was born Alice Ruth Moore in New Orleans, Louisiana. Her father never lived with the family, and her mother supported them as a seamstress. After attending public schools, Dunbar-Nelson graduated from the teachers' training program at Straight College (now Dillard University) in New Orleans in 1892. In 1895 *Violets and Other Tales*, her first collection of stories, essays, and poetry, was published.

In 1897 Dunbar-Nelson moved to New York City, where she taught public school in Brooklyn and helped to found a girls' school in Harlem. On March 8, 1898, she married the poet **Paul Laurence Dunbar** (1872-1906) and moved to Washington, D.C., where he lived. Their romance had been conducted through letters; he first wrote to her after seeing her picture alongside one of her poems in a magazine. At their first meeting they agreed to marry.

Although the couple had a stormy marriage, it helped Dunbar-Nelson's literary career. In 1899 her second collection, *The Goodness of St. Roque*, was published as a companion book to her husband's *Poems of Cabin and Field*. The couple separated in 1902, and Dunbar-Nelson moved to Delaware, where she taught English at the Howard High School. A second marriage to a fellow teacher also failed, and in 1916 Dunbar-Nelson married Robert J. Nelson, a journalist, with whom she remained until her death in 1935.

Dunbar-Nelson's writings, published continually throughout her life, displayed a wide variety of interests, including literary criticism, black education and history, and the Afro-American oral tradition. Dunbar-Nelson also wrote columns for two newspapers. She was a tireless advocate for the rights of women and blacks; in fact, in 1920 she lost her job at Howard High School because of her political activity. After leaving Howard High, Dunbar-Nelson promptly founded the Industrial School for Colored Girls in Marshalltown, Delaware, which she directed from 1924 to 1928. Her political activism continued throughout her lifetime.

Duncan, Robert Todd ▪▪▪

CONCERT SINGER
February 12, 1903–February 28, 1998

Baritone Robert Todd Duncan was the first black male to sing with a major American opera company. Born in Danville, Kentucky, Duncan was raised in Indianapolis, Indiana, where he attended Butler University, earning his undergraduate degree. Awarded his master's degree from Columbia University Teachers College in New York, he began teaching music at the college level in 1925. From 1931 to 1945 he was head of the music department at **Howard University** (Washington, D.C.).

Duncan is known best for singing the part of Porgy in American composer George Gershwin's (1898–1937) *Porgy and Bess*. Credited with creating the standard for the role, he sang it more than eighteen hundred times between its 1935 debut and 1944. In 1945 he sang with the New York City Opera, becoming the first African-American male singer to perform with a major U.S. opera company. Duncan also gave recitals (solo concerts), performing more than two thousand times internationally between 1940 and 1965, when he retired. Duncan received numerous awards during his lifetime.

Duncanson, Robert S. ▪▪▪

PAINTER
1821–December 21, 1872

Robert S. Duncanson progressed from a housepainter to an internationally known artist. He was one of the first African Americans to enter the predominantly Anglo-European art world, and one of the first to use the landscape as an expression of cultural identity. By 1841 Duncanson had moved to Cincinnati, Ohio, to learn the art of painting. Throughout the 1840s he worked painting portraits, historical subjects, and still lifes (paintings of nonmoving objects, such as a bowl of fruit).

While working in Detroit, Duncanson received a commission (or pay) to paint a landscape. This launched Duncanson's career and established him in a lifelong relationship with abolitionist (those who opposed **slavery**) arts supporters. In 1853 he became the first African-American artist to tour Europe with his art when a patron sponsored his journey. Upon his return, Duncanson became the principal landscape painter in the Ohio River Valley.

In the months preceding the **Civil War** (1861–65), Duncanson created the largest easel painting of his career, portraying the coming conflict. Deeply troubled by the war, Duncanson exiled himself from the United States and traveled to Canada in 1863, where he was warmly received. He remained there for two years and helped found a national landscape-painting school. He then toured the British Isles, where he was actively supported by the British upper class.

Upon his return to Cincinnati in 1866, Duncanson began a series of Scottish landscapes. In his final years he suffered from dementia (mental

Robert Duncanson: Selected Paintings

The Cliff Mine, Lake Superior
(1848)

Blue Hole, Flood Waters, Little Miami River
(1851)

Landscape with Rainbow
(1859)

The Land of the Lotus Eaters
(1861)

Ellen's Isle, Loch Katrine
(1870)

deterioration, or loss of sanity), perhaps caused by lead poisoning, which led him to believe that he was possessed by the spirit of a master painter. His illness, combined with the pressures of racial oppression and his lofty artistic ambitions, proved too great for the artist to manage; he collapsed while hanging an exhibition in October 1872, dying shortly thereafter.

Dunham, Katherine

CHOREOGRAPHER, DANCER
June 22, 1909–

A pioneer in the field of black dance, Chicago-born dancer and choreographer (dance composer) Katherine Dunham introduced audiences to authentic Caribbean dance and rhythms in popular American productions. She studied dance and anthropology at the University of Chicago (bachelor's degree in social anthropology, 1936) and at Northwestern University in Illinois (master's degree, 1947).

Dunham's research in the West Indies greatly affected her personal and professional focus. She would later live part-time in Haiti and become a priestess in the voodoo religion (a **religion** derived from African religions and ancestor worship, practiced mostly in Haiti). During 1937 Dunham founded the Negro Dance Group and premiered "Haitian Suite" in New York City. The choreography was taken from *L'Ag'Ya*, a longer work based on a folktale from the West Indian island of Martinique.

Dunham moved to New York City in 1939, where her production *Tropics and Le Jazz Hot: From Haiti to Harlem* was a big hit. In 1940 Dunham and her company appeared in the black Broadway musical, *Cabin in the Sky*, staged by the famous choreographer George Balanchine.

Beginning in the 1940s, the Katherine Dunham Dance Company appeared on Broadway and toured throughout the United States, Mexico, Latin America, and Europe. In Europe, Dunham was recognized as a serious anthropologist and scholar and admired as a glamorous beauty.

During the 1940s and 1950s Dunham fought segregation in hotels, restaurants, and theaters by filing lawsuits and criticizing these places publicly. In Hollywood she refused to sign a big contract when the producer said she would have to replace some of her company's darker-skinned members.

Dunham choreographed more than ninety individual dances and produced five revues (shows), including the critically acclaimed *Bal Negre* (1946). Toward the end of the 1950s, however, Dunham was forced to disband her company because of financial problems and a crippling knee condition.

Dunham operated two schools, the Dunham School of Dance and Theater in Manhattan (beginning in 1945) and the Performing Arts Training Center in East St. Louis, Illinois (beginning in 1967), a school that served children and senior citizens (now the Katherine Dunham Center for the Performing Arts).

In 1992, at the age of eighty-two, Dunham made news when she underwent a forty-seven-day fast to protest the deportation (sending home) of Haitian boat refugees by the United States. At the time of her ninetieth

birthday, a film and an educational video about the legendary dancer went unfinished owing to a lack of funding.

Du Sable, Jean Baptiste Pointe

FOUNDER OF CHICAGO
c. 1750–1818

As its first permanent non–American Indian resident, Jean Baptiste Pointe Du Sable is honored as the founder of Chicago. Du Sable (also spelled Au Sable, De Sable, and De Saible) was probably born in what is now the West Indian country of Haiti to an African mother and a French father. He was educated in Paris before working as a seaman on his father's ships.

How Du Sable got to North America is not known. By 1779 he had traveled to the Chicago River area and established several trading posts. One was at the mouth of the river, at a place called "Checagou" by local Indians. While at his post near modern-day Peoria, Illinois, his support of the Americans during the **American Revolution** (1775–83) led to his arrest by British authorities, who charged him with being a spy. After Du Sable was released the following year, the British used him as a supplier and hired him to manage their trading post.

In 1784, after the British left the region, Du Sable returned to Checagou. He built a cabin, which was to be the first house ever built in Chicago. He decorated it with French furniture and twenty-plus paintings. He lived in the region for sixteen years and married a Native-American woman from the Potawotomi tribe, with whom he had two children.

In 1800, after an unsuccessful try at being elected chief of the Potawotomi, Du Sable sold his business and property for about $1,200 and moved back to Peoria. Despite owning eight hundred acres there, he was bankrupt by 1814. Oddly enough, his former land holdings in Chicago are now worth more than $1 billion dollars.

Du Sable moved to St. Charles, Missouri, where he died in poverty in 1818. His grave in St. Charles was discovered in 1991. In 1961 the Du Sable Museum of African-American History opened, and it is now the oldest private nonprofit black museum in America. In 1987 Du Sable appeared on a postage stamp.

Ebony Magazine

Ebony Magazine was founded in 1945 and has grown to be the most widely circulated African-American periodical. It was the first magazine to highlight the achievements of blacks, rather than the negative effects of racism.

The idea for *Ebony Magazine* came from a few staff members who convinced publisher John H. Johnson to create a publication that displayed the positive developments within the African-American community. Johnson funded the idea and decided to include several photos on glossy paper, a style that had made Life magazine popular. *Ebony* gets its name from the beautiful, strong black wood. Johnson premiered the magazine in 1945 with the pledge that he would accept no advertising money until circulation reached 100,000.

After only one year, the goal was reached, and advertising money began filtering in. By 1947 circulation reached over 300,000; however, the publication began struggling financially. But as white businesses began to realize that they could profit from blacks as well as whites, they began advertising in black publications. The increased revenue from white advertisers helped relieve the magazine's financial problems, and the magazine began to grow again.

Some have been critical of *Ebony* over the years because it has focused on wealthy blacks and avoided political involvement. *Ebony* responded by

taking a more active position during the **Civil Rights movement** and including sections for the average person, such as cooking and health. Although several publications have attempted to rival *Ebony*, it remains the leading black publication and has branched out to other audiences with *Ebony Man* and *Ebony Fashion Fair*. In the early 1990s the circulation of *Ebony* was approximately 1.9 million, and the magazine appeared in forty different countries. To learn more about *Ebony Magazine*, visit their Web site at http://www.ebony.com.

Eckstine, William Clarence "Billy"

SINGER, BANDLEADER
July 8, 1914–March 8, 1993

Singer and bandleader Billy Eckstine worked with well-known African-American musicians during his career and became a sex symbol for black as well as white audiences. He was born in Pittsburgh, Pennsylvania, and moved several times in his childhood. He later attended the St. Paul Normal and Industrial School in Lawrenceville, Virginia, and **Howard University** in Washington, D.C. Eckstine began his career in show business as a singer and nightclub emcee (announcer) in Detroit, Michigan, and Chicago, Illinois. In 1939 he was hired as the main vocalist for the big band of **Earl "Fatha" Hines** (1903–1983). While with Hines, he introduced jazz greats **Dizzy Gillespie** (1917–1993), **Charlie Parker** (1920–1955), and **Sarah Vaughan** (1924–1990) to the Hines band. After a few hit recordings, Eckstine left Hines in 1943.

In 1944 Eckstine organized his own big band, which included many up-and-coming bebop (a peppy type of jazz) musicians, such as **Miles Davis** (1926–1991), Charlie Parker, Dexter Gordon (1923–1990), and **Art Blakey** (1919–1990). When he was obliged to abandon the band in 1947 for financial reasons, he became a solo singer. His smooth baritone was particularly well suited for ballads. He was one of the first black singers to transcend the race barrier and to become a national sex symbol.

Eckstine spent the next several decades as a performer in nightclubs, often accompanied by pianist Bobby Tucker. He also appeared in several films as "Mr. B," as he was widely known. He occasionally played the trumpet but was primarily known as a singer. He influenced several generations of African-American singers, including Arthur Prysock (1918–1999) and Lou Rawls (1936–). He died in Pittsburgh in 1993.

Billy Eckstine:
Selected Works

Jelly, Jelly
(1940; song)

Skylark
(1942; song)

Skirts Ahoy
(1953; film)

Let's Do It Again
(1975; film)

Jo Jo Dancer: Your Life Is Calling
(1986; film)

Economics

After the **Civil War** (1861–65), four million slaves were freed, joining one-half million free blacks in the North. Despite the federal government's intent, the nation's black population did not have the full rights of citizenship. Those rights would not be secured for many decades, until the height of the **Civil Rights movement** (during the late 1950s and 1960s). Without full voting rights and initially without property (which slaves had been forbidden by law to possess), African Americans struggled to earn a living, provide for their families, and make the transition to freedom.

The Post–Civil War Era

During **Reconstruction** (1865–77), the twelve-year period of rebuilding that followed the Civil War, the predominant occupation of blacks in the South was **sharecropping** or share-tenancy. In these farming systems, which were fraught with problems, African Americans planted, tended fields, and harvested crops on the promise that they would earn a share of the proceeds from the market sale of the crops.

In the late 1800s and early 1900s there was not significant movement by black people from one region of the United States to another. There were, of course, exceptions. After the Civil War, some African Americans in the South moved to the North where they mostly found service jobs in cities. They worked as waiters and maids in hotels, as servants in homes, and as clothes cleaners in laundries. A few were able to set up their own businesses, which catered to the black community. Because of persistent racism, they were usually unable to gain white customers.

Some blacks from the South seized the opportunity to gain government lands in the West, which was being opened up for settlement. Most were farmers who planted their fields and took their crops to market in the same way as white farmers. All growers were subject to poor weather conditions, however, which could ruin crops, and to changes in the marketplace, which could cause the prices paid for crops to drop.

The War Era

When the United States entered **World War I** (1914–18) in 1917, the military pulled thousands of men from their jobs and sent them into battle. At the same time, the war had caused a stop in the flow of immigrants from Europe to the United States. These conditions resulted in a shortage of workers in cities. Seeing the opportunity to secure jobs previously not open to them, many southern blacks moved to the North, where they found factory and service jobs. An estimated 525,000 African Americans migrated to the urban North between 1910 and 1920.

When the war ended, manufacturers continued to hire black workers to fill the many jobs that were created by growth. The automobile industry and its related businesses, such as steel and rubber, were flourishing. Furthermore, the U.S. population, boosted by immigration (which had by now resumed), continued to grow. The increased population put great demands on manufacturers to produce enough finished goods. Although job discrimination continued, for the first time in the nation's history, a sizable number of African Americans were employed outside of agriculture. Black populations of northern cities, such as Detroit, Michigan, Chicago, Illinois, and New York, swelled.

The movement to northern cities was halted by the **Great Depression** (1929–39), which swept the nation and hit the black population especially hard. Hundreds of banks and businesses failed, putting one in four Americans out of work. To ease the situation, government programs were created to put people back to work. But these same programs required businesses to pay a minimum wage to their employees. With racism still prevalent, this meant that some black workers, who were paid less than white workers, were forced to give up their jobs. The prevailing feeling among employers was that as long as they were required by law to pay a certain wage, they were going to pay it to white workers.

World War II (1939–45) lifted the nation out of its long economic depression. Americans who did not go off to war went to work. The defense industry, those manufacturers producing goods for the military, was required by law to integrate its workforce. As a result, African Americans, too, went back to work.

Discrimination at Work

The first decades of the 1900s were active years for organized labor in the United States. Unions, groups of workers joined together to safeguard their interests, actively signed up new members. They also staged demonstrations to increase public support for such issues as the minimum wage and a limited (usually eight-hour) workday. But many unions silently or outrightly barred black workers from joining. Some African Americans formed their own labor organizations to protect their rights as workers.

The combined effects of barring blacks from labor unions and discriminating against them in the workplace, which caused higher-paying jobs to go to white workers, kept black men and women at work for much lower wages than their white counterparts. Even educated black people found it difficult to secure work in their chosen field. Many were underemployed, meaning they worked in jobs that did not require their level of qualification.

These conditions began a terrible and, so far, lasting cycle in the black community. Youths observed adults working as hard as whites but for not as much money. Young African Americans also saw that those in their community who had graduated from high school or college often could not find suitable work. In the decades to come, this caused school dropout rates to soar. In turn, many black workers were then not prepared to secure good jobs in a workplace that increasingly demanded educated workers, at least through the high school level.

The Civil Rights Era

By the 1960s the reformers of the Civil Rights movement had made strides in securing the full rights of citizenship for black people. With black voters going to the polls in greater numbers, more black public officials were elected. These men and women worked for change on every level—local, state, and national. The Civil Rights Act of 1964, which was signed by President Lyndon Johnson (1908–1973; president 1963–68), included the establishment of the Equal Employment Opportunity Commission (EEOC). The EEOC has worked since to enforce a policy of nondiscrimination in the American workplace.

Government and increased awareness caused most employers to open their doors to African-American workers. On-the-job training programs were desegregated. There still were, and are today, exceptions. Some industries openly or quietly kept blacks out altogether, or at least out of positions of authority. Nevertheless, African Americans benefited from strong laws and a strong economy between 1963 and 1973. A black middle class emerged.

But many black workers found they were the victims of a more subtle form of racism. Although more jobs were opened to them, African Americans simply were not paid as much for the same work as their white counterparts. The nation has continued to struggle with this issue in the decades since.

Economic Recession

Just as the black community benefited from the booming economy of the 1960s, it was affected by the downturn of the 1970s. Between 1973 and 1975 oil and gas shortages caused fuel prices to soar. Since industry is dependent on these fuels, manufacturers' costs rose sharply. In turn, the prices consumers paid for goods rose. Americans were then unable to buy as much with their dollar, decreasing the demand for goods. In response, industry cut back production and cut jobs. The auto industry was hard hit and laid off many workers, among them African Americans. At the same time, European and Japanese economies had fully recovered from World War II (1939–45) losses and reparations (payment of damages). Foreign nations were exporting (shipping) their goods to the United States, where the products sold for a lower price than the same American products.

These circumstances produced the worst economic recession (slump) in the United States in the postwar era. During the 1980s poverty rates (the number of poor people) rose. By 1992 the poverty rate for blacks was 33 percent; for whites it was just under 12 percent.

Economic Recovery

The economy recovered after 1993. By the end of the 1990s, the United States was experiencing its strongest economy ever. Unemployment dropped steadily from about 7 percent in 1993 to 4 percent in 2000. Although African Americans benefited from overall prosperity, problems persisted. On the whole, black workers continued to earn less than their white peers. According to the U.S. Bureau of Labor Statistics, in 2000 the median (middle) earnings for full-time, white male workers was $672 per week; for white women it was $497 per week; for black men it was $496 per week; and for black women it was $422 per week.

With many African-American households headed by a single mother, this last statistic posed a serious threat to the well-being of the black community. In fact, in 2000 fewer black men than black women were in the workforce (5.9 million black men as opposed to 6.4 million black women). In 1998 the U.S. Census Bureau estimated that about 23 percent of all black families in the nation were living in poverty (compared with 8 percent of white families). Of the black families that were living in poverty, more than 40 percent of the households were headed by a woman. For the same year, the statistics continued to show that on the whole the nation's minorities continued to lived in poverty (26 percent of blacks compared with 10.5 percent of whites lived in poverty in 1998). While African Americans had made economic gains over the past hundred years, there was still progress to be made. (*See also* **Affirmative Action**.)

Edelman, Marian Wright

LAWYER, COMMUNITY ACTIVIST
June 6, 1939–

Marian Wright Edelman (AP/Wide World Photos. Reproduced by permission)

Born in 1939 in South Carolina, Marian Wright Edelman has devoted her life to helping children and their families who are in need. In 1973 she started the Children's Defense Fund (CDF), a group that helps children receive an education and proper health care. Because of her work with CDF, Edelman is now a member of the National Women's Hall of Fame.

Edelman graduated first in her class at **Spelman College** (Atlanta, Georgia). She decided to become a lawyer in order to help in the fight for civil rights. Edelman went to Yale University (New Haven, Connecticut) Law School on a scholarship and later became the first black woman in Mississippi to pass the bar (law) exam, a requirement to practice law. In 1968 she headed the **National Association for the Advancement of Colored People**'s Legal Defense and Education fund in Mississippi.

Edelman has received numerous honors and awards for her contributions to child welfare, women's rights, and civil rights, including the MacArthur Foundation Prize Fellowship (1985) and the Albert Schweitzer Humanitarian Prize from Johns Hopkins University. In August 2000 President Bill Clinton bestowed on Edelman the nation's highest civilian honor—the Presidential Medal of Freedom.

Edelman is also the author of several books, the most famous of which is *The Measure of Our Success*.

Edmondson, William

SCULPTOR
c. 1870–1951

Sculptor William Edmondson was untrained in sculpting, yet he created work that blended **folk art**, fine art, and African-American mythology. Edmondson was born in Tennessee to parents who were former slaves. Before 1908 he worked for the railroad; between 1908 and 1931 he was a custodian for the Women's Hospital in Nashville. The hospital closed in 1931 and Edmondson lost his job; shortly thereafter, he began sculpting. He claimed to be inspired by the voice of God, first to cut tombstones and later to carve animals, human figures, angels, and crucifixions. Edmondson, who had arthritis, fashioned chisels out of railroad spikes and used cast-off limestone (a type of rock often used in building) for his sculptures.

Edmondson and his work were discovered in 1937 by the photographer Louise Dahl-Wolfe, who arranged the same year for an exhibition of his work at New York's Museum of Modern Art–the first solo exhibition of the work of a black artist at the museum. The Works Progress Administration (a program established during the **Great Depression** to create jobs) commissioned him (paid him) to do two projects between 1939 and 1941. Edmondson's sculpture was shown in several more exhibitions before he died in Nashville in 1951. His work has since been displayed at the Tennessee State Museum, the La Jolla Museum of Contemporary Arts in California, the Hirshhorn Museum and Sculpture Garden in Washington, D.C., and the Musée du Jeu de Paume (tennis museum) in Paris.

Edmondson's mastery of abstract (reflecting the qualities or nature of something but not its outer appearance as would be seen in a photograph) sculptural forms enabled him to bypass the boundary between folk and fine art and gave his work a remarkably modern look. The geometric lines that characterize the faces of his figures give them a masklike quality. The animal forms he created often echo images found in African and African-American mythology and folktales. Although Edmondson was an untrained, nonprofessional artist, his style bears striking resemblances to contemporary art.

Education

The history of the education of African Americans is a history of the struggle for civil rights. Since colonial times, when most blacks were denied schooling, black people have fought for the right to be educated. While great advances were made during the 1900s, problems remain today.

The Antebellum South

In the South before the **Civil War** (1861–65), called the antebellum period, most masters made sure their slaves did not learn to read or write. White people feared that these skills would only help blacks organize and rise up against **slavery**. Therefore, most blacks living in the South before 1865 were illiterate, unable to read or write.

There were exceptions. An estimated 10 percent of blacks living in the South before **abolition** were literate. But they had acquired these skills informally—they had learned on their own, had received lessons from a sympathetic white person, or had been taught by missionaries. (Missionaries believed that in order to convert slaves to Christianity it was necessary to teach them to read the Bible.)

Nevertheless, the prevailing sentiment among whites in the South was to deny slaves any kind of education. By the time the Civil War began in 1861, this view had been made formal by state laws. Slave rebellions had inspired lawmakers to ban literacy among slaves. It was against the law for anyone to teach a black person to read or write. Many blacks who had gained these skills hid them. And it was not until 1865, after the Civil War, that it was discovered that hundreds of schools had already been established by black slaves. Although informal, these schools had operated secretly, teaching basic skills.

Schools for Free Blacks

Before 1860 formal education (meaning education received in established schools) was primarily open only to free blacks, who made up just 5 percent of the black population in the United States. Religious groups, abolitionist societies, and black reformers set up private schools in many cities, including New York, Boston, Massachusetts, and Philadelphia, Pennsylvania. But independent schools for black children faced serious problems. Most lacked funds and some met with violence from white people who opposed the education of blacks.

By 1850 reformers were struggling to integrate the public schools in the North. Since schools were funded by the government, many felt they should be open to black and white children alike. But most schools were segregated—separate schools had been set up for black students. Boston was the setting for a highly publicized battle for school integration. The city's public schools finally opened their doors to both white and black students in 1855, after a ten-year struggle.

After Emancipation

After the abolition of slavery in 1865, black people and reform-minded whites fully understood that for free blacks to become full members of society, it was necessary for them to be educated. The desire to learn was so strong among blacks that educator **Booker T. Washington** (c. 1856-1915) described it as "a whole race trying to go to school."

With federal government funding, by 1866 the percentage of former slaves attending schools in the South was equal to that of blacks attending schools in the North. By then there were nearly one thousand schools and more than fourteen hundred teachers for blacks in the South. While at first most teachers in the South's black schools were white women from the North, by 1900 most were African American.

The American Missionary Association (AMA), affiliated with the Congregational Church, also played an important role in black education. The AMA supported freedmen's schools and established its own network of schools in the South during Reconstruction, the period of rebuilding that followed the Civil War. Northern missionaries taught students to read and write; gave instruction in subjects such as Latin, history, geography, and science; and instilled in students the value of hard work and self-control. While the missionaries lacked an understanding of their students' cultural background, they took great risks to teach black students. Conditions in the South were generally poor, and many whites were openly hostile to people from the North.

Progress and Problems of the Early Twentieth Century

By 1900 the literacy rates among blacks in the South had risen to about 33 percent. The improvement was encouraging to educators, but there was still a long way to go. Efforts were frustrated by lack of government funds. Unable to afford good talent, black schools were forced to hire poorly trained or inexperienced teachers. Some classrooms were without books, maps, and other instructional tools. Schools often operated for just a few months a year, closing their doors when the money ran out. Worse, children in rural areas of the South were beyond the reach of the system since no schools had been established for blacks in remote areas. Only 36 percent of black children in the South attended school in 1900.

March on Washington protesting school segregation (Courtesy of the National Archives and Records Administration)

To address the problems of the public system, some communities set up their own primary education system. These elementary schools were usually supported by white charitable organizations or black community members themselves. Between 1913 and 1935 an estimated 17 percent of the total costs for school construction in the South was provided by black people. As a result, by the 1930s the majority of African-American children had access to an elementary school.

The Debate over Secondary Schools

State governments paid little attention to funding black schools beyond the elementary school level. This was caused by persistent discrimination. While most white people came to accept that black students needed to learn basic skills, they were unwilling to support secondary schools and colleges, where African Americans might be trained to work in jobs that were traditionally held by whites. As a result, most black public high schools in the South were not built until after 1920.

Furthermore, most black high schools (both public and private) were not academic schools, but rather vocational "common" schools, where students were trained to become laborers or work in other traditionally black jobs such as farming and service jobs. Common schools, modeled on Booker T. Washington's **Tuskegee Institute** (1881), were the center of a great debate. While supporters believed it was most important for young blacks to learn a trade, critics of the common schools charged that they pigeonholed graduates, who would be limited to work only in jobs for which they had been specifically trained.

The debate quieted during the severe economic downturn of the **Great Depression** (1929–39). Many black laborers lost their jobs only to be replaced by white workers who, desperate for employment, were now willing to work in menial (low) positions. By 1940 most common schools had converted to a standard high school curriculum (course work).

Desegregation Begins

In the 1920s blacks began migrating in great numbers from the rural South to cities in the North. In 1910 a full 90 percent of African Americans lived in the South; but by 1970, this figure had dropped to just over 50 percent. The population shift changed almost every aspect of African-American life, including education. In seven northern states (Illinois, Massachusetts, Nevada, New Jersey, New York, Ohio, and Pennsylvania), schools had already been desegregated by 1910. Consequently, blacks who relocated to these states found—and took advantage of—greater opportunities for education. By 1940 the percentage of black students (between the ages of five and twenty) who were attending school was about 64 percent; thirty years earlier it was just 44 percent.

However, the public school systems in most states remained segregated. In compliance with the 1896 court case of ***Plessy v. Ferguson,*** which upheld the law of "separate but equal" schools, many state and local governments had established separate schools for black students. The unfairness of this system was clear to the black community. Their school buildings were crowded and in poor condition, teachers were not paid as well as in white schools, and they lacked educational materials.

In May 1954 the policy of providing black students with separate facilities was successfully challenged by the Legal Defense and Educational Fund of the **National Association for the Advancement of Colored People (NAACP).** The U.S. Supreme Court ruled in the case of ***Brown v. the Board of Education of Topeka, Kansas*** that "in the field of education the doctrine [rule] of separate but equal has no place." The next year, American schools were ordered to desegregate "with all deliberate speed."

But the much of the white community was reluctant, if not completely unwilling, to integrate schools. For example, in 1957 the governor of Arkansas used the National Guard to forcibly prevent desegregation in the Little Rock schools. The federal government stepped in, passing the Civil Rights Acts of 1957 and of 1964. These laws promised investigation into cases where blacks were denied equal rights and helped districts to desegregate schools.

Persistent problems

Many schools still were not desegregated. Some systems tried to redraw the boundaries of their districts to create student bodies with a mix of black and white students. But settlement patterns in the North had clustered blacks into city neighborhoods and whites into suburbs. Some communities tried to bus students from one district to another, but this method met with great opposition from whites, particularly in South Boston, where protests in 1974–75 turned violent. Eventually, some cities, such as Indianapolis (Indiana), solved the problem by consolidating the city school district with those districts of the surrounding suburbs or county.

Poor inner-city, predominantly black schools remain a problem in many communities. Educators, parents, activists, and government officials struggle with how to correct the situation. Proposed solutions include (1) setting up "magnet schools" in inner cities, where the curriculum is so advanced that suburban (white) parents are willing to send their children outside their district; (2) allowing community control of local schools so that parents work with school administrators and teachers to decide school organization, curriculum, and staffing; and (3) providing for school choice, or giving parents vouchers (credits) that they can use to pay for their child's education in a private school of their choosing. Each solution has advantages and disadvantages.

Schools also struggle with how to revise their courses and textbooks to embrace and foster the heritage of not only a large and growing African-American population but also a growing Latino population. Until the late 1900s, most students were taught history and culture from a European perspective. The multicultural approach to teaching has worked to include the perspectives of other ethnic traditions, including the Afro-centric.

Challenges for Tomorrow

Today there is still much progress to be made. The emphasis has shifted to equality in education. In other words, the goal is to ensure that blacks and other minority groups receive an education that is on a level with that of white students. Those who have worked throughout history and activists who are working now to bring about reforms in public education have understood that without the benefit of excellent schooling, black graduates will be unprepared to take their places as workers in an economy that is always changing. (*See also* **Colleges and Universities; Economics.**)

Edwards, Melvin

SCULPTOR
May 4, 1937–

Mel Edwards's sculpture effectively blends political and social statements in a classical art form. Edwards was born in Texas in 1937 and received a bachelor of fine arts degree from the University of Southern California in 1965. Two years later, Edwards moved to New York City, and from 1968 to 1971 he worked on public art projects in Harlem with artists known as the Smokehouse Group. In 1972 Edwards joined the faculty at the art department at Rutgers University in New Jersey, and in 1980 he became a professor at the Mason Gross School of Creative and Performing Arts at Rutgers University.

Edwards employs African or African-American themes in his work. In the late 1960s he began using simplified geometric forms in his large-scale sculpture. He tells a story with each piece so that aspects of his work are filled with content, evoking personal memories from his life. He also has used half-circles and curves to describe various body parts. Edwards's travels in Africa have influenced his large-scale steel sculpture.

Slavery is a repeated theme in Edwards's work. In his work during the 1960s, he frequently used chains, often suspended in loops from wires set in the ceiling. Such chains are used in his collective works *Lynch Fragments* (1963–67), which represent specific historical incidents. The works feature intense collections of found objects (discarded objects or objects come across by accident) such as nuts, bolts, and metal tools used in forms that evoke the violence and brutality of the **lynching** of African Americans in the United States. In Edwards's hands, however, this sculptural statement stands out for its successful blending of formal technique with political and social commentary.

Edwards has taught art history, drawing, and sculpture at Rutgers University since 1977. He has received many awards, and his work has been featured in solo exhibitions at many museums, including the Santa Barbara (California) Museum of Art (1965); the Walker Art Center in Minneapolis, Minnesota (1968); the Whitney Museum of American Art in (1970); the Studio Museum in Harlem, New York (1978); the Sculpture Center Gallery, New York (1982); and the Oklahoma City Art Museum (1991). His first commercial show was held in 1990 in New York.

Selected Sculptures: Melvin Edwards

Lynch Fragments
(1963–67)

Chains
(1964)

Curtain for William and Peter
(1970)

Rockers
(1970)

Homage to Coco
(1970)

Elders, M. Jocelyn Jones

SURGEON GENERAL
August 13, 1933–

M. Jocelyn Jones Elders was a medical doctor who became the first black woman to be named surgeon general of the United States (1993–94). Although her involvement in politics was brief, she left a lasting impression because of her unwavering commitment to her beliefs.

Born in Schaal, Arkansas, Elders earned a bachelor's degree from Philander Smith College in Little Rock, Arkansas. She originally set out to

be a doctor and joined the U.S. Army, where she received medical training and later earned a medical degree from the University of Texas in 1960. In 1971 Elders became a professor of pediatrics (children's health care) for the University of Arkansas.

In 1987 Arkansas governor Bill Clinton named Elders as the health commissioner for Arkansas. Elders was heavily criticized for her support for making information about preventing unwanted pregnancies and sexually transmitted diseases (such as AIDS) available to schoolchildren. Although her intent was to educate young people about the importance of safe sex, some people thought it improper to distribute such information to school-age children. When Clinton became president, he appointed Elders to the position of U.S. Surgeon General (the chief U.S. medical officer). Once again, Elders was criticized for the policies she pursued. Many people were shocked when she ordered a study to determine the effect that legalizing drug use would have on reducing the crime rate. Although she was heavily criticized, she also earned the respect of thousands of Americans for the firm position she took. Elders resigned in 1994.

After serving in the public spotlight, Elders went back to teaching medicine at the University of Arkansas and wrote an **autobiography** in 1997 called *Jocelyn Elders, M.D.* In 1998 Elders made a speech at a conference for sexually transmitted diseases in which she indicated that she had no regrets for doing what she believed, and still believes, is right—educating youth on the dangers of unsafe sex.

Duke Ellington: Selected Compositions

"Mood Indigo"
(1930)

"It Don't Mean a Thing If It Ain't Got That Swing"
(1932)

"Sophisticated Lady"
(1932)

"I Let a Song Go out of My Heart"
(1938)

"Take the A Train"
(1941)

"I Got It Bad and That Ain't Good"
(1942)

"Satin Doll"
(1953)

A Drum Is a Woman
(1956)

"King Fit the Battle of Alabam"
(1963)

The Far East Suite
(1967)

Afro-Eurasian Eclipse
(1971)

Ellington, Edward Kennedy "Duke"

COMPOSER, BANDLEADER, JAZZ PIANIST
April 29, 1899–May 24, 1974

One of the most famous composers and bandleaders of the twentieth century, Edward Kennedy Ellington was born in Washington, D.C. He received the nickname "Duke" as a child because of the pride he took in his clothes. In addition to studying piano, he was also a talented painter as a high school student.

By 1918, when Ellington married Edna Thompson, he was leading a band that played at white "society" events. To support his wife and son, Mercer, Ellington also worked as a sign painter.

In 1923 Ellington moved to New York as pianist and arranger for The Washingtonians. He soon became the band's leader and led the group in his first recordings. Ellington was being influenced by trumpeter Bubber Miley, whose bluesy style added a new element to Ellington's compositions and arrangements. Miley's growling, mournful solos inspired Ellington's "East St. Louis Toodle-O," among other compositions.

In 1927 Ellington's band debuted at Harlem's **Cotton Club,** a nightclub for all-white audiences. The job lasted on and off for four years and made Ellington one of the best-known musicians in **jazz.** He became known for danceable tunes and for compositions that attracted the attention of the classical music world. During the 1930s the orchestra toured the United States and Europe.

Composer and bandleaderDuke Ellington (Archive Photos. Reproduced by permission)

During the late 1940s and early 1950s, Ellington's band declined in influence. However, their performance at the 1956 Newport (Rhode Island) Jazz Festival reaffirmed their reputation, and earned Ellington a cover article in *Time* magazine. The orchestra also made albums with some of the biggest names in jazz, including **Louis Armstrong** (1901–1971), **Count Basie** (1904–1984), and **Ella Fitzgerald** (1917–1996).

Ellington also composed film scores, music for ballets by choreographer **Alvin Ailey** (1931–1989), and in his last decade, religious music for three events he called "Sacred Concerts" (1965, 1968, 1973).

Ellington cherished the many awards and honorary degrees he earned, including the NAACP's Spingarn Medal (1959) and eleven GRAMMY Awards. In 1970 Ellington was awarded the Presidential Medal of Freedom, the nation's highest civilian honor, by President Nixon and was given a seventieth-birthday celebration at the White House. He died of cancer on May 24, 1974.

After Ellington's death, his orchestra was led by his son, Mercer, a trumpeter and composer, until his death in 1996. In 1986 Duke Ellington became the first African-American jazz musician to appear on a U.S. postage stamp.

Ellison, Ralph

WRITER
March 1, 1914–April 16, 1994

Ralph Ellison was born in Oklahoma City, Oklahoma, where he grew up in a lively local culture. He played in high school **jazz** bands and in 1933 enrolled as a music major at Tuskegee Institute (now **Tuskegee University**) in Alabama. He involved himself in the other arts as well, and on his own discovered British writer T. S. Eliot's (1888–1965) epic poem *The Waste Land*

(1922), a poem whose richness he described as being "as mixed and varied as that of **Louis Armstrong.**"

At the end of his third college year, Ellison went to New York City to earn money. There, he met the black writers **Langston Hughes** (1902–1967), whose poetry he had read in high school, and **Richard Wright** (1908–1960). Ellison wrote a book review for Wright's magazine *New Challenge* in 1937, his first published work. In 1938 he took a job with the New York Writer's Project, a government program for the support of artists, and worked at night on his own fiction. He launched his literary career passionately, writing many book reviews and short stories.

Ellison's first stories were realistic, presenting specific political solutions to the problems of African Americans. By 1940 he had begun to find his own direction with a series of stories about black youngsters who were achievers, rather than victims, in a land of possibility. "Flying Home" (1944) is a story about a man who helps a lonely youngster develop a healthier attitude toward his painfully divided world. It set the stage for Ellison's monumental 1952 novel *Invisible Man*, which the following year received the National Book Award, given annually by the National Book Foundation for the best work of fiction in the United States.

Set between 1930 and 1950, *Invisible Man* tells of the development of an ambitious young black man from the South who goes to New York in search of advancement. Rich in historical and literary references, *Invisible Man* is a brilliant reflection on American history. The novel represents black American life in the twentieth century; it names the modern American as centerless and invisible, but somehow surviving and getting smarter.

Later collections of nonfiction, including *Shadow and Act* (1964) and *Going to the Territory* (1987), established Ellison as a distinguished man of letters. His books offer a strong challenge to social scientists and historians to consider African-American life in terms of not just its struggles but also its ability to change and grow and to influence the nation and the world.

> *"I am invisible simply because people refuse to see me. Like the bodiless heads you see sometimes in circus sideshows, it is as though I have been surrounded by mirrors of hard, distorting glass. When they approach me they see only my surroundings, themselves, or figments of their imagination—indeed, everything and anything except me."*
>
> (Source: Ralph Ellison. *Invisible Man,* 1952.)

Emancipation

From the early seventeenth century, when African-born people were first brought ashore in Virginia as slaves to white plantation owners, the agony of **slavery** and the hope of emancipation, or freedom, haunted each generation of slaves. It would be 250 years before President Abraham Lincoln (1809–1865) would free them by signing the Emancipation Proclamation on January 1, 1863. Lincoln called emancipation the central act of his administration and the greatest event of the nineteenth century. But black freedom was not given; it was fought for by the slaves themselves, who left the plantations as fugitives making their way north to free states, who joined the Union (Northern) forces as soldiers or hired hands during the **Civil War** (1861–65), or who stayed behind on the plantations and prayed for freedom. Many of the twentieth-century triumphs in America's search for racial equality have roots in emancipation and the events that followed.

The Long Road to Freedom

One of the issues at the heart of the Civil War was slavery. Southern states depended on agriculture, and slaves were central to keeping their economy going. When Southern states seceded, or left, the Union (the United States), they did so to protect their way of life. As the war progressed, however, a policy to free slaves slowly took shape in the North. In the beginning, escaped slaves were turned away by the Union military, but as floods of refugees began to enter Union lines in Virginia, Tennessee, and on the Southern coasts, they were hired as laborers, camp hands, and even spies.

The first of a string of laws that led to emancipation was passed in 1861—the First Confiscation Act. It allowed Union soldiers to seize all Confederate (Southern) property used in the war effort, and since slaves were "property," they were also taken. While not technically free, many slaves were at least away from their masters' plantations. Other slaves ran away from plantations and hid in forests or swamps, begging or stealing food and supplies. In 1862 Congress abolished (did away with) slavery in the District of Columbia (Washington, D.C.) and in the western territories. It also passed the Second Confiscation Act, which freed slaves of all persons "in rebellion" against the Union, including all parts of the slaveholding South.

President Lincoln was committed to eliminating slavery, but even more he wanted to reunite the North and the South. If this meant compromising with the South, then he was willing to do so. In September 1862 he issued the first Emancipation Proclamation and tried to bargain with the South to stop the war and rejoin the Union. If it did, he would let slavery stay much as it was. He also suggested a gradual emancipation, where the government would pay a slave owner in exchange for a slave's freedom. But none of these approaches worked. He signed the official Emancipation Proclamation on January 1, 1863, declaring that all slaves in the Confederacy were to be "forever free."

The proclamation did not, however, free slaves in the Northern states, which means that approximately 800,000 Northern blacks were not free. Freedom for all blacks did not come until 1865, when the Thirteenth Amendment to the U.S. Constitution was passed.

Emancipation Day Jubilees

When Emancipation Day came, "jubilee" meetings were held all over black America. At Tremont Temple in Boston, Massachusetts, a huge gathering of blacks and whites met from morning until night, awaiting the news that Lincoln had signed the Emancipation Proclamation. Among the many **free black** leaders who spoke that day was **Frederick Douglass** (1817–1895), a former slave who had escaped to freedom to become an abolitionist, lecturer, and writer.

New Freedom and the Reconstruction Period

After emancipation, thousands of slaves lived in contraband camps (centers for refugee former slaves), struggling and sometimes starving as they attempted to adjust to life on their own. Women and children were often left behind as men went to find work or served in the military.

LETTER FROM A FUGITIVE SLAVE, 1862

After emancipation, many African-American families were torn apart as men left their homes in search of better opportunities. The following is an excerpt from a letter written in January 1862 by John Boston, a fugitive slave living in Upton, Virginia, to his wife, Elizabeth, who stayed behind in Maryland:

It is with grate [great] joy I take this time to let you know Whare [where] I am I am now in Safety in the 14th regiment of Brooklyn this Day I can Adres [address] you thank god as a free man I had a little truble [trouble] in giting [getting] away But as the lord led the Children of Isrel [Israel] to the land of Canon [Canaan] So he led me to a land Whare Fredom [where freedom] Will rain in spite Of earth and hell ... I am free from al [all] the Slavers Lash. . . .

Dear wife I must Close rest yourself Contented I am free. . . . Write my Dear Soon. . . . Kiss Daniel For me.

Slowly, the freed slaves gained a sense of dignity, mobility, and identity. They were especially eager to learn to read and to own their own land. Many former slaves returned to their old plantations after the war as hired workers or as sharecroppers, receiving a portion of the crops in exchange for their work. Along with freedom from slavery came new rights, including **suffrage** (the right to vote), citizenship rights, and the ability to hold public office. Many of these gains in racial democracy were lost by the late nineteenth century, but emancipation and the period that followed remain among the most significant in African-American history. (*See also* **Abolition; Slavery.**)

Emanuel, James A. Sr.

POET, TEACHER, CRITIC
June 14, 1921–

James A. Emanuel was born in Alliance, Nebraska, and educated at **Howard University** (Washington, D.C.; bachelor's degree, 1950), Northwestern University (Evanston, Illinois; master's degree, 1953), and Columbia University (Ph.D. degree, 1962). He has worked for the Civilian Conservation Corps and the U.S. War Department. He taught at the City University of New York and was a Fulbright professor at the University of Grenoble, France (1968–69) and the University of Warsaw, Poland (1975–76).

As a poet, Emanuel has performed readings and lectures throughout the world, including Europe and Africa. Hel has also done poetry readings on both BBC (British Broadcasting Corporation) radio and "Voice of America" radio. His themes are broad, the titles of his poems reflecting some of his focus: "White Power Structure," "Black Poet on the Firing Line," and "Kickass." His published works include *The Treehouse and Other Poems* (1968),

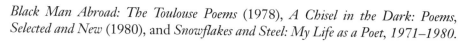
Black Man Abroad: The Toulouse Poems (1978), *A Chisel in the Dark: Poems, Selected and New* (1980), and *Snowflakes and Steel: My Life as a Poet, 1971–1980*.

Emanuel also coedited *Dark Symphony: Negro Literature in America* (1968) and published a collection of essays, **Langston Hughes** (1967). He has written numerous critical articles and addressed such subjects as blackness, literary theory, and the black aesthetic (artistic sensibility).

Embry, Wayne

BASKETBALL PLAYER
March 26, 1937–

Wayne Embry was a skilled **basketball** player and became the first African-American vice president and general manager of the National Basketball Association (NBA). Embry was rewarded for his achievements by being elected to the Basketball Hall of Fame in 1999.

Born and raised in Ohio, Embry attended Miami University (Oxford, Ohio). After graduating, he began a basketball career with the Cincinatti Royals in 1958. During his career he was named to the NBA All-Star team five times. After his retirement from basketball in 1969, Embry worked for the Milwaukee Bucks and the Indiana Pacers. As manager of operations, Embry helped the struggling Cleveland Cavaliers become one of the most successful teams in the NBA. Because of these accomplishments, Embry received the NBA Life Achievement Award in 1991.

Engineering

African Americans have contributed to engineering from America's earliest days to the present. Applying science and math, and using energy and the properties of nature, engineers develop structures (such as skyscrapers and bridges) and machines (such as harvesters and printing presses) as well as systems and processes. Engineering fields include electrical, mechanical, civil, architectural, chemical, industrial, and computer engineering.

Black Invention before the Civil War

By law, slaves were expressly forbidden to develop products or hold patents (official licenses giving inventors the sole right to make, use, or sell their inventions) under their own names. But some free blacks in the North were successful in registering their inventions. The first to do so was Thomas Jennings (1791–1859), who developed a method of dry cleaning clothes; he received his patent in March 1821. There were other African-American inventors at work during the 1800s. One was **Granville T. Woods** (1856–1910), who patented more than thirty-five electrical devices and more than sixty nonelectrical inventions between 1884 and 1907. His first registration was for a fuel-efficient steam boiler furnace. He is sometimes called "the black Edison," since, like inventor Thomas Edison (1847–1931), he was always busy working out a new idea.

Some black engineers contributed mightily to war effort, completing airfields in record time, building roads for transport vehicles, and constructing docks

Educational Firsts

In 1892 Robinson Taylor was the first black engineer to graduate from the Massachusetts Institute of Technology (MIT), which was among the first universities to open their doors to African-American engineering students. Howard University graduated its first engineering student, Manuel A. Agosto, in 1914. Howard was also the first to graduate a black female engineer, La Bonnie Ann Bianchi. In 1933, the first African American to earn a doctoral degree in any engineering field was Marron William Fort, who earned his Ph.D. in chemical engineering from MIT.

Engineering Programs Open Doors to Black Students

In the late 1880s northern colleges and technical schools, including prestigious universities such as the Massachusetts Institute of Technology (MIT; Cambridge, Massachusetts), began admitting African-American students into engineering programs. Black universities also established their own courses of study for engineering. The first to do so was **Howard University** (Washington, D.C.) in 1910. North Carolina Agricultural and Technical College and **Hampton Institute** (Virginia) soon followed. By the mid-1940s these schools had graduated their first African-American engineers.

The War Effort and the Postwar Era

When the United States entered **World War II** in 1941, there were many African-American engineers in the army. Although racial prejudices were still at work in the military, and many black soldiers worked as laborers, some black engineers contributed mightily to the war effort, completing airfields in record time, building roads for transport vehicles, and constructing docks.

After World War II (1939–45) the development of sophisticated technologies including radar, aeronautics, nuclear reactors, and computers, fueled the growth of many new industries. Eventually these industries combined with the demands of the "space race" between the United States and the Soviet Union to increase the overall demand for engineers. The black scientific community eventually benefited from this. Although in 1960 less than 1 percent of the five hundred thousand engineers at work in the United States was black, by 1986 this number reached forty-one thousand, and in 1992 American industry employed more than sixty-eight thousand black engineers.

During the same period engineering programs at colleges and universities began recruiting minority students, including African Americans, to increase the pool of trained engineers in the nation. Black women also began enrolling in engineering programs, and by 1986 more than four thousand were employed as engineers in the United States. Although the numbers of African- American men and women studying engineering or employed as engineers have remained relatively low, they continue to rise. The technol-

ogy revolution under way at the close of the 1900s promised to involve the next generation of engineers, and the sheer size of that revolution means that it will need to draw engineers from all races.

Entrepreneurs

The rise in the number of black entrepreneurs (business owners) in the United States has been slow and gradual. Social change, fueled by the abolition of slavery, the **Civil Rights movement**, and the emergence of several prominent black leaders, has blunted some of the effects of racism and helped a greater number of African Americans fulfill "the American Dream." Today there is a robust community of wealthy African-American business leaders offering evidence of the extent to which American society has progressed since the time of slavery.

Black Entrepreneurs up to the Civil War Era (1619–1865)

Early in American history, black entrepreneurs became successful in certain areas, such as food production and personal services. In the 1600s black slaves grew food and tobacco and traded in local markets. Slaves that earned enough money on their own could buy their freedom; however, it was extremely difficult to do (in Mississippi only one thousand out of four hundred thousand were able to buy their freedom). In the 1700s Anthony Johnson opened a successful tobacco farm, and Emanuel Manna Bernoon opened the first African-American catering business. Bernoon opened his business in Rhode Island, which became the early haven for black business development. Many blacks opened resort areas in Rhode Island, the most famous of which was Samuel Fraunces (1722–1795). Fraunces ran a hotel resort that was among the best in colonial America.

In the eighteenth century, blacks began setting up trading posts in the American frontier (areas west of the American colonies). Others developed sports and music businesses. Most prominent among these entrepreneurs was Occramer Marycoo, a musician who helped established the African Union Society, which was designed to help blacks improve their lives. In the period leading up to the **Civil War** (1861–65), blacks began to open successful business in the transportation, personal services, catering, and construction fields. The personal service and craft fields were popular business enterprises for blacks because they did not require much money to get started. By the beginning of the Civil War, twenty-one blacks had raised over $100,000 in personal wealth, a considerable amount of money for that time. Many black business leaders, such as Stephen Smith and William Whipper, used their influence to help with the **abolition** movement (the effort to bring an end to **slavery**).

Black Entrepreneurs up to the Civil Rights Movement (1865–1963).

By the end of the Civil War there were only twenty-five hundred black business owners. After the war however, the first African-American millionaires emerged. The primary industries in which blacks earned their wealth were food and personal service. The development of banks, insurance companies, and real estate businesses helped the number of blacks involved in business grow from thirty-one thousand in 1890 to seventy-four thousand in 1920. Certain areas began to develop as centers for black business, including Durham, North Carolina, and Atlanta, Georgia.

The social conditions of the time influenced the type of businesses in which blacks participated. Slavery and racism prevented blacks from getting the same education as whites. Many successful blacks often got their start as laborers, farm helpers, or slaves. Junius C. Graves ran a large farm and became known as "the Negro potato king." Joseph Davis, who was the brother of the Confederate president Jefferson Davis, ran a cotton plantation and a retail store. Richard H. Boyd, a minister, began a publishing company in Tennessee that printed religious materials and became one of the largest black businesses in the nation. Boyd also established a transportation company for blacks to rival the segregated streetcar policy in Tennessee.

In the 1900s a black consumer market began to develop. Cities such as Chicago, Illinois, New York, and Durham, North Carolina, took the lead as centers of black business. Durham became known as "the capital of the black middle class." Although some risky business ventures such as real estate and insurance led to bankruptcy, the period leading up to **World War I** (1914–18) was a boom era for blacks. During and after the war blacks began branching out into the publishing and media industries. However, the primary area of business development for blacks remained the service industry (food, hotels, and hair salons).

Although the **Great Depression** (a period of severe economic hardship in the 1930s) reduced the number of black-owned businesses, food production and real estate continued to be areas of growth. By the 1940s blacks began to establish big businesses in food and cosmetic products. Black entrepreneurs also began to open manufacturing and food-processing enterprises, such as potato chip and ice cream plants. During **World War II** (1939–45) S. B. Fuller became one of the richest black businessmen when he introduced a line of health and beauty products. Although the 1940s and 1950s saw the door open for blacks in manufacturing, it was not until the 1960s that blacks began to own large-scale business operations.

Black Entrepreneurs in the Modern Era (1964–Present).

The Civil Rights movement opened doors for blacks both economically and socially. More laws against racial discrimination and new government financial programs made it easier for blacks to obtain funds to start new businesses. The federal government created programs such as the Small Business Administration (SBA) to encourage black and other entrepreneurs to start business ventures. Blacks began to penetrate the entertainment business, the most prominent of which was Berry Gordy's Motown Records in Detroit, Michigan. Black entrepreneurs also began publishing businesses, such as John H. Johnson's *Fashion Fair* magazine. Athletes and entertainers became some of the first blacks to enter into large-scale business ventures. In the 1970s basketball star **Earvin Johnson** and actor **Bill Cosby** purchased the Coca-Cola Bottling Company.

Perhaps the most famous and successful black person in business in modern times is **Oprah Winfrey**, who created an enormously successful television and motion picture business through her talk show. In the late 1980s Carl Jones became the first black to enter the clothing industry on the manufacturing side, and Henry F. Henderson broke into the technology industry by securing contracts with the U.S. military.

During the past three centuries, American business has opened up opportunities for black participation in nearly every industry. However, the number of black entrepreneurs remains low. Approximately 3 percent of the companies in the United States are owned by blacks, and only 1 percent of black businesses are involved in manufacturing. These numbers suggest that although black entrepreneurs have made considerable progress in the business arena, there are still improvements to be made in one of the most important indicators of social equality—personal wealth.

Episcopalians

Although not as numerous as black Baptists or Methodists, African-American Episcopalians' history is a long one, dating back to colonial times. As early as 1695 the first blacks were baptized in the Church of England, the faith of their masters. Many English planters living along the eastern (Atlantic) shore of what became the United States wanted to introduce Christianity to their slaves. Some masters actively encouraged slaves to become baptized and enter the church. Others did not pay any attention to, or even were against, the spiritual lives of blacks.

After the **American Revolution** (1775–83), the Church of England was reorganized into a separate American denomination, or religious group, called the Protestant Episcopal Church (1787). But the new church had fewer members, both black and white, than its predecessor. Some had left after the British lost the war, and others joined new churches, such as the Baptist and Methodist, which were more welcoming. The Episcopal Church required its members to be able to read and to learn the catechism (religious lessons). Most black Episcopalians were free blacks living in the North, not slaves.

Following the **Civil War** (1861–65), the Episcopal Church Freedman's Commission, set up to meet the needs of the freed slaves, operated schools, hospitals, and churches. But still, the Episcopal Church did not draw as many black people as the Baptist or the Methodist. In some areas, black Episcopal membership not only failed to grow, but declined. For example, in South Carolina the number of black Episcopalians in 1868 was less than three hundred; before the Civil War it was ten times that, or about three thousand.

The problem of black membership in the church worsened in 1883 when a conference of bishops (church officials) met in Tennessee and decided to segregate the church, or divide it into black churches and white churches.

An African-American F I R S T

In 1794 St. Thomas African Episcopal Church, Philadelphia, Pennsylvania, became the first black Episcopal church in the United States. Its minister, **Absalom Jones** (1746–1818), was the Episcopal Church's first black priest. No black priest was named bishop until 1918, when the Episcopal Church conferred that office on Edward T. Demby and Henry B. Delany. In 1976 Pauli Murray became the first black female Episcopal priest; and in 1980 Barbara Harris was named the first female Episcopal bishop (a black woman).

Alienation within the Church

Black Episcopalians did not enter the 1900s in a position of strength. Members in a predominantly white church, black priests and church members were not given full voting rights within the church. For the first two decades of the 1900s, black and white Episcopalians in the North and South struggled with how the church should be organized, funded, and run. By 1921 there were only 31,851 black members, 288 black congregations, 176 black ministers, and 2 black bishops.

Even with African-American migration to the North following **World War II** (1939–45), the number of black Episcopalians did not increase. Black Episcopalian scholars attacked the spontaneous, emotional music and folk traditions of the rural black southern church, especially as found in the Baptist and Methodists churches. Excluded from and criticized by the Episcopal Church, black people turned away from it.

Reforms Boost African-American Membership

With many African Americans feeling alienated by the Episcopal Church, at the height of the **Civil Rights movement** church officials decided to do something about it. A special program, the Episcopal Society of Cultural and Racial Unity, was founded in 1967 to care for the needs of African-American parishioners and to attract more blacks to the church. Twenty chapters of the society were set up to minster to an estimated 150,000 black Episcopalians.

Since then, the church has established an Office of Black Ministries (1973); published an official hymnal (a collection of church hymns), *Lift Every Voice and Sing: A Collection of Afro-American Spirituals and Other Songs* (1981); and drew new members from an influx of black Anglicans (members of the Church of England) from Caribbean island nations. These efforts have combined to increase the presence of African Americans in the Episcopal Church.

Equiano, Olaudah Gustavus Vassa

AUTOBIOGRAPHER
c. 1750–April 30, 1797

Olaudah Equiano was born the son of a chieftain in Benin, now part of Nigeria, Africa. He was eleven when he and his sister were kidnapped and sold to white slave traders on the coast. He was shipped to the island of Barbados in the West Indies and later to Virginia, where he was sold to a British naval officer. On board ships and during brief times in England, he learned to read and write and converted to Christianity.

Equiano's **autobiography** tells of his several adventures at sea off the Canadian coast during the Seven Years' War (1756–63) and with a Mediterranean fleet. To his dismay, his master, who had promised him his freedom, sold him to an American shipowner. He was put to work making

trading runs—sometimes with slaves as cargo—between the islands of the West Indies and the North American coast. From these experiences Equiano wrote about murders and cruel injustices inflicted on blacks, both free and enslaved.

In 1766 Equiano was able to purchase his freedom, but he chose to remain a seaman. He sailed on an expedition to the Arctic and later worked as an assistant to a doctor with the Miskito Indians in Nicaragua. After 1777 he remained in the British Isles and became increasingly involved in the antislavery movement. In 1787 he was appointed commissioner of stores (supplies) for the resettlement of free Africans in Sierra Leone, but was dismissed after accusing a naval agent of mismanagement. His efforts to join an African expedition group or to do African missionary work also met with failure.

In 1789 Equiano published his autobiography under the title *The Interesting Narrative of Olaudah Equiano, or Gustavus Vassa the African, written by himself.* Three years later he married Susannah Cullen, an Englishwoman, by whom he would have two children. Although several of his accounts have since been questioned, nine editions of his autobiography were printed in his lifetime, and he received invitations to lecture throughout the British Isles. Because Equiano's autobiography contains antislavery views and compares enslaved blacks with biblical Hebrews enslaved in Egypt, his work is generally regarded as a more genuine precursor of **slave narratives** written between 1830 and 1860 than other eighteenth-century African-American autobiographies.

Erving, Julius Winfield II "Dr. J"

BASKETBALL PLAYER
February 22, 1950–

Julius Winfield Erving II, better known as "Dr. J," is one of the most famous professional basketball players in history. Erving is best remembered for his soaring jumping abilities. The National Basketball Association (NBA) named him one of the fifty greatest players of all time.

Erving was born in East Meadow, New York, in 1950 and was a standout in high school, for his academic abilities as well as for his basketball playing. He attended the University of Massachusetts on a scholarship but left college after his junior year to play professional basketball. He first joined the American Basketball Association (which later became the National Basketball Association) on the Virginia Squires team and won Rookie of the Year in 1972. Erving joined the Philadelphia 76ers in 1976. During his career Erving made the All-Star team eleven times, and twice was the All-Star team's Most Valuable Player. In 1980 the NBA named him to the All-Time Team.

Erving retired from professional basketball in 1987, the same year he became the third player in NBA history to score 30,000 points. After retirement Erving devoted his time to developing businesses, including the Erving Group and the Philadelphia Coca-Cola Bottling Company.

Julius Erving, "Dr. J.," in flight to the hoop
(AP/Wide World Photos. Reproduced by
permission)

Erving's nineteen-year-old son, Cory, disappeared on May 28, 2000. On July 6, 2000, after searching for weeks, investigators found Cory Erving dead in his car at the bottom of a pond near his family's home in Kissimmee, Florida. Cory Erving had a history of drug use, but his family believed that he had turned his life around. A family spokesman released a statement reading, "The Erving family will go forward from here. We have no other choice."

Espy, Michael "Mike"

GOVERMENT OFFICIAL
November 30, 1953–

Michael Espy was the first African American to head the U.S. Department of Agriculture. He was also the first black to represent Mississippi in the U.S. House of Representatives, where he made a significant impact on public policy. Espy may be best known for the 1995 investigation into the claim that he took gifts in exchange for political favoritism. Espy was acquitted of all criminal charges by a Mississippi jury in 1998.

Born in Yazoo City, Mississippi, Espy attended Catholic high schools before earning a bachelor's degree from **Howard University** (Washington, D.C.) and a law degree from the University of Santa Clara (California). After serving as the assistant state attorney general, Espy ran for Congress. He won by a narrow margin, but he earned a healthy majority of Mississippi voters in later elections. His work in Congress concentrated on agriculture policy, but he also supported antipoverty programs, upheld abortion rights, and supported prayer in public schools.

In 1992 Espy was a prominent early supporter of Arkansas governor Bill Clinton's successful presidential candidacy. Clinton responded in 1993 by appointing Espy U.S. secretary of agriculture, making him not only the first African American but also the first southerner to hold the post. As secretary of agriculture, Espy fought for aid to farmers after the terrible 1993 Mississippi River floods, and he revised the department's food inspection process. He also visited China in an effort to persuade Chinese leaders to import American wheat.

In October 1994, following rumors of bribery and corruption, Espy resigned as secretary of agriculture and opened a law office in Jackson, Mississippi. Donald Smaltz was engaged as a special prosecutor to investigate Espy. In 1995 Espy was indicted (charged with a crime) by a federal grand jury on thirty counts of accepting gifts—totaling $34,000 in transportation and ticket expenses to sporting events—from Tyson Foods and other companies regulated by Espy's department. Meanwhile, Smaltz was widely criticized for pursuing Espy because the evidence against him was weak. In December 1994 Espy was found innocent of all criminal charges by a Mississippi jury.

Estes, Simon Lamont

OPERA SINGER
February 2, 1938–

Simon Lamont Estes's bass-baritone voice brought him international recognition. The son of a coal miner, he was born in Centerville, Iowa. At the University of Iowa he studied medicine, theology (religion), and other subjects before a music professor introduced the singer to opera (classical music for the stage). Showing great promise, he was awarded a scholarship to the Juilliard School (New York), where he completed his studies.

In 1965 Estes made his debut, singing in the famous opera *Aida* (1871) in Berlin, Germany. In 1978 he was the first African-American man to sing at the Bayreuth Festival, a long-standing and prestigious classical music event in Germany. He made his American concert debut in 1980, performing at New York's Carnegie Hall. Two years later, he sang at the Metropolitan Opera (New York). Estes has performed nearly ninety operatic roles, including leading parts in German composer Richard Wagner's (1813–1883) *The Ring Cycle* (1848–74) and American composer George Gershwin's (1898–1937) *Porgy and Bess* (1935).

Europe, James Reese

COMPOSER, CONDUCTOR
February 22, 1881–May 9, 1919

Pioneering musician James Europe was hailed as America's "jazz king" for incorporating **blues, ragtime,** and **jazz** elements into his band arrangements. Born in Mobile, Alabama, he was raised in Washington, D.C., where his father worked for the U.S. Postal Service. His brother John became a noted ragtime pianist, and his sister Mary was an accomplished concert pianist and music teacher. In high school Europe studied violin, piano, and composition.

In 1903 the young Europe moved to New York City. He began working as a composer and music director in black musical theater, contributing to various productions until 1910. In April of that year he cofounded the Clef Club, a union and booking agency for black musicians. Europe became conductor of the club's 125-member concert orchestra. In 1912 the orchestra performed at New York's Carnegie Hall. Called the "Concert of Negro Music," the event met with rave reviews and was repeated in 1913 and 1914.

By 1914 Europe had built the Clef Club into a great force for organizing the efforts of black musicians in New York. Club members played in orchestras, hotels, cabarets, and dance halls, as well as for private society parties and dances. In 1913 Europe was recruited as musical director for the legendary dance team of Vernon (1887–1918) and Irene Castle (1893–1969). Together, Europe and the Castles revolutionized American social dancing. They made formerly objectionable dances, such as the turkey trot and the fox-trot, acceptable to mainstream America. Europe's talent won him a recording contract with Victor Records, the first ever for a black orchestra leader.

With World War I (1914–18) being waged, late in 1916 Europe enlisted in the National Guard. As part of a recruitment effort, he organized a brass band. Overseas he was a company commander and is credited with being the first black American officer to lead troops into combat. Returning to the United States in 1919, Europe began a nationwide tour. During a performance in Boston, Massachusetts, he was fatally injured during a struggle with a mentally disturbed band member. He was buried with full military honors in Arlington National Cemetery (Virginia).

EUROPE'S INFLUENCES

Early in his musical career James Europe was influenced by singer/composer Harry T. Burleigh (1866–1949) and musician-composer **Will Marion Cook** (1869–1944). Both Burleigh and Cook had studied with celebrated Czechoslovakian composer Antonín Dvořák (1841–1904), who believed African-American folk music could provide the basis for an American national music. Europe clearly subscribed to this idea.

In turn, Europe was a strong influence on the careers of jazz pianist-composer **Eubie Blake** (1883–1983); musical great **Noble Sissle** (1889–1975; he wrote the landmark musical *Shuffle Along*); and composer George Gershwin (1898–1937; whose works include the folk opera *Porgy and Bess*).

Evans, Ernest. *See* Checker, Chubby

Evers, Medgar Wylie

CIVIL RIGHTS ACTIVIST
July 2, 1925–June 12, 1963

Born in Decatur, Mississippi, Medgar Evers served in **World War II** (1939–45), graduated from Alcorn Agricultural and Mechanical College, and became an insurance agent. Refused admission to the University of Mississippi's law school, he became the first Mississippi field director of the **National Association for the Advancement of Colored People (NAACP)**.

Evers's job entailed investigating murders of blacks that local police generally dismissed as accidents. A clear target for violence, Evers bought a car big enough to resist being forced off the road and powerful enough for quick escapes. He received daily death threats but always tried reasoning with callers.

Evers led voter registration drives and fought segregation; organized consumer boycotts to integrate schools; and won a lawsuit integrating Jackson, Mississippi's privately owned buses.

In the middle of the night on June 12, 1963, Evers arrived home. His wife heard his car door slam, then gunshots. He died that night; his accused murderer was found not guilty, despite compelling evidence. The man suspected of killing Evers, Byron De La Beckwith, was ultimately convicted of murder in 1994. Evers's murder and the fight to bring his killer to justice are the subjects of the movie *Ghosts of Mississippi* (1996).

Exodusters

The decade following the American **Civil War** (1861–65), known as the **Reconstruction** period, was a good time for African Americans. When

slavery was outlawed in 1865, they became free and soon gained many new rights, such as the right to vote, to hold public office, and to send their children to school. But in the spring of 1879 Democratic whites were about to regain control of state governments in the South. Blacks in Mississippi, Louisiana, Texas, Kentucky, and Tennessee feared they would lose the precious rights they had gained and might even be forced back into slavery. Some whites had already used violence and threats to reverse the progress made for blacks during Reconstruction. Many African Americans saw only one way to preserve their freedom: to leave the South and go elsewhere to live. Blacks throughout the South sought new homes in Kansas, Indiana, and West Africa. The twenty thousand who went to Kansas in 1879 are known as the Exodusters (from "exodus," meaning a mass departure or emigration).

Benjamin "Pap" Singleton of Kentucky and Henry Adams of Louisiana were said to be leaders of the Exodusters, although it was really a mass movement in which people trusted in God and depended on the federal government for a share of the free land waiting to be homesteaded (claimed and settled) in Kansas. To people who had been slaves, owning their own land meant being their own masters.

Only a few of the Exodusters got to keep land as homesteaders, but they achieved much more economic and political freedom than they would have in the South. Although some black leaders called the Exodusters cowards for leaving, many blacks and whites supported the migration, and it is generally considered a success.

Expatriates

An expatriate is someone who gives up citizenship in his own country to become a citizen of another country. According to law, a person is considered an expatriate for a number of reasons, including the fact that he or she has lived outside the United States for a certain number of years. In general, however, the term "expatriate" is used only for those individuals who make a real and public decision to live outside the United States for political or social reasons. For example, some African Americans choose to live somewhere else to escape the racism of American society; others move to other countries to find political and artistic freedom.

Most of the first African-American expatriates were abolitionists who were motivated to leave America during the 1800s for political reasons. They wanted not only to escape racism but also to find a place where they could safely continue their fight to end **slavery**. They also wanted to spread the message to the world that slavery in America must be stopped. Abolitionists such as **William Wells Brown** (c. 1814–1884) and William and Ellen Craft fled to England during the mid-1800s, and newspaper editor John Brown Russwurm (1799–1851) worked as an editor in the African nation of Liberia until his death in 1851.

Into the twentieth century, African Americans continued to leave the United States for political reasons. Following **World War I** (1914–18),

Marcus Garvey (1887–1940), founder of the **Universal Negro Improvement Association,** began a "Back to Africa" movement in hopes of establishing a black-governed country in **Africa.** Garvey inspired many African Americans to move to Liberia. Political leaders such as **W.E.B. Du Bois** (1868–1963), who lived most of his life in the United States, eventually settled elsewhere. Du Bois moved to Ghana in 1961, where he spent the rest of his life.

The turbulent years of the **Civil Rights movement** (1950s and 1960s) caused many African-American political leaders to flee the United States to avoid criminal charges. Former Black Panther **Eldridge Cleaver** (1935–1998) escaped to Algeria, in northwestern Africa, in 1969 and lived there until 1979, while activist **Stokely Carmichael** (1941–1998) lived in the West African nation of Guinea from 1969 until his death in 1998.

African Americans have also chosen to leave the United States for artistic reasons. Writers, musicians, entertainers, and artists have moved to other countries because they have been welcomed, accepted, respected, and allowed to create. As early as 1773, poet **Phillis Wheatley** (c. 1753–1784) traveled to Europe, and by the mid-1800s entertainers such as dancer William Henry "Juba" Lane (c. 1825–c. 1852) and actor **Ira Aldridge** (1807–1867) were living in England and France. Probably the best known of all African- American expatriates was **Josephine Baker** (1906–1975), who moved to Paris in 1925 and quickly became the most popular entertainer in Europe. Baker became a French citizen in 1937 and died in Paris in 1975.

France has been a particular destination of many African-American expatriates, especially writers, musicians, and artists. Just as the **Harlem Renaissance** was peaking in the United States (1920s to the 1930s), a similar movement, called the French Negritude movement was taking place across the Atlantic. **Claude McKay** (1889–1948), one of the central writers of the Harlem Renaissance, lived from 1922 to 1934 in France, Spain, and Morocco. Other writers, including novelists **Richard Wright** (1908–1960) and **James Baldwin** (1924–1987) lived most of their adult lives in Paris: Wright from 1947 until his death in 1960, and Baldwin from 1948 until his death in 1987.

Although the majority of African Americans choose to live in other countries for political or artistic reasons, there are other motivating factors as well, including opportunities for a better education or better jobs. In particular, African-American athletes have historically lived in Europe and other parts of the world. Many early African-American baseball players spent large portions of their careers playing both winter and summer ball in Latin America, where they were untroubled by segregation or American racism. In more recent decades, African-American baseball players such as Roy White and Cecil Fielder have starred in Japanese leagues, while black basketball players have been lured to European teams.

African Americans continued to live outside the United States toward the end of the twentieth century; however, the reasons seemed to be more for personal choice and less to escape racism. As racial and political tensions lessened into the 1980s and 1990s, fewer and fewer considered themselves to be expatriates. As James Baldwin put it, they preferred to be called "transatlantic commuters."

France has been a particular destination of many African-American expatriates, especially writers, musicians, and artists

Fagan, Garth

DANCER, CHOREOGRAPHER
1940–

Dancer and choreographer (dance composer) Garth Fagan was born in Jamaica, West Indies. After training and performing with the Jamaica National Dance Theater in his teens, he moved to the United States at age twenty to attend college.

In the United States, Fagan first settled in Detroit, Michigan. He studied with Martha Graham, José Limón, Mary Hinkson, and **Alvin Ailey** before accepting a professorship at the State University of New York (SUNY) at Brockport in 1969.

In 1970 Fagan started his own dance company based in Rochester, New York. Because the dancers consisted of inner-city students who began dance lessons at a late age, the company was originally called The Bottom of the Bucket, But . . . Dance Theater. As the dancers improved and the company gained in stature, the name was changed to The Bucket Dance Theater in 1981. By the company's twentieth year, it had become simply Garth Fagan Dance.

Fagan developed a unique style combining elements of modern dance and **ballet** with African and Caribbean rhythms and postures. Fagan's dancers gain a certain look, regardless of the body they started with: long, lean, leggy, and muscular.

Fagan has been famous for his dances for couples, in which the dancers often wrap around each other, such as the 1990 *Until, By & If.* The music for Fagan's work is often performed live and has included collaborations with jazz pianist Don Pullen and jazz composer and trumpeter **Wynton Marsalis.**

In 1998 Fagan won a Tony Award for his choreography for the extraordinarily popular Broadway musical *The Lion King*, which was based on an animated film with the same name.

Fard, Wallace D.

RELIGIOUS LEADER, POLITICAL LEADER
Unknown–Unknown

Mystery surrounds Wallace D. Fard, who is credited with founding the **Nation of Islam (NOI).** Just before 1930 he appeared in Detroit, Michigan, where he spoke to the city's black community about salvation and freedom through **Islam.** The religion of Islam is the faith of Muslim people, who believe in one god, called Allah, and in the prophet Muhammad (c. 570–632). Fard claimed that, like Muhammad, he was born in Mecca (Saudi Arabia) and that he was a member of the same tribe as Muhammad. Some people believed that Fard was a prophet, a spiritual leader who foretells the future. In 1930 he founded the Temple of Islam in Detroit.

In his preaching, Fard asserted that black people were the first on earth. He called for African Americans to set up their own independent nation inside the United States, saying that only through separation from white people, whom he fiercely disliked, could black people achieve self-determination—the freedom to decide their own future. In addition to the temple, Fard also organized a civil defense corps and an unconventional elementary and high school for Muslim children. He began the practice of substituting "X" for Black Muslims' last name. This was a way to cast off the legacy of slavery (most slaves were given the last names of their owners).

After converting an estimated eight thousand Detroit blacks to the NOI, Fard suddenly left Detroit in 1934. His followers believed his disappearance was evidence that he was a prophet sent by Allah. Others claimed Fard was deported by government officials. (His critics further charged that prior to his arrival in Detroit he was jailed in California for dealing drugs.) Nevertheless, members of the NOI continued to revere him. Fard's whereabouts since 1934 are unknown.

Farmer, James

CIVIL RIGHTS LEADER, EDUCATOR
January 12, 1920–

Dedicated to nonviolent protest as a way to bring about change, James Farmer was one of the chief leaders of the **Civil Rights movement.** Born in Mississippi, he was raised in Marshall, Texas, where his father, a minister, was a college professor. He graduated from **Howard University** (Washington, D.C.) with a bachelor's degree in divinity in 1941. But he chose not to become a minister because the position he was offered in the Methodist Church was to lead an all-black congregation. Farmer believed churches should be integrated (include black and white members).

During **World War II** (1939–45), Farmer opposed the draft because the U.S. military was segregated. Influenced by the example set by Indian nationalist leader Mohandas Gandhi (1869–1948), Farmer committed himself to peaceful protest. In 1942 he organized a civil rights group, the **Congress of Racial Equality (CORE)**. CORE was committed to bringing about integration by staging nonviolent demonstrations. As CORE's national director, Farmer was one of the Civil Rights movement's most powerful speakers, and he participated in its various forms of protest, including **sit-ins**, strikes, **freedom rides**, and voter education programs.

Farmer was an early advocate of programs that would require employers and government to hire African Americans in numbers proportionate to their makeup of the general population. His ideas provided the basis for **affirmative action** policies, which gave jobs to and trained more black workers.

By 1966 CORE had turned away from its original goals, and Farmer left the organization. During the late 1960s and early 1970s he became involved in politics, running for Congress (he was defeated by African-American Democrat **Shirley Chisholm**) and serving as assistant secretary of the Department of Health, Education, and Welfare (HEW) during the administration of President Richard Nixon (1969–74). During the 1970s Farmer was active in various nonprofit organizations. In 1982 he began teaching at Mary Washington College (Virginia), where he remained into the early 1990s. In 1998 he was awarded the Presidential Medal of Freedom, the nation's highest nonmilitary award, for his civil rights work.

Farrakhan, Louis Abdul "Louis X"

RELIGIOUS LEADER
May 17, 1933–

Dynamic yet controversial, Louis Farrakhan has many followers. He has also attracted harsh criticism for his words and actions. Born Louis Eugene Walcott, he was raised in Boston, Massachusetts, by his mother, who was from the West Indies (the Caribbean). Deeply religious, he became involved in the Episcopal church as a youth. He was active in high school, running track and playing violin in the orchestra, and he graduated with honors. In 1953 he dropped out of Winston-Salem Teachers College (North Carolina) to pursue a career in music. Returning to Boston, he performed calypso in nightclubs.

In 1955 Louis Walcott was recruited by **Nation of Islam (NOI)** leader **Malcolm X** (1925–1965). He converted to the Muslim faith and, according to custom, dropped his last name, becoming known as Louis X. After assisting and learning from Malcolm X at the Harlem (New York City) temple, Farrakhan was given his own pastorate in Boston. When Malcolm X left the NOI in 1964, Louis X was named leader of the important Harlem temple. In May 1965 NOI leader **Elijah Muhammad** (1897–1975) gave him his Muslim name, Abdul Farrakhan.

A powerful speaker, Farrakhan emerged as a charismatic leader. Many believed he was the obvious successor to Elijah Muhammad. But upon Muhammad's death in 1975, one of his sons was chosen as "supreme minister." The NOI shifted its emphasis toward orthodox (Sunni) Islam, a fundamentalist faith. Cut off from his own religion, for the next three years Farrakhan traveled in Muslim countries. He became convinced that the NOI must return to its original teachings, including its emphasis on race.

Returning to the United States in 1978, Farrakhan founded a new Nation of Islam and began rebuilding his following by speaking to black communities around the country. (The original Nation of Islam was renamed the American Muslim Mission.) He preached that African Americans should hear the "final call"—to convert to the NOI, which he proclaimed represented the last chance for black people to be liberated. He also talked about the importance of knowing oneself (self-identity), doing for oneself (self-reliance), and establishing union among black people.

In the 1980s Farrakhan, by then a nationally known figure, was criticized for making anti-Jewish statements. He maintained that his remarks had been wrongly interpreted. Nevertheless, he has continued to be controversial. For example, in 1996 he traveled in the Middle East and later announced that Libyan leader Mohamar Khadaffi had donated $1 million to the NOI. Since Khadaffi is a known dictator with close ties to terrorism, Farrakhan was strongly rebuked by many American leaders for accepting the gift.

The NOI has an estimated twenty thousand followers and branches in Ghana (western Africa), England, and the Caribbean. Farrakhan draws large crowds at his speaking engagements. As an organizer of the Million Man March on Washington in 1995, he delivered the keynote speech, calling on African-American men to place high priority on their families and to organize in their communities to bring about positive change.

The NOI has been credited with giving women important roles in the religion, working to organize peace agreements between inner-city gangs, establishing an AIDS treatment center, and ridding some housing projects of drug dealers. The movement continues to be criticized, however, for its message of racist separatism.

Father Divine

MINISTER

c. 1880–September 10, 1965

Father Divine created a religious movement that appealed to those suffering from poverty and hardship. Born George Baker in Maryland, he began his religious career at age twenty. He moved to Baltimore, where he taught Sunday school and preached in storefront churches. In 1912 he worked as a traveling minister in the American South. He attracted a small following and purchased a home in the exclusively white community of Sayville, New York. He opened his doors to the unemployed and homeless.

By 1931 thousands were flocking to worship services in his home, and his white neighbors grew hostile. In November they summoned police, who arrested him for disturbing the peace. Four days later after Father Divine was found guilty, the sentencing judge died. The judge's death gave Father Divine a great deal of attention. Some saw it as evidence of the Father's great powers; others viewed it as a sinister form of revenge. Although Father

Divine denied responsibility for the death, news media continued to report on his activities through the 1930s.

Father Devine relocated the headquarters of his growing movement to **Harlem, New York,** where he conducted worship services and helped the unemployed find jobs. During the **Great Depression** (a time of great economic hardship in the 1930s), the movement furnished thousands of poor people with food, clothes, and jobs.

Father Divine's appeal derived from his unique approach to religion. He used a mixture of African-American folk religion, Christianity, and a belief in the power of positive thinking. He encouraged followers to believe that he was God, and that they could use his spirit to generate health, wealth, and salvation. Disciples left their families and assumed new names. Father Divine's followers found a new sense of order in their lives that contrasted with the racism and poverty that many of them suffered.

Father Divine's social programs also drew followers. Although rigid rules governed the movement's shelters, they were heavily used. Father Divine spoke out for integration. He required his followers to live and work in integrated pairs.

When the economy improved in the 1940s, Father Divine's message lost much of its appeal. In 1946 he married a white disciple named Sweet Angel. He spent his last years preparing her for leadership. Upon his death in 1965, she assumed control of the movement, stating that Father Divine had not died but had surrendered his body, preferring to exist as a spirit. The movement continues with a small number of followers and businesses in the Philadelphia, Pennsylvania, area.

Fauset, Arthur Huff

FOLKLORIST, EDUCATOR
January 20, 1899–September 2, 1983

Arthur Fauset studied the customs and beliefs of African-American communities. He was born in New Jersey and completed a Ph.D. degree in anthropology in 1942 at the University of Pennsylvania. From 1918 to 1946 Fauset was a teacher and administrator in the Philadelphia public school system. Arthur Fauset was married for almost ten years but divorced in 1944.

Fauset's first important essay appeared in 1925, when he published "American Negro Folk Literature" in philosopher **Alain Leroy Locke**'s (1885–1954) famous collection *The New Negro* (1925). Fauset also won first prize in a short story competition sponsored by *Opportunity* magazine in 1926. He is best known, however, for his anthropological works, which remain an important contribution to understanding the history and culture of African-American life.

Fauset published *Folklore from Nova Scotia* (1931), which includes folktales, ballads, rhymes, riddles, and verses as related by black Nova Scotians (Canadians). He also collected material on **folklore** (the customs, beliefs, tales, sayings, dances, and art forms of a people, passed down from one generation to the next) from the Mississippi Delta.

Arthur Fauset: Selected Publications

Folklore from Nova Scotia
(1931)

For Freedom: A Biographical Story of the American Negro
(1927)

Sojourner Truth: God's Faithful Servant
(1938)

Black Gods of the Metropolis: Negro Religious Cults of the Urban North
(1944)

America, Red, White, Black, and Yellow
(with Nella Bright, 1969)

Fauset's best-known work focuses on religious cults and leaders, such as Father Divine of the Father Divine Peace Mission Movement (1880–1965) and Prophet F. S. Cherry (1880–1965) of the Church of God (a sect of the Black Hebrews or Black Jews). His work remains one of the most important efforts to explore African-American urban culture. Fauset died at the age of eighty-four.

Fauset, Jessie Redmon

WRITER, TEACHER
April 27, 1884–April 30, 1961

As literary editor of *The Crisis,* the official journal of the **National Association for the Advancement of Colored People (NAACP),** Jessie Fauset is best known for encouraging and publishing the early efforts of such writers as **Arna Bontemps** and **Langston Hughes.** However, she was also among the most productive authors of the **Harlem Renaissance,** an exciting period of cultural achievement in early 1900s Harlem, New York. In addition to her work for *The Crisis,* she published four novels in less than ten years.

Born in what is now Lawnside, New Jersey, in 1884, Fauset grew up in Philadelphia, Pennsylvania. She attended Cornell University (Ithaca, New York), where she was elected to Phi Beta Kappa (an honor society for students who achieve excellent academic marks), and graduated in 1905. She taught high school French and earned a master's degree from the University of Pennsylvania. In 1919 **W. E. B. Du Bois** hired her to work for *The Crisis.* Her contributions to *The Crisis* were numerous and diverse: biographical

---

EXCERPT FROM "SOME NOTES ON COLOR"

Being colored in America at any rate means: Facing the ordinary difficulties of life, getting education, work, in fine getting a living plus fighting everyday against some inhibition of natural liberties.

Let me see if I can give you some ideas. I am a colored women, neither white nor black, neither pretty nor ugly, neither specially graced nor at all deformed. I am fairly well educated, of fair manners and deportment. In brief, the average American done over in brown. In the morning I go to work by means of the subway, which is crowded. Presently somebody gets up. The man standing in front of the vacant place looks around meaning to point it out to a women. I am the nearest one, "But oh," says his glance, "you're colored. I'm not expected to give it to you." And down he plumps. According to my reflexes that morning, I think to myself "hypocrite" or "pig." And make a conscious effort to shake the unpleasantness of it off, for I don't want my day spoiled.

Jessie Fauset in *The World Tomorrow* (New York), March, 1922, pp. 76-77.

sketches, essays, translations from French, and reports on activists and political causes.

Each of Fauset's novels conveys a strong message. *There Is Confusion* (1924) depicts the struggle of a young woman to become a singer without compromising her personal and racial pride. Fauset's most critically acclaimed novel, *Plum Bun* (1929), explores issues of race and sexual identity. Her third and fourth novels were *The Chinaberry Tree* (1931) and *Comedy: American Style*. In the foreword to *The Chinaberry Tree*, Fauset explains that her purpose is to write about the "breathing-spells, in-between spaces where colored men and women work and love and go their ways with no thought of the 'problem'" (the "problem" being racial conflict between blacks and whites.)

After resigning from *The Crisis* in 1926, Fauset returned to teaching. In 1929 she married and later moved to Montclair, New Jersey. After her death in 1961, her work continued to inspire future generations of writers.

Festivals

African Americans have been celebrating their own festivals since colonial times. These usually centered around the desire to be free from **slavery** and to govern themselves. After **emancipation** (freeing of slaves) in 1863, festivals called jubilees were held to celebrate this new freedom. Rich in symbol and meaning, African-American festivals give blacks a chance to express themselves through costume, ritual, singing, dancing, feasting, speaking, and educating their community about black history and culture.

One of the earliest African-American festivals was the coronation festival. It was observed by both slaves and **free blacks** in the North, who held an annual ceremony to choose their own leader. This person was usually African-born, perhaps with royal African ancestors. He was named "king" or "governor" and was often the slave of an important master—the wealthier the slave owner, the more elaborate the election ceremony.

African-American kings served throughout the year by giving opinions on issues concerning slaves, seeing that justice was done, and by serving as a peacekeeper and bargainer between blacks and whites, helping to meet the needs of his people. This custom continued through the 1850s and paved the way for emancipation by expressing the slaves' desire to have their own communities and leaders.

Another festival in which blacks gathered around a leader was Pinkster, an old Dutch festival that was adopted by African Americans in New York during the late eighteenth century. In Albany, New York, the festival was held on top of a hill, near a place where blacks accused of starting a fire had been executed. It was also near an all-black burial ground and the graves of black soldiers who had fought in the nation's wars. The hill symbolized a place where blacks could look down on the world for a change, and it also represented the hills on which African kings once built their capitols.

Pinkster was so popular that American Indian, German, Dutch, and French residents also attended the festival.

After the **American Revolution** (1775–83) and during the years leading up to the American **Civil War** (1861–65), African Americans in the North held yearly emancipation celebrations at which they marched in parades or appeared at state fairs and expositions to give speeches or preach sermons about freedom for their fellow African Americans enslaved in the South. These celebrations were meant to build racial pride and let all citizens know that African Americans had helped to build the nation, had a right to freedom, and were capable of governing themselves.

Big Quarterly was a religious festival that became popular in Wilmington, Delaware, in 1814 and was observed in the mid-Atlantic region along the eastern coast of the United States until the late twentieth century. It was held near the end of the harvest season to honor the founder of the Union Church of Africa, Peter Spencer. At this festival, blacks prayed, sang, beat drums, and played modern and traditional instruments. The celebration began inside the church, then moved outside to the churchyard and later out into the streets, where thousands of people attended. Slaves, given a pass to attend the festival, were often tempted to escape to freedom in the North on the **Underground Railroad**.

January 1 became a day for general celebration of emancipation after it was proclaimed on that day in 1863, but African Americans in many states celebrated freedom from slavery on the day their state enacted the law granting freedom. In Massachusetts that was July 13; in New York it was July 5, and in Texas and surrounding states it is the still-popular "Juneteenth" (emancipation was not announced there until June 19, 1864, eighteen months after it was proclaimed by President Abraham Lincoln).

In New Orleans, Louisiana, African Americans—at first not allowed to participate in carnival celebrations—formed their own "krewe," or secret Mardi Gras society, called the Zulus, after an African tribal people. The Zulus mock the white Mardi Gras king, Rex, and his court by appearing in the parades wearing African masks and costumes and throwing coconuts and other symbolic African trinkets to the crowds. They combine this masking with brass bands, song and dance, and some Caribbean and Latin American carnival customs.

In Brooklyn, New York, and Toronto, Canada, blacks celebrate West Indian festivals in honor of the many slaves that arrived in the United States from islands such as Haiti during the nineteenth century. A migration of many people from the West Indies during the late twentieth century has also contributed to the culture and observance of the festivals. Participants use costumes, masks, music, and dance to re-create the history of blacks in the islands.

Since its creation in 1966, the African-American holiday of **Kwanzaa**, celebrated from December 26 through January 1, has steadily grown in popularity. It establishes a connection between African ancestry and culture and the principles by which African Americans live and work today to strengthen their community and its individual members.

Fetchit, Stepin

ACTOR
May 30, 1902–November 19, 1985

Stepin Fetchit made more than forty films between 1927 and 1976, becoming one of the first black Hollywood stars

Lincoln Theodore Monroe Andrew Perry became a major actor as "Stepin Fetchit." His career continues to be controversial. Some people see him as a pioneering actor who had an amazing career. Others see him as one who profited through his negative African-American characters.

Perry was born and raised in Key West, Florida, and left home in 1914 to pursue a career in show business. He and comic Ed Lee developed a vaudeville act ("vaudeville" refers to popular traveling stage shows of the early 1900s featuring song, dance, acrobatics, and magic acts) entitled "Step 'n' Fetchit: Two Dancing Fools from Dixie." When Perry and Lee split, Perry adopted the name "Stepin Fetchit" as his own.

Stepin Fetchit spent years on the vaudeville circuit, developing his stage character as a lazy, dim-witted, slow, shuffling black servant. Stepin Fetchit arrived in Hollywood in the 1920s, and his first appearance, in the 1927 film *In Old Kentucky*, playing his stereotyped black character, earned him positive reviews.

Stepin Fetchit went on to make more than forty films between 1927 and 1976, becoming one of the first black Hollywood stars. Nonetheless, Stepin Fetchit's heyday in Hollywood came to an end in the late 1930s. Black audiences were uncomfortable with the stereotypes, and white audiences became tired of them. Stepin Fetchit left Hollywood in the early 1940s and moved to Chicago, Illinois. It was not until the late 1960s that he resurfaced as a member of boxer **Muhammad Ali**'s staff.

In 1972 Stepin Fetchit was awarded a Special Image Award by the Hollywood chapter of the **National Association for the Advancement of Colored People (NAACP).** Stepin Fetchit died in Los Angeles, California, in 1985.

Fifteenth Amendment

According to the Fifteenth Amendment to the U.S. Constitution, voting rights cannot be denied by the federal government or any state "on account of race, color, or previous condition of servitude." The amendment reflected the federal government's growing role as the enforcer of civil rights.

Having granted most Southern black men the right to vote, at least temporarily, by the Military Reconstruction Acts of 1867, the Republican majority in Congress wanted to make black **suffrage** (voting rights) nationwide and permanent. Congressman George S. Boutwell of Massachusetts proposed a constitutional amendment in January 1869.

Other Republicans, however, insisted that northern states must remain able to restrict voting rights on the basis of literacy (the ability to read and write). In addition, the argument involved states' rights: some congressmen were against granting unrestricted authority, especially voting rights, to the federal government. In response to such concerns, a relatively limited form of the amendment passed Congress in February 1869, over strong Democratic opposition. It was approved by the states in March 1870.

As feared, Southern state governments almost eliminated black voting through poll taxes (taxes placed on voters), literacy tests, residency requirements, and similar means. The Fifteenth Amendment permanently secured voting rights in the Northern states, several of which still did not permit black voting at the time. It was not until the Voting Rights Act of 1965 that the vast majority of eligible blacks in the South were registered to vote.

Fifty-fourth Regiment of Massachusetts Volunteer Infantry

The Fifty-fourth Massachusetts Regiment was an all-black army unit created by the North during the American **Civil War** (1861–65). It was the first of its kind. "The eyes of the whole world are upon you," one black newspaper announced to members after the regiment was formed. "Civilized man everywhere waits to see if you will prove yourselves."

Massachusetts governor John A. Andrew, who was opposed to **slavery,** organized the regiment in 1863. For officers, he chose white men with military experience who also opposed slavery. Members of the unit came from all over the North, and members of many black communities braved the threats and assaults of racist mobs to collect money and supplies for the troops.

The Fifty-fourth quickly proved its courage in the South Carolina Sea Islands, saving a white regiment under attack. The unit also led the attack on Fort Wagner, a key Confederate stronghold in Charleston harbor, South Carolina. Although the regiment lost nearly half of its men and did not win the fort, the unit's bravery won blacks the right to serve in the army. Nearly 178,000 African Americans enlisted and played an important role in the victory over slavery and the South.

The unit continued to fight throughout the war. Members also led other black regiments in a pay strike against the government. Although they were promised the same pay and benefits as whites, all blacks, regardless of rank, received less pay than the lowest-paid white soldiers. The pay strike was successful, however, and in 1864 Congress passed a law granting equal pay for black and white troops.

Film

When the making of motion pictures began in the late 1800s, African Americans were only half a century removed from slavery and were portrayed in books, on the stage, and in advertisements as the typical poor, grinning black eager to please a white "master." This stereotype carried over into the first movies made by white filmmakers, but from the early 1900s blacks attempted to make films that would give a true picture of their race. Since that time, the number of African Americans in film has increased steadily, and today there are dozens of popular black actors and actresses and a growing number of successful black filmmakers in the United States.

Early Films Featuring African Americans

Some of the first motion pictures shown in the United States were simple documentary (based on facts) films played at the Cotton States Exposition in Atlanta, Georgia, in 1895. African Americans were realistically pictured in these films, before the stereotypes found in books and stage musicals made their way into the movies. After the turn of the twentieth century, filmmakers developed techniques for making longer movies, and with this new type of film the old African-American stereotypes returned. One example was *His Trust* (1911), an American **Civil War** (1861–65) tale about a slave who is trusted with managing his master's estate while he is away at war.

African Americans soon began making their own films designed for black audiences. One of the earliest was William Foster's *The Railroad Porter* (1912). As movies became more popular throughout the United States, however, larger motion picture companies controlled most of the business, making it nearly impossible for small-time filmmakers to pay for making and marketing a film.

When white filmmaker D. W. Griffith released his Civil War movie *The Birth of a Nation* in 1915, it portrayed blacks during the **Reconstruction** period (the decade following the war) as seeking revenge over whites in the broken South by cheating and scheming against them. The fact that the movie was nationally advertised angered blacks, and the **National Association for the Advancement of Colored People (NAACP)** demanded that scenes wrongly depicting blacks be cut from the movie.

Blacks began making their own movie to tell their story. Educator and leader **Booker T. Washington** (1856–1915) helped provide resources to make the film *The Birth of a Race*. But Washington died in 1915, and **World War I** (1914–18) had a tremendous influence on the country and the movie. By the time it was released, the theme had changed from one about African Americans to a movie about the United States entering the war.

Movies of the 1920s and 1930s

During the prosperous 1920s some black and white moviemakers produced "race" films that were about blacks and appealed to black audiences. **Oscar Micheaux** was one of the best known. A few white-owned studios made well-known black classics, like *The Sport of the Gods* (1921). The white company David Starkman's Colored Players produced *The Scar of Shame* in 1927, addressing the concerns of the black middle class and encouraging them to strive for good things in life in spite of discrimination.

During the **Great Depression** of the 1930s, Hollywood, California, moviemakers produced some good films with black characters, including *Hearts in Dixie* (1929). Hollywood movies still often included the clownish black man, such as **Stepin Fetchit,** and Hollywood's censorship system had many rules concerning blacks in motion pictures, limiting their performances to a few types of roles with smaller parts. However, black actress **Hattie McDaniel** became the first African American to win an Academy Award, for her role as "Mammy" in the classic film *Gone with the Wind* (1939).

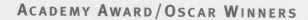

ACADEMY AWARD/OSCAR WINNERS

The Oscar is an award given annually by the Academy of Motion Picture Arts and Sciences for individual or group excellence in more than twenty different categories of motion picture making. The Annual Academy Awards Presentation is televised and has been held each year since 1929. Up to five nominations are made in each category, and final winners are chosen by vote of the entire academy membership.

Although African Americans have participated widely in motion pictures since about the 1940s, they have received few Academy Awards. Among the African Americans who have won Oscars are Hattie McDaniel (1939); Sidney Poitier (1963); Lou Gossett, Jr. (1982); and Denzel Washington (1990).

World War II Creates Big Changes

World War II (1939–45) affected moviemaking more than any other political event. Hollywood cut racist parts out of movies and made films such as *Lifeboat* (1944) that showed an integrated (blacks and whites sharing the same facilities) armed forces. The United States needed black soldiers and war workers, so the government made short films featuring blacks with important roles in the war effort.

After the war was over, the NAACP encouraged the government to send these films to schools, trade unions, and civil rights groups to educate whites about the role of blacks in the armed forces. Peacetime Hollywood movies made about the war also featured black soldiers, such as Stanley Kramer's *Home of the Brave* (1949).

Films of the 1950s and 1960s

The 1950s saw some African-American actors and actresses star in popular Hollywood films. Actor **Sidney Poitier** made *The Blackboard Jungle* (1954), *The Defiant Ones* (1959), and *Lilies of the Field* (1963), and Dorothy Dandridge starred in the all-black film *Carmen Jones* (1954).

Television coverage of civil rights activities during the 1960s forced Hollywood to give a more realistic portrayal of blacks. Independent and foreign filmmakers rose to the challenge before Hollywood did, and filmmaker Michael Roemer's *Nothing but a Man* (1964) was called by a popular magazine the greatest of all black movies.

Blaxploitation Films

As television programs of the 1960s and 1970s showed blacks in roles as social workers, policemen, and attorneys, Hollywood had no choice but to follow. However, many of the movies fell into the category of what came to be called "blaxploitation" films. Young blacks flocked to these movies. Although violent and political in content, they showed "cool" black heroes. Probably the most popular was *Shaft* (1970).

AFRICAN-AMERICAN FILMMAKERS

African Americans have been producing films since the early 1900s. Brothers George P. and Noble Johnson, impressed with the film *The Birth of a Race,* formed the Lincoln Company, which produced several films with black themes between 1916 and 1922. This inspired other African-American filmmaking ventures, including the Frederick Douglass Company and the Norman studio.

Oscar Micheaux (1884–1951) was one of the earliest well-known black film-makers. He worked from 1919 through the 1940s, producing films that were referred to as "race" films. These were about blacks and appealed to black audiences. Among them were *Within Our Gates* (1921) and *Body and Soul* (1924).

During the Great Depression **jazz** musician **Duke Ellington** (1899–1974) produced short musical films like *Black and Tan* (1929) and *The Symphony in Black* (1935). In 1941 **Walter Francis White,** of the NAACP, helped adapt the movie *Sundown* to fit the changing politics brought on by World War II.

During the 1960s and 1970s filmmakers Gordon Parks Jr. and Melvin Van Peebles created "blaxploitation" films about black heroes in violent city settings, like Parks's *Shaft* (1970) and Peebles's *Sweet Sweetback's Baadasssss Song* (1971).

By the 1970s and 1980s many young blacks had enrolled in film schools, and independent filmmakers produced some excellent films. Among them were St. Clair Bourne (*Let the Church Say Amen!,* 1973), **Charles Burnett** (*Killer of Sheep,* 1977), and Ayoka Chenzira (*Hair Piece: A Film for Nappyheaded People,* 1984).

Filmmaker "Spike Lee"'s (1957–) movies, such as *Jungle Fever* (1991), were so successful that he was granted a chance to make a movie about the life of the great black leader **Malcolm X** (1925–1965). *Malcolm X* (1992) appealed to both black and white audiences. Lee's most recent films include the documentary *4 Little Girls* (1997), about the 1963 bombing of an African-American church in Alabama, and *He Got Game* (1998), about a high school basketball star.

Black filmmakers enjoying success at the beginning of the twenty-first century include John Singleton (1968–), who at age twenty-four was the youngest person ever to be nominated for an Academy Award for best director; actor-filmmaker Forest Whitaker (1961–); the actress, talk-show host, and producer Oprah Winfrey; actor-filmmaker Eddie Murphy; and comedian-filmmaker brothers Shawn, Marlon, and Keenan Ivory Wayans. Some of the popular films created by Singleton are *Boyz N the Hood* (1991), *Poetic Justice* (1993), and *Shaft* (2000). Whitaker's movies include *Waiting to Exhale* (1995) and *The Green Dragon* (2000). The Wayans brothers created *Don't Be a Menace to South Central While Drinking Your Juice in the Hood* (1996) and *Scary Movie* (2000). Murphy's films include *Vampire in Brooklyn* (1995) and *Nutty Professor II: The Klumps* (2000). Winfrey produced *Beloved,* based on the novel by black author **Toni Morrison,** in 1998.

Modern Film

During the late twentieth and early twenty-first centuries, black actors, actresses, and filmmakers quickly rose to success and fame. Among the

biggest stars were actors Samuel L. Jackson, **Morgan Freeman**, **Denzel Washington,** Cuba Gooding Jr., Wesley Snipes, **Danny Glover,** Laurence Fishburne, Will Smith, LL Cool J, Omar Epps, Taye Diggs, and Djimon Hounsou. Black actresses with starring roles included **Whoopi Goldberg**, **Oprah Winfrey,** Angela Bassett, Halle Berry, Vanessa L. Williams, Queen Latifah, and Nia Long.

Fisher, Rudolph John Chauncey

FICTION WRITER, DRAMATIST, ESSAYIST
1897–1934

The youngest child of a Baptist minister, Rudolph Fisher was born in Washington, D.C., in 1897. He was raised mostly in Providence, Rhode Island, where he graduated from Brown University. He wrote his first published short story, "The City of Refuge" (1925), in his final year at **Howard University** Medical School (Washington, D.C.), launching careers in both literature and science. When Fisher's internship ended at Freedman's Hospital in Washington, D.C., a fellowship took him to New York City in 1925 to work in bacteriology (the study of bacteria and other very small living things, especially those that cause disease) at Columbia University.

During the **Harlem Renaissance**, an exciting period of cultural achievement in early 1900s Harlem, New York, he published both scientific articles (in medical publications such as the *Journal of Infectious Diseases*) and short stories (in such magazines as the *Atlantic Monthly* and *McClure's*.).

One of the more productive writers of the Harlem Renaissance, Fisher produced in less than a decade fifteen published and seven unpublished short stories, two novels, half a dozen book reviews, a magazine feature article, and a play—while maintaining a medical practice, administering a private X-ray laboratory, and overseeing the radiology (X-ray) department at the International Hospital in Manhattan (New York). The *Walls of Jericho* (1928), his first novel, weaves together the lives of people who are attending a Harlem ball. His other novel, *The Conjure Man Dies* (1932), is regarded as the earliest example of a detective novel by an African-American author.

Fisher's reputation rests, however, on the excellence of his short fiction. The varied focus of his short stories creates a rich and varied image of Harlem life. Two stories in particular, "The City of Refuge" and "Miss Cynthie" (1933), are Fisher's most highly regarded achievements. In "Miss Cynthie," Fisher's last published work, the main character struggles to accept her grandson, who she hopes will be a doctor but who turns out to be a song-and-dance whiz.

In 1934 Fisher underwent a series of operations for an intestinal disorder and died on December 26.

Fisher produced in less than a decade fifteen published and seven unpublished short stories, two novels, half a dozen book reviews, a magazine feature article, and a play—while maintaining a medical practice

Fisk Jubilee Singers. *See* Fisk University

Fisk University

Founded: Fisk was established in 1866 with funds from the American Missionary Association, the **Freedmen's Bureau,** and from Gen. Clinton Bowen Fisk, assistant commissioner of the Freedmen's Bureau for Tennessee and Kentucky. (The Freedmen's Bureau was a government agency formed after the Civil War (1860–65) to protect the rights of former slaves.)

History Highlights:

- 1866: The Fisk School, or the Fisk Free Colored School, is established as an elementary school for **free blacks** in the Nashville, Tennessee, area.

- 1867: The Fisk School becomes Fisk University, with the goal of being a first-class college for educating black teachers.

- 1871: Because the school is experiencing severe financial difficulties, Fisk's treasurer and music instructor, George L. White, along with nine students, sets off on a fund-raising singing tour. The group is named the Fisk Jubilee Singers.

- 1873: Groundbreaking ceremonies are held for the erection of Jubilee Hall. It is the first permanent building on the forty-acre campus; the land was bought with the $20,000 the Jubilee Singers raised during their first singing tour.

- 1875: The first four students graduate from Fisk, and black professors first join the staff.

- 1926: Thomas Elsa Jones becomes the last white president of Fisk.

- 1944: The Institute of Race Relations (IRR) is established with the goal of promoting better race relations worldwide.

- 1947: Charles Spurgeon Johnson, founder of the IRR, becomes Fisk's first black president.

- 1983: Long plagued by financial difficulties, the university is $2.8 million in debt (which includes a $157,000 overdue gas bill). Fisk alumni and leaders across the United States rally, and through donations the crisis is averted.

Location: Nashville, Tennessee

Known For: Many historic black college and university firsts, including the first black college to be fully accredited by the Southern Association of Colleges and Schools and to be granted a chapter of Phi Beta Kappa (the most prestigious college honor society). Fisk University is also home to the famous Fisk Jubilee Singers, who have performed throughout the world since 1871.

Number of Students (1999–2000): 826

Grade Average of Incoming Freshman: 3.0

Admission Requirements: Recommended two years of math (including algebra and geometry), four years of English, one year of science, one year of foreign language, one year of history; SAT or ACT scores; letter of recommendation from a teacher, counselor, or principal.

Mailing Address:
Fisk University
Office of Admission
1000 17th Ave. North
Nashville, TN 37208

Telephone: (800) 443-3475

E-mail: admit@dubois.fisk.edu

URL: http://www.fisk.edu

Campus: Fisk's forty-acre campus is located just outside downtown Nashville. The library contains over 200,000 documents and includes many valuable research collections and rare books. The Carl van Vechten Gallery is home to Fisk's $10 million Alfred Stieglitz Collection of Modern Art, presented to the university in 1949 by Georgia O'Keefe, artist and widow of Stieglitz.

Special Programs: The Fisk Race Relations Institute, which is a forum for scholars and leaders throughout the world to explore racism and race relations, provides training about race relations and hosts an intensive seminar each summer that draws black and white leaders to the campus; combined programs in medical technology and nursing with Rush- Presbyterian-St. Luke's Medical Center (Chicago); combined programs in business administration and science/engineering with Vanderbilt University; combined program in pharmacy with **Howard University** (Washington, D.C.).

Extracurricular Activities: Student government; student newspaper; literary magazine; four sororities and four fraternities; organizations, including the famous Fisk Jubilee Singers, the Modern Mass Choir, and the Orchesis Dance Club; athletics (men's baseball, basketball, cross-country, tennis, track-and-field; women's basketball, cross-country, tennis, track-and-field, volleyball).

Fisk Alumni: Historian and editor **W. E. B. Du Bois** (1868–1963); historian Charles H. Wesley (1891–1967); novelist **Frank Yerby** (1916–1991); Hazel O'Leary (1937–), former U.S. secretary of energy.

Fitzgerald, Ella ▪▪▪

JAZZ VOCALIST
April 25, 1918–June 15, 1996

Hailed as "the first lady of song," Ella Fitzgerald was one of the great American voices of all time. Born in Virginia, as a child she moved with her mother to Yonkers, New York. Her career in music began almost by accident. Attending an amateur-night contest in the New York City neighborhood of Harlem, on a dare Fitzgerald took the stage, intending to dance. Frozen by stage fright, she sang instead. She was awarded first prize.

The next year, 1935, she appeared at Harlem's famous **Apollo Theater**, where many black performers got their start. She was spotted by a member of Chick Webb's (1909–1939) band, the great swing orchestra. Fitzgerald sang with Webb's ensemble for the next six years. Her breakthrough came in

ELLA'S SONGBOOKS

Fitzgerald made numerous recordings during her fifty-year career. Among her best known are her series of "songbooks." In 1956 she released the first, *The Cole Porter Songbook,* and later turned her attention to recording the music of other great American composers, including **Duke Ellington** (1899–1974) and Irving Berlin (1888–1989). The songbooks have been acclaimed as the ultimate showcase of the art of popular singing.

1938 with the recording of "A-Tisket, A-Tasket," which she cowrote. The hit song made her a national celebrity.

During the 1940s Fitzgerald built her reputation as a solo performer, releasing many popular records that demonstrated her versatility. With excellent pitch, clear diction, and an always-present sense of rhythm, she could sing swing, jazz, and popular songs with great style. She became known for scat singing. (In scat, sounds take the place of words, and the singer makes them up as she goes.) No one "scatted" better than Ella, as she was fondly known by fans around the world.

The recipient of numerous Grammy Awards and other honors, Fitzgerald was single-mindedly devoted to her music. Not even her failing health kept her from the stage. After undergoing heart surgery in 1986, she continued to give concerts and record on a limited basis for the last ten years of her life.

Flack, Roberta

POPULAR SINGER
1939–

Born in North Carolina but raised in Virginia, Roberta Flack is a singer whose smooth, romantic songs touch the hearts of her listeners. She began playing music at an early age on a piano salvaged from a junkyard. At fifteen she won a full scholarship to **Howard University** (Washington, D.C.), and she graduated in 1958 with a degree in music education. After teaching for several years, she began performing in 1967 at a Washington, D.C., nightclub. She was signed to a record contract in 1969 and later that year released her debut album, *First Take,* which included a song that would become her breakthrough recording three years later, "The First Time Ever I Saw Your Face" (1972).

"The First Time" became the number one hit song in the United States for six weeks and won a Grammy Award for Record of the Year and for Best Female Pop Vocal Performance. In 1973 Flack recorded another number one single, "Killing Me Softly With His Song," which topped the charts for five weeks and won Flack a Grammy for Song of the Year. She also won a trophy for Best Female Pop Vocal Performance for "Killing Me Softly."

Ella Fitzgerald, the "First Lady of Song" (Archive Photos. Reproduced by permission)

Besides doing solo work, Flack also recorded several hit duets with singer Donny Hathaway, including "Where is the Love," from 1972, and "The Closer I Get to You," from 1978. In the early 1980s Flack teamed up with Peabo Bryson for a number of recording duets, producing in 1983 a top twenty single, "Tonight I Celebrate My Love." Flack continues to release albums full of romantic vocals.

Fletcher, Thomas "Tom"

PERFORMER, MINSTREL
May 16, 1873–October 13, 1954

Tom Fletcher was a minstrel entertainer, and he later wrote about his experiences in his autobiography. He was born and raised in Portsmouth, Ohio, a town that was frequently visited by minstrel shows. Minstrel shows were performances that included music, songs, and jokes. Fletcher developed an early love for the theater and sang at local talent shows and festivals. As a teenager he traveled with some of the best-known minstrel groups of the time. Fletcher had a variety of skills, and he often served as singer, dancer, drummer, comedian, and stage manager. He performed in vaudeville shows (traveling theater shows at the beginning of the 1900s that featured a variety of short acts), in private homes, and in films.

In 1919 he toured with musician **Will Marion Cook**'s (1869–1944) New York Syncopated Orchestra in Europe. Fletcher remained active as a performer and bandleader in the 1920s and 1930s for various summer resorts, at New York City-area affairs, and at the Mount Washington Hotel in New Hampshire. In the 1940s he performed on Broadway and assisted with the **Katherine Dunham** Company's *Ballet Negro* (1946).

Fletcher is best known for his partly autobiographical *100 Years of the Negro in Show Business* (1954), one of the few books describing black entertainment history before 1930. His book recalls the day-to-day life of black theater performers in the late nineteenth and early twentieth centuries. *100 Years* is a basic source for the still largely untold history of blacks in show business.

Flipper, Henry Ossian

ARMY OFFICER
March 21, 1856–May 3, 1940

Henry Ossian Flipper was the first African American to graduate from West Point

Henry Ossian Flipper was the first African American to graduate from West Point, the most prestigious military academy in the United States. This important achievement opened the door for future black students to receive some of the best military training in the country. Flipper is perhaps just as well known for his dismissal from the army as he is for his pioneering efforts at West Point. However, fifty-nine years after his death, Flipper's name was cleared and the dignity of his achievement was restored.

Flipper was born in Thomasville, Georgia, to parents who were both slaves. He began his college education at **Atlanta University** and later transferred to West Point. After four years of harsh racial treatment and hard work, Flipper graduated in 1877. He later wrote a book describing his experiences, *The Colored Cadet at West Point*. In 1881, while working for the army in Texas, he was charged with stealing money and behaving improperly. Although it was proved that Flipper did not steal anything, he was expelled from the army for improper behavior. Flipper believed he was a victim of racism and spent the rest of his life trying to clear his name.

Flipper worked for the U.S. Department of Justice after his discharge and became an expert on Spanish and Mexican land law. In 1919 he earned a position as translator for the Senate and worked his way into a position with the U.S. Department of the Interior (which at that time was in charge Indian affairs). Although Flipper did not live to see his name cleared, in 1976 West Point granted him an honorable discharge and had a statue of him created in his honor. Then, in 1999, President Bill Clinton held a ceremony during which he pardoned Flipper, officially clearing his name and recognizing his important achievement.

Flood, Curtis Charles "Curt"

BASEBALL PLAYER

January 18, 1938–January 21, 1998

Curtis "Curt" Charles Flood was a gifted outfielder whose influence on professional **baseball** extended beyond his athletic abilities. He made a stand for players' rights in trading situations by taking major league baseball to court.

Born in Houston, Texas, Flood moved to Oakland, California, where he developed a passion for baseball at a young age. After graduating from high school, he signed with the Cincinnati Reds (1956). At the time racism dominated the league, which prevented Flood from proving his abilities with the Reds. However, when he was traded to the St. Louis Cardinals in 1958, Flood took full advantage of the increased playing time he received. In St. Louis, Flood won seven Golden Glove awards for his fielding, had a .293 batting average, and helped the Cardinals win two World Series championships (1964 and 1967).

In 1969 the Cardinals announced that Flood was to be traded to Philadelphia. Flood was hurt by this decision and decided to fight it. He took the league to court, arguing that it was unfair that players did not have a say in trading decisions. Flood's legal defense challenged the league's ability to make players the property of a team, because it prevented players from seeking better opportunities. Flood's position was shared by the majority of players, and the case was ultimately heard by the U.S. Supreme Court. Although Flood lost the case, his efforts paved the way for future advances in players' rights.

After retiring from baseball, Flood opened a bar in Spain. He returned to the United States in 1976 and earned a management position with the Oakland Athletics. Flood also became involved in youth baseball programs and published an **autobiography** called *The Way It Is* (1998).

Florida

First African-American Settlers: Blacks have lived in Florida since shortly after the founding of St. Augustine by Spain in 1565.

Slave Population: Spain offered freedom to runaway slaves from the British colonies in Georgia. In 1763 Spain surrendered Florida to Britain, and practically all of its inhabitants—including at least 600 slaves and 23 **free blacks**—departed for Havana, Cuba, and other places. More enslaved blacks began arriving in 1781, and their population rose from 2,000 to more than 10,000 in a short time. After Florida was sold to the United States in 1819, the state developed an agricultural economy based on slave labor. It became the twenty-seventh state in 1845.

Free Black Population: When Spain regained the state in 1783, St. Augustine developed a large free black population, and in 1795 the colonial governor ruled that slave owners had eight days to claim slaves or they would be considered free.

Civil War: When in 1862 Union (Northern) troops took over St. Augustine, they fortified the town with the hired labor of the town-s free black population and of slaves who had fled to freedom behind Union lines. A battle between federal forces and Confederate soldiers near Olustee in 1864 resulted in the death of 300 black soldiers occupying the North's front line.

Reconstruction: Reconstruction brought a reordering of Florida's political system, allowing African-American males the right to vote and providing for public schools. When Democrats regained control of the state in 1876, however, blacks quickly lost the scant legal protections they had managed to build. Most blacks, unable to purchase or retain land holdings, were forced to seek agricultural work or to accept dangerous jobs. Although commercial development brought employment to many African Americans around the turn of the century, many blacks left Florida; between 1900 and 1940 blacks dropped from 44 percent to 27 percent of the total population.

The Great Depression: Florida entered a sustained depression in the 1920s that lasted until the coming of **military** bases and the growth of the citrus industry during **World War II** (1939–45). The expanding economy drew African Americans southward and also led to an increase in the migration of Caribbean blacks. The struggle for equality took on new life in the 1940s, with important court victories (for example, ordering the registration of thousands of black voters and forcing the integration of public schools and universities). The Tallahassee Bus Boycott of 1956 was a significant turning point in civil rights struggles in Florida.

Civil Rights Movement: The **sit-in** movement began in Florida in 1950, sparking local whites to riot and causing some public areas to close rather than admit blacks. Large protests against racial discrimination during the 1960s drew heavy white resistance and police brutality. Florida's tense race relations led to several racial uprisings during the period, including seven in 1967 alone.

Current African-American Population: According to U.S. Census Bureau estimates, the total black population in Florida was 2,267,753 (15 percent of the state population) as of July 1, 1998.

Key Figures: Josiah T. Walls (1842–1905), prominent attorney and U.S. representative; Thomas Fortune (1856–1928), journalist and civil rights activist; composer J. Rosamond Johnson (1873–1954); writer **Zora Neale Hurston** (c. 1891–1960); **Mary McLeod Bethune** (1875–1955), founder of **Bethune-Cookman College**; **Howard Thurman** (1900–1981), minister and educator.

Folk Arts and Crafts

Before the industrial era of the late 1800s and 1900s, most people made their own tools, containers, clothes, and toys. Slaves on the plantations had

few household items, so they either made them or did without. After slavery ended, the folk arts and crafts that blacks had learned on the plantations continued to be useful as they struggled in poverty as free men and women. Folk arts and crafts have always served as both a means of providing goods and an outlet for creative self-expression.

The names of only a handful of early African-American folk artists have survived. Most contemporary folk artists come from South Carolina, Georgia, Alabama, Mississippi, Louisiana, and Texas, and most produce their best works late in life. A thread of African inspiration can be found in traditional black arts and crafts of the South, revealing a link to African heritage. African-American folk art is brightly colored, without the use of techniques learned in art schools, such as perspective and scale. But because it is so spontaneous and free of outside influences, a number of trained African-American artists have used folk art forms in their work.

Most contemporary folk artists come from South Carolina, Georgia, Alabama, Mississippi, Louisiana, and Texas, and most produce their best works late in life

Basketry

Black artisans in the United States have been making coiled-grass baskets for more than three hundred years. These were especially popular along the "rice coast," the Atlantic coastline from North Carolina to the Florida border, where African slaves introduced basketry as part of their rice-harvesting skills. Today, baskets are made and sold at outdoor stands by hundreds of "sewers" around Charleston, South Carolina. They use sweetgrass, rushes, pine needles, and strips of palmetto leaves to make an endless variety of "show baskets." More delicate than the old-time "work baskets," these can be used as decorative containers for all kinds of objects, from flower pots to umbrellas.

Musical Instrument Making

Plantation slaves made instruments like fiddles and banjos from gourds and animal hides, as well as rattles, gongs, scrapers, fifes, whistles, pan pipes, and drums. Drumming was an ancient African tradition that slaves continued in America for musical performances as well as religious and healing rituals. Slaveholders, believing slaves were using drums to send secret messages, passed a law in 1739 banning the beating of drums, but slaves continued to make drums from animal skins and hollow logs or gourds.

Pottery

For decades historians who found fragments of round-bottomed clay vessels at old plantation sites thought they were made by American Indians. They later discovered that slaves made these pots. A mysterious "X" carved into the bottom of many of the pots is believed to represent a Central African symbol that slaves might have used to call on the spirits of African ancestors.

Around 1810 a white South Carolina potter named Abner Landrum began training slaves to produce pottery in his successful shop in the Edgefield district. The best-known slave potter was "Dave," who had learned to read and write by working at Landrum's newspaper. He signed the bottom of his pots and wrote a few words describing the pot and its maker. Dave's most famous pot is a forty-five-gallon jar, thirty inches high, which he called "Great and Noble Jar." Black potters in Edgefield also decorated their pottery with faces, using a white clay for the eyes and teeth, similar to Central African styles used on statues and masks. White objects were used in Africa to represent the ancestors and the dead.

Woodcarving

The most decorative of African-American woodcarving forms is the cane, or walking stick, often carved with African symbols like snakes and other reptiles, as well as figures of humans, signifying communication between people and the spiritual world. Southern canemakers also decorate their work with bits of metal, glass, beads, and other shiny materials, much the way African craftsmen use mixed media to create artworks.

Two of the most impressive examples of nineteenth-century African-American carved walking sticks were in Missouri made by a slave blacksmith named Henry Gudgell (c. 1826–1895) during the 1860s. The snake, lizard, and tortoise carvings on the sticks are unmistakably African. These figures were sometimes related to African beliefs in witchcraft and folk healing.

Quilting

Early women slaves learned the art of quilting from their white mistresses, but the oldest form of African-American quilt patterns are those using long strips like the kente cloth of Ghana, suggesting the quilters' African heritage. Late-nineteenth-century African-American quilter Harriet Powers, of Athens, Georgia, used images that appeared to come from Dahomey, a kingdom on the West African coast.

Twentieth-Century and Contemporary African-American Folk Art

Tombstone carver **William Edmondson** (1882–1951) of Tennessee was the first African–American folk artist to earn national recognition, when his limestone sculptures were shown in 1937 at the Museum of Modern Art in New York. Painter **Horace Pippin** (1882–1946) of Pennsylvania was the most famous early-twentieth-century folk artist. Most of his paintings are now in the permanent collections of major museums.

New interest in African-American folk art began in 1982, when the Corcoran Gallery of Art in Washington, D.C., displayed an exhibit called "Black Folk Art in America, 1930–1980." It included the works of twenty African-American artists and was the first such exhibit at a major museum.

Using thrown-away objects and scraps is another characteristic of black folk art. Some of the objects used are chewing gum, styrofoam, mud, fish bones, broken glass, umbrella frames, bottle caps, and aluminum cans.

Elderly artists often create scenes from slavery or their rural childhood. Louisiana artist Clementine Hunter (1885–1988) rarely depicted whites in her paintings, showing a great deal of black pride. Folk artist John Landry (1912–1986) grew up in New Orleans and was always fascinated by Mardi Gras floats. He created miniature, shoebox-size floats out of wire and plastic beads.

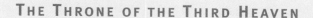

THE THRONE OF THE THIRD HEAVEN

Most modern African-American folk art shows the artist's deep religious beliefs. Many artists are ministers or missionaries or say that God guided them in their work. One of the most mysterious of these religious works is *The Throne of the Third Heaven of the Nation's Millennium General Assembly,* created in a downtown Washington, D.C., garage by James Hampton (1911–1964) over a period of fourteen years. The throne is made from furniture, light bulbs, and other thrown-away objects that were carefully covered with silver and gold foil. Few people knew about the throne before Hampton's death, but it has now been placed in the Smithsonian Institution, National Museum of American Art.

Folklore

African-American folklore includes tales, songs, proverbs, greetings, gestures, rhymes, rituals, and ways of making and using objects. Folklore has always served to communicate shared cultural beliefs and values within the African-American community. It continues to provide individuals with a rich creative outlet for expression and performance.

Scholars once thought African slaves left their native cultures behind when they were forced to come to America. Now they know that the slaves created a new culture based on common ideas they shared from a blending of their African cultures. They adapted these ideas to fit their situation in the new land.

African-American folklore was passed down orally (through the spoken word) until the late nineteenth century, when the first attempts were made to write it down. White missionaries who flocked to the South after the American **Civil War** (1861–65) to help educate and train freed slaves were the first to gather and record African-American folklore. Their focus was mainly on spirituals (religious songs about freedom), animal-trickster tales, and folk beliefs.

Spirituals

The first book-length collection of African-American folklore published was a collection of spirituals, *Slave Songs of the United States* (1867). Spirituals developed around biblical Old Testament figures whose faith in God allowed them to be freed from slavery and persecution. The songs were modeled after an African song type, the "call and response," which has a lead singer and a chorus.

Animal-Trickster Tales

Tales about clever animals who posed as humans to communicate an important lesson about survival were found everywhere in Africa. African-American slaves adapted these tales to fit the conditions of **slavery**. In African-American folktales the trickster uses cleverness, quick words, and

Books of African American Folklore

native wit to outsmart the fox or wolf (who represents the slavemaster) and get food or material goods.

With the publication of author Joel Chandler Harris's (1848–1908) *Uncle Remus, His Songs and Sayings: Folklore of the Old Plantation* (1880), which is based on African-American folktales, the collection of animal-trickster tales increased. By the end of the nineteenth century, hundreds had been published. Brer Rabbit, made famous in Harris's stories, was the most common animal trickster in the United States.

Folk Beliefs

At the center of African-American folk beliefs was the "conjurer," or one who had a special gift for either causing or curing illness. Based on African medicine men, he was known as the root doctor, hoodooer, or "two-heads." Some people believed the conjurer's power came from an evil source; some said it came from God; and still others believed it was a practice that could be learned.

Like their African ancestors, many African-American slaves believed that someone could cast a "spell" to cause another to be sick. Slaves believed only the power of a conjurer could make the person well again. Conjurers used charms, amulets, curses, and spells in their practice, but they most often used herbal medicines to cure illness.

Other Types of Folklore

In the late nineteenth and early twentieth centuries, the trickster was transformed into the badman, a character who was often celebrated in legends and ballads. His enemy is the law, usually the white policeman or sheriff. The badman in folklore tries to get members of the black community to join in illegal activities and then finds himself in trouble with the law. When the folktale badman is caught and punished, his community shows him sympathy. An example is the story of Stackolee, who shoots a man who was cheating him in a card game.

The most common types of folktales performed by African Americans since the end of slavery try to identify reasons for blacks' difficulties in society. These often-humorous tales address ways that blacks might have caused their own troubles through negative attitudes. Learning about these attitudes gives them the power to change them and improve their lives. Some of these tales deal with physical characteristics of the black race, such as dark skin, nappy hair, or big feet or hands. They are often set at the beginning of time, when God is supposedly giving out human traits. Black people are said to have received their traits because they arrived late, were playing cards and did not hear God calling them, or were too impatient to wait for God.

The character "Colored Man" is central to another large group of folktales that tries to explain why African Americans experience the hardships they do. These tales were popular in the early to middle twentieth century. In this group of tales, Colored Man is in a contest with men of other races. God gives the men a task, like choosing packages of different sizes. Colored Man makes the wrong choice because he is greedy, lazy, easily deceived by appearances, or is trying too hard not to be outsmarted.

Verbal play is another form of African-American folklore that was popular in the late twentieth century. Known by the characteristics of signifying, marking, and loud talking, this activity is creative and artistic because it uses humorous and witty forms to convey serious messages.

Folk Music and Singers

African-American folk music includes sacred songs, called spirituals, and many kinds of vocal and instrumental secular (nonreligious) music. Among these are "work" songs, which helped workers get into a rhythm and work more smoothly; street cries; field "hollers" that let plantation workers communicate over long distances; lullabies; and many kinds of dance music. All of these were known before the American **Civil War** (1861–65) and all had roots in the music of Africa.

The ability to make and play African instruments such as the banjo, drums, a "flute," and the balafo, a kind of xylophone was also brought to America by slaves. Some slave-ship captains even collected native instruments before leaving Africa and provided them throughout the voyage to keep the slaves' spirits up, hoping to prevent a revolt. Slaves also learned to play European instruments such as the fiddle, the French horn, and the flute, and they sometimes played for white dances.

Traditional African music uses strong rhythms, hand clapping and foot stomping, and the common "call-and-response" form of singing, in which the leader and the chorus overlap. All of these became part of African-American folk music.

As white evangelists began to convert slaves to Christianity during the mid-eighteenth century, African Americans adapted secular work tunes to sacred songs in church and also learned Protestant hymns. African dances were held less often, except in New Orleans, Louisiana, where they continued into the nineteenth century. One religious dance, called the "shout," was permitted in most black communities after church services were over. It was a circle dance in which the feet edged backward and forward or right and left without being lifted from the floor.

Spirituals probably rose out of a mixing of European hymns and African singing styles when blacks and whites attended church meetings and revivals together at the beginning of the nineteenth century. They became the most popular form of black music after the Civil War. The public in the North first became aware of spirituals through concert tours in the 1870s by groups like the Fisk Jubilee Singers and the Hampton Singers.

In spite of the suffering that slaves endured, they continued to sing and dance. Whites began to imitate them during the early 1800s. They put on "minstrel shows" dressed as slaves, with their faces painted black. After the Civil War talented black performers began to play in minstrel shows and popular theater themselves.

Another form of African-American folk music was the **blues**. Its origins are unknown, but it probably developed among rural blacks during the late 1800s. In contrast to the spiritual, which was usually a group performance with solo and chorus alternating, the blues was a solitary expression of loneliness and misery. It combined some characteristics of the field holler with notes and the rhythm used in African music. Most early blues songs were improvised, or made up on the spot, and so were never written down. By the time the blues became popular enough to be recorded, musicians had developed a professional blues style.

Collections of secular black folk songs began to be published after **World War I** (1914–18), when Natalie Curtin Burlin edited the *Hampton Series of Negro Folk Songs* (1918–19), based on the singing of students at the **Hampton Institute**, Hampton, Virgina. John Wesley Work III produced an important collection, *American Negro Songs and Spirituals*, in 1940, and Lawrence Gellert published *Negro Songs of Protest* in 1936.

The **Civil Rights movement**, which began with the Montgomery, Alabama, bus boycott in December 1955, produced a group of folk songs that played an important role in the movement. Two of the most famous are "We Shall Overcome" and "No More Auction Block for Me."

In southern Louisiana, French-speaking blacks had made their own folk music, called "zydeco," for many years before it was noticed by the outside world. The first **zydeco** recordings were made after **World War II** (1939–45).

Every form of music in the United States has been influenced in some way by black folk music's rhythm and unique notes. This influence has spread worldwide during the late twentieth century. (*See also* **Gospel**)

Football

American-style football is a variation of the English sport of rugby, which developed in the late 1800s. Unlike the case with other sports, African Americans were able to participate in organized football early in American history. However, discrimination prevented blacks from making it into the upper ranks of organized football until the early 1940s. Today, the most prestigious league in the world, the National Football League (NFL), is a reflection of how far the United States has come in granting equal opportunity to African-American athletes.

Blacks in Football, 1890–1920

During the late 1800s and early 1900s, blacks were far more welcome in football than in the majority of other sports. This did not mean, however, that racism was not present. In college football, blacks who played on white college teams had to be taken off the roster if an all-white team did not want to play against them.

Although the majority of blacks were prevented from attending white schools and universities in the late 1800s, certain exceptions were made for athletes. Among the blacks who managed to play football at predominantly white colleges were William Henry Lewis and William Tecumseh Sherman Jackson. Both played for the starting squad at Amherst College in Massachusetts. The first football game between two all-black colleges occurred in 1892. However, the majority of black colleges did not have the funding to establish a football program early on. It was not until the 1920s

that football programs began to develop at all-black schools. It was not until the 1940s that blacks began being accepted into professional football, although there were a few early exceptions. The first black to play professionally was Charles Follis, who played from 1902 to 1906. Follis experienced harsh racist treatment, particularly from fans, and eventually decided it was not worth it anymore and quit the game.

Blacks in Football, 1920–1945

After **World War I** (1914–18) more blacks were showing a talent for the game. However, racism still prevented blacks from entering the game without harassment. At some white universities, blacks were forced to live off campus. In 1923 a black player named Jack Trice was the target of an extreme beating during a game and died of internal bleeding. In addition, several black players, including Duke Slater and Woodrow "Woody" Strode, were not recognized for their skills even though many believed they were All-American candidates. However, several blacks managed to have outstanding football careers, such as running backs Oze Simmons and Bernard Jefferson. In the 1930s the dominant black schools were Morgan State University, the Tuskegee Institute, Wiley University, and Langston College, all of which produced outstanding players.

In 1919 the American Professional Football Association was created, which was the early form of the National Football League (NFL). The first blacks to enter the newly formed league were Robert "Rube" Marshall and Fritz Pollard. Racial incidents were common in the NFL, primarily from the fans. Although NFL coaches and management could have hired blacks, they often claimed that there was a lack of black college talent. Blacks were forced to either create their own teams or play on the West Coast, which created integrated leagues.

Famous Blacks in Modern College Football

After **World War II** (1939–45), the color barrier began to crumble. More blacks began showing their athletic skills on college and professional football fields. Yale University opened its doors to black players in 1949, and blacks began making appearances in college bowl games. The play of running back **Jim Brown** proved that blacks could play as well as whites.

The **Civil Rights movement** helped secure African Americans' place on the football field. During this era Ernie Brown became the first black to win college football's most cherished prize, the Heisman Trophy. By the 1970s and 1980s it became common for white colleges to recruit black players. From 1970 to 1993 blacks won the Heisman Trophy seventeen times. Black colleges began finding the necessary funding to improve their football programs as well. Two of the greatest players in the history of the NFL came from all-black colleges: **Walter Payton** (Jackson State) and Jerry Rice (Mississippi Valley State).

Famous Blacks in Modern Professional Football

In 1946 the Cleveland Browns hired black players **Marion "Tank" Motley** and Bill Willis, who helped them win four consecutive champi-

THE BROWN BOMBERS

In the absence of a professional league in which to play, blacks formed their own teams. The effort was led by Harlem sports promoter, Hershel, "Rip" Day. Blacks put together extremely talented teams such as the New York Brown Bombers (1935), who took their name from heavyweight champion Joe Louis (nicknamed the "Brown Bomber.") The team was coached by **Fritz Pollard,** who eventually became the first black to coach in the NFL. The Brown Bombers was an assembly of all of the outstanding black players that the NFL refused to let play. Pollard coached the Bombers to three winning seasons, playing against semi-professional white teams across the country

onships. Both Motley and Willis were named All-Pros and eventually inducted into the Football Hall of Fame. The success of the Browns opened the floodgates for blacks. Professional teams realized that if they wanted to remain competitive they would have to include blacks in their recruiting. The San Francisco '49ers signed Joe Perry, who became the first black to rush for over one thousand yards two seasons in a row (1953 and 1954).

In 1959 the American Football League (AFL) was created, which presented even more opportunities for blacks to play. In the 1960s players such as Roosevelt Brown and Jim Parker were All-Pro offensive linemen and Willie Davis and Herb Adderly were standout defensive players. In the 1960s the NFL was lit up by the elegant running style of **Gale Sayers.** Sayers won Rookie of the Year honors in 1965 and led the league in rushing the following year before his career was cut short by a knee injury. Paul Warfield and Charlie Taylor revolutionized pass-receiving in the 1960s and were both later elected to the Hall of Fame.

In 1970 the AFL merged with the NFL, which set the stage for the emergence of professional football as America's most popular sport to watch. The NFL was later split into two parts: the National Football Conference (NFC) and the American Football Conference (AFC). By the time of the merger blacks showed particular skill at the running back, wide receiver, and defensive back positions. **"O. J." Simpson** and **Walter Payton** were two of the greatest running backs during the 1970s and 1980s and have become legends. In the 1980s Erick Dickerson, Earl Campbell, and Tony Dorsett also showed remarkable skill as running backs. The 1990s produced several more outstanding running backs, such as Therman Thomas, Barry Sanders, and Emmitt Smith.

Blacks have proved themselves at every position on the football field. However, very few blacks have managed to secure management positions. In 2000 there were no black owners and very few black head coaches. Some exceptions have been Dennis Green of Minnesota and Tony Dungy of Tampa Bay. The small number of blacks on the business and coaching side of football suggests that full equality on the football field has yet to be achieved.

BLACK QUARTERBACKS DISPROVE AN OLD MYTH

Because so few blacks had managed to become successful quarterbacks, there was speculation that blacks did not have the intelligence for the mentally demanding position. Although a number of blacks made it to the NFL at the quarterback position, very few were able to prove themselves as starters. However, in 1988 Doug Williams displayed remarkable poise and expertise as he led the Washington Redskins to a victory in Superbowl XXII. In the 1990s Randall Cunningham and Warren Moon shattered the myth by helping turn their respective teams around. Steve McNair led the Tennessee Titans all the way to the Superbowl with his exceptional running and passing abilities.

Ford, Harold Eugene

POLITICIAN
May 20, 1945–

Harold Eugene Ford was the first African American from Tennessee to be elected to the U.S. Congress. Ford is a sharp politician who is respected for his speaking and organizing skills. Although his political career has been successful, that success has not come easily. Ford has been accused of dishonesty, but that has never been proved. Ford claims that the accusations against him were racially motivated.

Born in Memphis, Tennessee, Ford earned a bachelor's degree from Tennessee State University in 1967 and worked at his family's funeral business before entering politics. He entered the Tennessee state legislature in 1970 and soon earned an important position called majority whip (who is responsible for communicating party positions to other members and determining "where the votes are" for proposed laws).

Ford entered the U.S. Congress in 1974 and became the youngest member to head a subcommittee for the House Ways and Means Committee (one of the most powerful committees in Congress, responsible for determining how tax money is spent). While in Congress, Ford concentrated on issues such as welfare reform, education, and increasing jobs.

Ford retired from Congress at the end of 1996. After leaving office, he worked as a lobbyist and political organizer in Memphis and helped his son Harold Ford Jr., who took over his seat in Congress. In November 1999 Ford served as his brother's campaign manager in an unsuccessful race for mayor of Memphis.

Foreman, George Edward

BOXER, MINISTER, ACTOR
January 22, 1948–

George Edward Foreman was the World Heavyweight Boxing Champion at the age of twenty-five (1973) and again at the age of forty-five

George Foreman flexes his muscles for the camera (AP/Wide World Photos. Reproduced by permission)

(1994). After making a name for himself as a great boxer in his early years, Foreman made an amazing comeback later in life, which many people believed was a publicity stunt.

Born in Marshall, Texas, Foreman led a troubled early life in Houston, getting into fights and drinking heavily until he entered the Job Corps in 1965. He found a focus for his energy in boxing. Foreman won the gold medal in the 1968 Olympics and caught the world's attention by waving the American flag in the ring after the fight. At the time, some athletes were making political statements at the Olympics in protest of racial injustice in the United States. Foreman made a bold statement that, in effect, said that he loved his homeland in spite of its faults.

Foreman entered professional boxing with impressive results, winning his first thirty-seven matches and knocking out the reigning heavyweight champion, **Joe Frazier,** in two rounds in 1973. One year later, however, Foreman lost his title to **Muhammad Ali** in a fight dubbed "The Rumble in the Jungle" (the fight took place in the African nation of Zaire). Foreman took the loss to Ali hard and stopped boxing professionally in 1977.

Foreman spent his retirement years preaching, and he opened a youth center in 1984. He returned to boxing in 1987 at the age of thirty-nine. Few boxing fans took the comeback seriously, yet Foreman's second attempt as a professional boxer was very successful. He won the World Heavyweight Championship against Michael Moorer at the age of forty-five. Foreman's comeback made him a celebrity, and he appeared in television commercials and starred in a television show, *George*, based on his life.

In 1997 Foreman retired from professional boxing for a second time and began work as a boxing commentator for televised fights. He endorsed various products on television, including a popular cooking appliance called "George Foreman's Lean, Mean Grilling Machine." Foreman has also continued to promote the development of young people, expanding his youth centers and supporting worthy causes. He donated $600,000 to the Progressive Amateur Boxing Association in April 2000. The gift enabled the organization to continue helping young athletes fulfill their dreams.

Forman, James

CIVIL RIGHTS ACTIVIST
October 4, 1928–

James Forman was a scholar and political activist dedicated to the **Civil Rights movement.** He helped organize political movements, worked on African-American economic development, and wrote books on civil rights.

Born in Chicago, Illinois, Forman spent his childhood in Mississippi before returning to Chicago to embark on a lifelong war against racial injustice. After serving in the U.S. Air Force (1945–51), he earned a bachelor's degree from Chicago's Roosevelt University and worked for an African-American newspaper, the *Chicago Defender.* In 1960 Forman's commitment to the Civil Rights movement was solidified when he was arrested and beaten for participating in a political demonstration called **Freedom Rides.** He then began working for the **Student Nonviolent Coordinating Committee (SNCC),** which he transformed into an influential political force.

However, SNCC members later became divided over how the organization should be run, which led to Forman's resignation. Forman tried to help the SNCC define its goals and develop its structure, including attempting to merge the group with the **Black Panther Party** in 1967. However, the SNCC continued to lack focus. Forman then concentrated his efforts on the economic development of blacks with the National Black Development Conference (NBDC), which resulted in raising $1 million in donations for the damage caused by **slavery.** Forman used the funds to promote economic development and the civil rights of blacks

Forman spent later years on scholastic projects. In 1980 he earned a master's degree in African-American studies from Cornell University (Ithaca, New York) and earned a Ph.D. degree from the Union of Experimental Colleges and Universities in Washington, D.C. From his studies he produced a book titled *Self Determination: An Examination of the Question and Its Application to the African American People* (1984). In 1990 he received the National Coalition of Black Mayors' **Fannie Lou Hamer** Freedom Award.

Forrest, Leon

NOVELIST, EDUCATOR
1937–1997

Writer Leon Forrest was born and raised in Chicago's South Side. He attended Roosevelt University (Chicago, Illinois) and the University of Chicago before entering the U.S. Army in 1960. His army service as a public information specialist helped launch a career in journalism. In 1969 he became an editor of *Muhammad Speaks,* the newspaper of the Black Muslim movement, and four years later he was appointed associate professor of African-American studies at Northwestern University (Evanston, Illinois), where he later became director of the African-American studies program.

Like **Ralph Ellison** and **Toni Morrison,** Forrest was an African-American writer of the second half of the twentieth century who combined modern literary forms and techniques with the traditions of African-American fiction. He wrote with a stream-of-consciousness style that resembled the work of American author William Faulkner (1897–1962), whose writings had a great influence on Forrest.

Forrest's most important literary creation is the Forest County series, which consists of four novels published from 1973 to 1992. These novels are interrelated in setting, characters, and themes. As a whole, the Forest County novels—*There Is a Tree More Ancient Than Eden* (1973), *The Bloodworth Orphans* (1977), *Two Wings to Veil My Face* (1983), and *Divine Days* (1992)—depict a rich vision of African-American life and culture in Chicago's South Side during the 1960s and 1970s.

Divine Days, a 1,138-page book, is about one week and one day in the life of an aspiring playwright, Joubert Jones. It is considered to be Forrest's masterwork.

In addition to his novels, Forrest wrote several plays and librettos (opera texts), as well as a collection of essays (*Relocations of the Spirit*, 1994) on such subjects as William Faulkner, singer **Billie Holiday,** religious leader **Elijah Muhammad,** and basketball player **Michael Jordan.** Forrest died of cancer in 1997.

Forten, James

BUSINESSMAN, ABOLITIONIST
September 2, 1766–March 15, 1842

Born free in Philadelphia in 1766, James Forten attended a Quaker school in Philadelphia, Pennsylvania. At the age of fourteen he went to sea and became a powder boy (carried gunpowder) on the ship *Royal Louis.* Forten later began to work for a Philadelphia sailmaker, and his skill and aptitude guaranteed his success in the industry. Eventually, Forten became the master of the shop and developed a reputation for excellent service and innovative sail-handling techniques.

Forten used both his fortune and his fame to fight **slavery** and was a lifelong advocate of immediate **abolition.** In 1800 he requested that the U.S. Congress change the terms of the 1793 Fugitive Slave Law, which permitted suspected runaways to be seized and arrested without a warrant. Forten also refused to rig sails for ships that participated (or were suspected of participating) in the **slave trade.**

In 1832 Forten and several other African Americans forwarded another petition to the Pennsylvania legislature asking it not to restrict the number of **free blacks** that were allowed to move to the state and not to begin more rigorous enforcement of the 1793 federal Fugitive Slave Law. Their argument was based on two main principles: a moral argument against the evils of slavery, and an economic argument—that free blacks were extremely productive members of the Philadelphia community and other Pennsylvania towns.

As one of the organizers of the American Anti-Slavery Society in 1833, Forten provided support, especially economic, to abolitionist activities. Even before his death in 1842, Forten's deep belief in abolition was carried on by his family. Forten's children, and later his grandchildren, were prominent abolitionists and civil rights activists throughout the nineteenth century.

Forten, Robert Bridges

ABOLITIONIST, BUSINESSMAN
c. 1814–April 1864

Robert Bridges Forten was born in Pennsylvania, the son of James Forten, a **free black**, a successful businessman, and a dedicated abolitionist (opponent of slavery). Young Forten inherited his father's abolitionist beliefs and prosperity. As a young man, he spoke at abolitionist rallies and joined his father's sail-making business. Just before the **Civil War** (1861–65), Forten moved his wife, son, and business to Great Britain in order to escape discrimination in the United States. His daughter, Charlotte, lived with friends in Massachusetts.

When the Civil War began, however, Forten felt it his duty to return and fight for the **emancipation** (freedom) of African Americans. Although educated, prosperous, and fifty years old, Forten enlisted as a private in the 43rd U.S. Colored Infantry. He was quickly promoted to the rank of sergeant-major. In April 1864, approximately one month after his enlistment, Forten died of a skin infection. He was buried with a full military ceremony in Philadelphia, Pennsylvania, the first African American to receive such an honor. (*See also* **Charlotte Grimké**.)

Foster, Robert Wayne "Bob"

BOXER
December 15, 1938–

Robert "Bob" Wayne Foster was a light heavyweight **boxing** champion known for his powerful left hook. Foster was six feet three and a half inches tall and weighed 173 pounds. Although he was too light to compete for a heavyweight championship, he dominated the light heavyweight class from 1966 to 1970.

Born in Albuquerque, New Mexico, Foster started out in football before he picked up boxing in the U.S. Air Force. While in the military, he won the light heavyweight championship four times and won the All-Service championship once. He began his professional boxing career in 1961 but was unsuccessful at first. Then, in 1966, after taking a year off, Foster came back to win a record twenty consecutive matches (nineteen of which were knockouts). In 1968 he won the light heavyweight title and defended his crown a record fourteen times.

Despite his size, Foster later made a run at the heavyweight title against **Joe Frazier** and **Muhammad Ali**, losing both times. In 1973 he became the first black to step inside the ring with a white boxer in South Africa, when he defeated Pierre Fourie. Foster retired from boxing in 1978 with a career record fifty-six wins, eight losses, and one draw. In 1990 he was elected to the Boxing Hall of Fame.

Four Step Brothers

ACROBATIC TAP DANCE ACT

The Four Step Brothers electrified audiences with their flashy and exciting style of **tap dancing.** Unlike many other brother acts of the mid-1900s, the Four Step Brothers were not blood brothers but a group of talented dancers who worked together. While working as a newsboy in New York City in the mid-1920s, Maceo Anderson (1910–) spent most of his spare time at the Hoofers Club in Harlem, headquarters of tap dance. Anderson saw Al Williams (1910–1985) and Happy Johnson perform at an amateur night competition at the **Apollo Theater.** The three formed a trio in 1925.

They convinced musician **Duke Ellington** (1899–1974) to introduce them during an intermission at the **Cotton Club.** The Cotton Club of Harlem catered mostly to whites but featured talented black performers. The trio ended up staying there as performers for several years. By 1930 Sherman Robinson joined the group, and they became a quartet. Their electrifying style of tap used the "tap challenge," a form of one-upmanship, during which they egged each other on and set dance speed by clapping their hands and stomping their feet. The act was famous for its trademark "bottle dance" and for an exciting ending in which the dancers jumped over each other in wild flips and splits. They performed in Europe and worked in many U.S. nightclubs and theaters. They also appeared in a number of films.

The Four Step Brothers was one of the longest-lived of acrobatic tap dance acts. Over the years new members joined the act in addition to Maceo Anderson and Al Williams, who remained with the group until it disbanded in the mid-1970s. The quartet incorporated into its performances a wide variety of comedy, song, Afro-Cuban movement, acrobatics, and a boogie-woogie style of rhythm tapping.

Four Tops, The

POPULAR MUSIC GROUP

The Four Tops were a legendary soul group whose classic songs for Motown Records in the 1960s helped to establish the Detroit, Michigan, recording company's reputation and success. At first called the Four Aims, they changed their name to the Four Tops in 1956. The members of the quartet—Renaldo "Obie" Benson (1947-), Abdul "Duke" Fakir (1935-), Lawrence Payton (d. 1997), and lead singer Levi Stubbs (1936-)—were boyhood friends in Detroit. They first played together at another friend's birthday party.

Performing in genuine Detroit Sound-**Motown** tradition, the Four Tops recorded songs about love, happiness, and romantic heartbreak. The group released a steady stream of hits between 1964 and 1967, including "Baby, I Need Your Loving" (1964), "Standing in the Shadows of Love" (1966), and "Bernadette" (1967). Two of their songs reached the top of the national pop charts: the bouncy "I Can't Help Myself" (1965) and "Reach Out, I'll Be There" (1966), widely considered to be a pop masterpiece.

The Four Tops recorded the hit song "Ain't No Woman" in 1973. In the 1980s and 1990s they continued their busy international touring and recording schedule and released several albums, including *Tonight!* (1981), *Magic* (1985), and *Indestructible* (1988). In 1990 they were inducted into the Rock and Roll Hall of Fame.

Lawrence Payton died in 1997, and the remaining group members began performing as "The Tops." They celebrated their 45th anniversary in 1999-2000 and were still active in community projects in Detroit. In March 2000 the Public Broadcasting Service (PBS) aired *The Four Tops in Concert*, featuring some of the group's greatest hits.

Motown legends the Four Tops (Archive Photos. Reproduced by permission)

Franklin, Aretha Louise

SINGER
March 25, 1942–

Known as "Lady Soul" and "the queen of soul," Aretha Franklin brought the power of black gospel singing to American popular music beginning in the late 1960s. Franklin's formative years were spent singing in her father's church choir and traveling to perform in **gospel** concerts. At fourteen she recorded a selection of gospel songs. At eighteen Franklin was brought to the attention of Columbia Records. She signed a recording contract with Columbia but achieved only limited success as a singer.

The "Queen of Soul," Aretha Franklin (AP/Wide World Photos. Reproduced by permission)

Franklin's breakthrough came in 1966 when her Columbia contract expired and she signed with Atlantic Records, where she was teamed with veteran producer Jerry Wexler. He created songs for her based on her own piano playing. In these comfortable musical settings, her true voice emerged with intensity and emotion. Franklin's first record with Wexler was "I Never Loved a Man (The Way I Love You)" in February 1967. It was an immediate success and topped *Billboard* magazine's charts. Her second hit, "Respect," was sung with such conviction that it became a call for black and feminist pride and empowerment.

Franklin next produced a series of top records, including "Chain of Fools," "Think," and "Don't Play That Song." Franklin continues to record and perform and had hits in the 1970s, 1980s, and 1990s. She has won fifteen Grammy Awards (the record industry's most prestigious prize), three American Music Awards, and a Grammy Living Legend Award. With thirty-five albums to her credit, Franklin has had seventeen number one **rhythm-and-blues (R&B)** singles and more million-selling singles than any other female singer.

Franklin, John Hope

HISTORIAN, EDUCATOR
January 2, 1915–

A pioneer in the field of African-American history, John Hope Franklin was born in Rentiesville, Oklahoma, a completely African-American town. From an early age, Franklin saw many discriminatory white practices in the South. He went to high school in Tulsa, where a supposedly "separate but equal" education meant inferior facilities and a sharply limited curriculum. He went on to receive his bachelor's degree from **Fisk University** (Nashville, Tennessee) in 1935 and his Ph.D. degree in history from Harvard University in 1941.

Franklin's career combined scholarship with social activism. He served on the research team whose work led to the Supreme Court's ***Brown v. Board of Education of Topeka, Kansas*** decision outlawing school segregation. In 1965 he joined more than thirty other historians on the civil rights march into Montgomery, Alabama.

Franklin helped prove that the history of black Americans was a legitimate field for scholarly research. His first book, *The Free Negro in North Carolina, 1790-1860* (1943), explored the unique position of **free blacks** in the slaveholding South. Franklin's *From Slavery to Freedom* (1947) introduced hundreds of thousands of students to African-American history.

In his books and his teaching, Franklin showed the unique quality of the history of African Americans. At the same time, he viewed the subject as inseparable from American history. Regarding the need to include African Americans in historical accounts, he warned against replacing old distortions with new myths and one-sided presentations of heroes and heroines.

Franklin taught at several colleges before he became the chairman of the history department at Brooklyn College (New York) in 1956. In doing so, he became head of a department of fifty-two white historians, an accomplish-

ment that made the front page of the *New York Times*. From 1964 to 1982 Franklin was part of the history faculty of the University of Chicago. He later taught legal history in the law school at Duke University in Durham, North Carolina.

Franklin retired in 1992. In 1995 he was awarded the Presidential Medal of Freedom, the nation's highest civilian honor, and he also received the Spingarn Medal from the **National Association for the Advancement of Colored People (NAACP).** In 1997 Franklin was called out of retirement to chair President Bill Clinton's Initiative on Race.

Fraternities and Sororities

African-American fraternities (for men) and sororities (for women), have played an important role in college campus life. The social groups are also called Greek-letter organizations, since each took letters from the Greek alphabet to form its name.

The first black Greek-letter organization, the Alpha Phi Alpha fraternity, was founded in 1906 at New York's Cornell University. By 1922 all eight of the major societies had been formed. Five of the groups were organized at **Howard University** in Washington, D.C.: Alpha Kappa Alpha sorority (1908), Omega Psi Phi fraternity (1911), Delta Sigma Theta sorority (1913), Phi Beta Sigma fraternity (1914), and Zeta Phi Beta sorority (1920). Kappa Alpha Psi fraternity was founded in 1911 at Indiana University; and Sigma Gamma Rho sorority was founded at Butler University (also in Indiana) in 1922. Chapters, or local units of the organizations, were then opened on other college campuses around the nation.

Pros and Cons

Founded primarily for social purposes, so that students could become acquainted and forge friendships in small groups, fraternities and sororities have been perceived as having both positive and negative influences. Open only to members, who must meet certain requirements before being invited to join, Greek-letter organizations have been criticized for reinforcing class and color divisions within the African-American community. Furthermore, the groups' initiation rites (which would-be members must perform before fully joining) and secret rituals (such as passwords or handshakes) have been called silly and snobbish. Opponents have also charged that the groups distract students from their studies and from more worthwhile campus pursuits.

But the Greek system has champions as well. Many African-American leaders were members of fraternities or sororities during their college days. They and others have pointed out that in addition to teaching valuable social skills, the groups encourage good scholarship (by requiring members to meet certain levels of academic achievement) and foster a sense of community service. For example, black Greek-letter organizations have contributed to health projects, organized bookmobiles in rural areas of the South, founded homes for troubled youths, provided agricultural assistance to com-

PROMINENT MEMBERS OF THE BLACK GREEK-LETTER SYSTEM

African-American leaders who were members of college sororities include activist **Dorothy Height** (1912–); congresswoman **Barbara Jordan** (1936–1996); and singers **Marian Anderson** (1897–1993), **Lena Horne** (1917–), and **Leontyne Price** (1927–).

Black fraternity members included **Countee Cullen** (1903–1946); historian and educator **W. E. B. Du Bois** (1868–1963); Supreme Court justice **Thurgood Marshall** (1908–1993); congressman Ralph Metcalfe (1910–1978); and Olympic athlete **Jesse Owens** (1913–1980).

munities in Africa, and sponsored educational programs that increased awareness of black accomplishments.

Historically, too, the system had advantages for African-American students. On predominantly white campuses, these fraternities and sororities sometimes offered black students their only opportunities to socialize. They also provided housing at a time when university dormitories were all-white.

Nevertheless, administrators at the nation's black colleges saw no need for fraternity and sorority chapters to form on their campuses. Fearing the exclusive societies would divide student bodies and distract students from other activities (such as religious or literary pursuits), some black universities barred them. Eventually these bans were lifted.

In the 1940s most of the groups removed references to color or race from their membership requirements. Nevertheless, the fraternities and sororities have remained overwhelmingly African American and committed to work in the black community.

Frazier, Joseph William "Smokin' Joe"

BOXER
January 12, 1944–

Joseph William Frazier, better known as "Smokin'" Joe Frazier, was the World Heavyweight Boxing Champion from 1970 to 1973. Frazier used a unique fight style that took advantage of his relatively small frame (five feet eleven and a half inches tall and 205 pounds). He is perhaps best known for his exciting matches against **Muhammad Ali,** the most famous of which took place in Manila in the Philippines and was dubbed "The Thrilla in Manila."

Born in Beaufort, South Carolina, and raised in Philadelphia, Pennsylvania, Frazier began **boxing** in the Police Athletic League. His career was ignited by three Golden Glove titles (1962–64) and an Olympic gold medal in 1964. Frazier was undefeated in the early part of his career, beginning with nine straight knockouts and thirty-one consecutive victories. Frazier picked up the heavyweight title in 1970 when Muhammad Ali was suspended from boxing for refusing to serve in the U.S. Army during the war in Vietnam.

When Ali was cleared of the charges, he returned to boxing in a title match with Frazier. Their fight in 1971 at New York's Madison Square Garden is considered to be one of the most exciting matches in boxing history. Frazier defeated Ali in a fight that put both men in the hospital. The fighters had two rematches, both of which Ali won. In 1973 Frazier lost the title to **George Foreman.**

Frazier retired from boxing in 1976, and after a comeback attempt in 1981 he retired again. He finished his career with thirty-two wins (twenty-seven knockouts) and five losses and was elected to the Boxing Hall of Fame in 1980.

Frazier began an unsuccessful singing career after boxing and managed his son's short boxing career. His daughter, Jacqui Frazier-Lyde has also taken up boxing as a career and hopes to one day face Laila Ali, Muhammad Ali's daughter, who also boxes. Frazier spends the majority of his time in his gym in Philadelphia, Pennsylvania, where he helps young boxers prepare for competition.

Frazier, Walter II

BASKETBALL PLAYER
March 29, 1945–

Walter Frazier II is considered one of the best defensive players in the history of **basketball.** He is perhaps best known for stealing the ball while opponents were dribbling. Frazier was so skillful at "stealing" the ball that he was nicknamed after the famous bank robber Clyde Barrow.

Born in Atlanta, Georgia, Frazier was a stand out in both basketball and football. Scouts for both sports sought his skills when he graduated from high school. He decided to accept a scholarship to Southern Illinois University to play basketball, partly because he was concerned about racism preventing him from succeeding as a professional quarterback (at the time blacks were not accepted at this position). In 1967 Frazier led Southern Illinois to a National Invitational Tournament and was named the tournament's Most Valuable Player.

In 1967 the New York Knicks drafted Frazier in the first round. He was voted to the NBA's All-Defensive team seven consecutive seasons (1968–75). He was also an outstanding offensive player, leading the Knicks in scoring five seasons and leading in assists every year he was with the team. Frazier was elected to the Basketball Hall of Fame in 1986. After retiring from basketball in 1980, Frazier began a business called Walt Frazier Enterprises, which represented athletes, and later he began a career as a radio commentator for the Knicks. He adds flavor to his broadcasts by using rhyme and colorful words to describe the action on the court.

Although slaves were not freed in America until 1865, prior to that time there were blacks who were not slaves living in various parts of the country. They were known as free blacks, free Negroes, free people of color, or free people. By 1860 free blacks accounted for approximately 2 percent of the entire population of America and about 9 percent of all black people.

Before the American Revolution

Before the **American Revolution** (1775–83), there were relatively few free blacks living in the colonies. Most of them were light-skinned children of mixed parents (one parent white and one parent black). Others had been freed by their owners, some were considered too old or physically unable to work, and a very small number won freedom from their masters in court or purchased their freedom. According to a 1775 Maryland census (official count of the population), free blacks made up less than 2 percent of the population. The numbers were even fewer in other colonies.

Most free blacks in Florida (controlled by the Spanish until 1763) and Louisiana (controlled by France and Spain) achieved freedom through different means: they became soldiers. The Spanish began hiring black men, many of them runaways from English colonies, by the late 1600s. They were hired to help protect the Spanish colonies from foreign invaders. Over the years, they eventually became craftsmen, sailors, and laborers.

The French began hiring black soldiers in Louisiana as early as 1730, and when Spain took control in 1763, the Spaniards continued to rely on the black army for support. Black soldiers bought freedom for their families, and some eventually became successful in business and trade.

After the American Revolution

Shortly after the American Revolution, **slavery** was abolished in all of the Northern states: New Hampshire, Massachusetts, Rhode Island, Connecticut, New York, New Jersey, Pennsylvania, and Delaware. This did not mean, however, that freedom came instantly. It took years for some states to officially pass laws that would grant freedom, and some slaves remained in bondage until well into the 1800s. Still, the North was considered a free society, and many changes happened for free blacks who lived there. The North also attracted slaves who fled from the Southern states (Maryland, Georgia, Virginia, North Carolina, South Carolina), where slavery continued.

Free blacks in the North did not have many political rights (for instance, they were not allowed to vote). They were also given few job opportunities and often faced racism and open hostility. In most states, however, they could travel where they wanted, they were allowed to create their own organizations, they could publish newspapers, and they could even protest against slavery. This limited amount of freedom allowed African churches, schools, political groups, literary societies, and the **Underground Railroad** to spring up and flourish into the 1800s. During this period black leaders also emerged, including **Richard Allen** (1760–1831) and **Frederick Douglass** (1818–1895).

In the South, blacks did not enjoy the same freedoms. The majority of blacks remained slaves, and those who were freed by their masters were given very few rights. They could not travel without permission, and free blacks could not meet in groups without being supervised by whites. There were no black newspapers, no black organizations, and no strong black leaders surfaced. When free blacks did meet, they did so in secret.

Free blacks in the South did a little better economically than free blacks in the North, who not only faced discrimination in the workplace but were also forced to compete for jobs against immigrants coming into the country. Few European immigrants settled in the South, so free blacks had more opportunities to become tradesmen and craftsmen. In some places, such as Charleston, South Carolina, and New Orleans, Louisiana, over three-fourths of free men of color were skilled craftsmen. A handful of free blacks became wealthy planters and even purchased their own slaves.

The majority of blacks, however, remained slaves until another war took place, this time one that divided the states rather than united them. Two years into the **Civil War** (1861–65), President Abraham Lincoln (1809–1865; president 1860–1865) ended slavery in the Southern states by signing the Emancipation Proclamation; in 1865 the Thirteenth Amendment abolished slavery in all of the states. The need to define an individual as "free" or "slave" was no longer necessary.

Freedom Rides

Organized initially by the **Congress of Racial Equality (CORE)** in 1961, the "Freedom Rides" consisted of interracial groups riding throughout the South on buses to test southern compliance with desegregation laws. The Freedom Riders attempted to galvanize the Justice Department into enforcing federal desegregation laws in interstate travel, and especially in bus and train terminals. White riders sat in the back of the bus, and black riders in the front, challenging long-standing southern racist transportation practices. Once at the terminal, white Freedom Riders proceeded to the "black" waiting room, while blacks attempted to use the facilities in the "white" waiting room.

Freedom Rides were a continuation of the student-led **sit-in** movement that was sparked in February 1, 1960, by four African-American college freshmen in Greensboro, North Carolina. When these students remained at a Woolworth's lunch counter after being refused service, they inspired hundreds of similar nonviolent student demonstrations. Essentially, Freedom Rides took the tradition of sit-ins on the road.

The idea for the 1961 Freedom Rides was conceived by Tom Gaither, black, and Gordon Carvey, white, who were field secretaries of CORE. In light of the 1960 *Boynton v. Virginia* Supreme Court judgment that banned segregation in bus and train terminals, Gaither and Carvey decided that compliance with the law should be gauged. The two activists were additionally inspired by the 1947 Journey of Reconciliation. Also motivated by a Supreme Court ruling, the Journey of Reconciliation was an interracial group of sixteen activists that traveled through the South to test *Morgan v. Virginia*, the federal case that resulted in the legal ban of segregation on interstate buses and trains in 1946. In the spirit of the Journey of Reconciliation, CORE began organizing and planning for the first Freedom Rides.

In early 1961, CORE, headed by its director and cofounder **James Farmer**, began carefully selecting the thirteen original Freedom Riders. The chosen group consisted of seven blacks and six whites, from college students to civil rights veterans, including a Journey of Reconciliation participant, white activist James Peck. The journey for the riders began on May 4; they were to travel from Washington, D.C., to Atlanta, Georgia, on two buses. The plan was to continue through Alabama, Mississippi, and finally to New Orleans, Louisiana, on May 17 for a desegregation rally.

The first episode of violence occurred in Rock Hill, South Carolina, where twenty-one-year-old **John Lewis,** future **Student Nonviolent Coordinating Committee (SNCC)** national chairman, and Albert Bigelow, an elderly white pacifist, were knocked unconscious by young white men. On May 14, 1961, the Freedom Riders boarded a Greyhound and a Trailways bus in Atlanta and headed for Birmingham, Alabama. The Trailways bus met six Ku Klux Klansmen in Anniston, Alabama, who threw the African Americans into backseats and hit two white riders on the head. In Birmingham, the bus encountered about twenty men with pipes who beat the riders when they disembarked.

In Anniston, the Greyhound bus faced two hundred angry whites. The bus retreated, but its tires had been slashed. Once the tires blew out, a firebomb was tossed into the bus through the glass. The riders managed to escape before the bus went up in flames. The following day, another mob prevented the Freedom Riders from boarding a bus in Birmingham. With the help of John Seigenthaler, Attorney General Robert Kennedy's assistant, the riders took a plane to New Orleans instead. The bus journey was continued under the leadership of the SNCC, with the coordination efforts of SNCC members **Diane Nash** and John Lewis.

Birmingham Police Commissioner "Bull" Connor used many tactics, including incarceration, to try to stop the students, but to no avail. Finally, the governor of Alabama, John Patterson, very reluctantly promised Robert Kennedy to protect the riders. As the new Freedom Riders left for Montgomery on May 20, 1961, it appeared that Governor Patterson had kept his word. However, by the time the bus arrived in Montgomery, all forms of police protection had disappeared. A mob of over one thousand whites viciously attacked the riders and John Seigenthaler.

On May 24 twenty-seven determined Freedom Riders, with the protection of National Guardsmen, headed for Jackson, Mississippi. In Mississippi they were arrested for sixty days. A new group of riders came to Jackson, and were also arrested. Eventually, 328 Freedom Riders had been incarcerated in Jackson. The riders chose jail over bail to publicize their efforts.

The Freedom Rides brought international attention to the southern struggle of desegregation, which put pressure on the authorities. Finally, on November 1, 1961, a huge victory for the Freedom Riders and all integrationists was won when the Interstate Commerce Commission made segregated travel facilities illegal.

Freedom Summer

In the summer of 1964 a Mississippi civil rights organization, the Council of Federated Organizations (COFO), invited white college students from northern states to come to Mississippi to help carry out a black voter registration and education campaign. This campaign, which became known as "Freedom Summer," had a lasting effect for African Americans throughout the South. It also influenced many other political movements of the 1960s, including the Black Power movement, the women's liberation movement, and the anti–**Vietnam War** movement.

The COFO was made up of members from three other civil rights organizations: the **Congress of Racial Equality (CORE)**, the **Student Nonviolent Coordinating Committee (SNCC)**, and the **National Association for the Advancement of Colored People (NAACP)**. Its goal was to focus national attention on the disfranchisement (denial of legal rights, especially voting rights) of blacks in Mississippi and to force the federal government to protect the civil rights of African Americans in the South. The SNCC had the largest role in the Freedom Summer project and provided most of its funding.

About one thousand white college students participated in Freedom Summer. They helped create community centers that provided health care and other basic services to blacks, and they started voter education and literacy classes aimed at encouraging Mississippi blacks to register to vote. The COFO also created "freedom schools," directed by Staughton Lynd, a white **Spelman College** history professor. One of the schools' main goals was to develop student leadership and interest black students in activism by discussing current events, black history, and ideas behind the **Civil Rights movement**. More than three thousand African-American students attended the freedom schools.

SNCC activists supported the Mississippi Freedom Democratic Party, which provided African-American candidates for Mississippi government offices and sent black representatives to the Democratic National Convention in Atlantic City, New Jersey, in the summer of 1964.

As the COFO worked for African-American rights, many whites in Mississippi used violence to try to halt the organization's activities. They bombed or burned sixty-seven homes, churches, and black businesses over the summer, and at least three civil rights workers were killed. Many others were beaten and arrested.

Freedom Summer programs lived on when the project ended and the COFO disbanded. Its community centers provided a model for federally funded clinics, Head Start programs, and War on Poverty programs. Freedom schools served as models for alternative schools. By publicizing barriers to black voting in Mississippi and elsewhere, the COFO helped to bring about the federal Voting Rights Act of 1965, which made literacy tests and voting taxes illegal.

After Freedom Summer ended, at least one-third of the white student volunteers stayed on in Mississippi to continue the struggle for black equality. Many who returned to other parts of the country became activists in the antiwar movement. Freedom Summer's most important contribution was

"Before the 1964 summer project there were people who wanted change, but they hadn't dared to come out. After 1964 people began moving. To me it's one of the greatest things that ever happened in Mississippi."

(Source: Fannie Lou Hamer, Mississippi civil rights activist and a leader of the Mississippi Freedom Democratic Party, 1966.)

Actor Morgan Freeman, holding his Golden Globe Award, which he won for his performance in the film *Driving Miss Daisy* (AP/Wide World Photos. Reproduced by permission)

the change in thinking among black Mississippians. Thousands of African Americans became active in political matters, and thousands of black children became aware of racial issues.

Freeman, Morgan

ACTOR
June 1, 1937–

Morgan Freeman is an accomplished actor whose impressive career has spanned more than thirty years. He grew up in Mississippi, where he began acting in elementary school. In junior high he won a statewide acting competition. Upon graduating from high school, Freeman worked in the U.S. Air Force. He eventually moved to California, where he took acting lessons at the Pasadena Playhouse and dancing lessons in San Francisco. In 1964 Freeman moved to New York, where his first Broadway appearance was in an all-black production of *Hello, Dolly!* in 1967. From 1971 until 1976 he portrayed the character Easy Reader on Public Television's *The Electric Company.*

Freeman made his film debut in 1980 and began playing many minor roles. He gained recognition for his work in the movie *Street Smart* (1987), for which he received an Oscar nomination. In 1989 he had starring roles as the school principal Joe Clark in *Lean on Me;* as the chauffeur in the movie *Driving Miss Daisy,* for which he received another Oscar nomination; and as the first black sergeant of a Northern black regiment during the **Civil War** (1861–65) in *Glory.* In 1992 Freeman fulfilled a lifelong ambition to play a cowboy by starring in the Oscar-winning western *Unforgiven,* opposite the actor Clint Eastwood.

In the fall of 1993 Freeman made his debut as a director with *Bopha!,* a film about the1976 Soweto uprisings in South Africa. Freeman's career continued to lead him to strong roles through the 1990s. In 1997 he costarred in the movie *Amistad,* and in 1998 he appeared in the film *Deep Impact.*

Freeman, Paul Douglas

CONDUCTOR
January 2, 1936–

Paul Freeman has led orchestras around the world and worked to bring greater recognition to music composed or performed by African Americans. Born in Richmond, Virginia, Freeman began piano lessons at age five. He also played the clarinet and cello in his youth. Studying at the Eastman School of Music (Rochester, New York), he earned his bachelor's, master's, and doctoral degrees by 1963. He also studied in Berlin, Germany.

Freeman began his professional career in 1961 as conductor of the Opera Theater of Rochester. In 1966 he joined the San Francisco (California) Conservatory Orchestra. By 1970 Freeman was installed as a conductor-in-residence with the Detroit Symphony Orchestra. For most of

the 1980s Freeman worked in Canada, with the Victoria (British Columbia) Symphony Orchestra. In 1988 he founded the Chicago Sinfonietta, an ensemble with many minority members. Throughout his career Freeman worked as a guest conductor for major symphony orchestras in the United States and Europe.

Freeman was a founder of *CBS Records' Black Composers Series*. Recorded between 1974 and 1979, the nine-album (CD) collection documents the Classical contribution of black composers from three centuries and three continents. The landmark anthology was reissued in 1987 by the College Music Society in conjunction with the Center for Black Music Research.

Fugitive Slaves

From the time of slavery in the American colonies (mid-1600s to late-1700s) until the adoption of the Thirteenth Amendment to the U.S. Constitution (1865), which outlawed slavery, black slaves tried to escape from bondage. During the 1800s many thousands made their way to free states in the North or as far as **Canada.** Others escaped to nearby plantations in the South to visit relatives and then returned to their masters. Many of the slaves who reached freedom in the North during the period before the **Civil War** (1861–65) became legendary figures in American history, even though they represent only a small percentage of the slaves who escaped.

Slave owners made an effort to recapture fugitive slaves, which were considered their "property," and the U.S. Congress passed laws regarding the capture and return of these slaves. However, the laws were mostly unsuccessful and further divided citizens of the Northern and Southern states on the issue of **slavery.** Southern slaveholders believed Northern residents should obey federal laws and return runaway slaves, but most Northerners were against slavery and were unwilling to act as slave catchers for Southern plantation owners.

In many cases, plantation owners waited as long as six months before reporting slaves as runaways, hoping they would come back to the plantation on their own. If a slave remained missing, the owner placed advertisements in newspapers, giving a complete physical description of the slave, including any speech flaws and variations in skin color, work skills, names of previous owners, and other attempts to run away. A reward was offered for the slave's return.

These fugitive slave advertisements help historians study the issue of runaway slaves. They have learned that most slaves who escaped were single men in their twenties. Successful escape called for planning, bravery, and the right opportunity. Because it was so difficult to avoid capture and because being captured meant certain punishment, including whipping, many women, especially those with children, were discouraged from running away.

Some white people helped slaves to escape, but the main source of assistance in attempts to escape was other slaves. In most Southern states the law provided that any black person could be stopped and checked for papers showing he or she was free. If a slave, the black person had to show a "free

A poster warning blacks to beware of slave catchers (Courtesy of the Library of Congress)

CAUTION!!

COLORED PEOPLE

OF BOSTON, ONE & ALL,

You are hereby respectfully CAUTIONED and advised, to avoid conversing with the

Watchmen and Police Officers of Boston,

For since the recent ORDER OF THE MAYOR & ALDERMEN, they are empowered to act as

KIDNAPPERS

AND

Slave Catchers,

And they have already been actually employed in KIDNAPPING, CATCHING, AND KEEPING SLAVES. Therefore, if you value your LIBERTY, and the *Welfare of the Fugitives* among you, *Shun* them in every possible manner, as so many *HOUNDS* on the track of the most unfortunate of your race.

Keep a Sharp Look Out for KIDNAPPERS, and have TOP EYE open.

APRIL 24, 1851.

pass," given by the owner, which allowed the slave to travel. Any slave found to be a certain distance from home without a free pass could be captured and returned to the owner for a reward. Many slaves who escaped were those who had been hired out to provide services as river boatmen, laborers, carriage drivers, or house servants. Away from the plantation, they found a means to escape, often after getting a pass to go to town. Slaves who could read and write helped others escape by forging passes that allowed them to get away to larger towns or cities, where there was less chance of being discovered and greater opportunities for work.

All slave states passed laws to prevent slaves from running away and to aid in their capture and return if they did escape. Before the **American Revolution** (1775–83), fugitive slave laws in the colonies were especially harsh. Runaways could be shot, dismembered, or whipped when caught. People accused of stealing slaves or encouraging them to run away were also severely punished. The Fugitive Slave Act of 1793 allowed slave owners or

those working for them to seize runaways and bring them before any federal, state, or local judge and give oral or written proof that the slave belonged to the owner. This law was declared unconstitutional in some Northern states, which passed laws protecting blacks from being captured by mistake.

During the 1800s owners tried harder to catch slaves they thought were headed to Northern states. Professional slave catchers in the Deep South often used hounds to hunt down fugitive slaves. In spite of great efforts of state and national governments to keep slaves from running away, the flow of fugitives to the North, many via the **Underground Railroad**, continued. Although slaves escaping to the North made up only a small percentage of the total number of fugitive slaves, they had a great impact on the African-American and white communities in the North and played a critical role in the antislavery movement before the Civil War.

In 1850 Congress amended the Fugitive Slave Act, providing for federal commissioners to enforce the law. These men were paid $10 for finding blacks to be runaway slaves but only $5 for finding them to be free. Northern opposition to this law increased after the publication of white abolitionist Harriet Beecher Stowe's (1811–1896) novel *Uncle Tom's Cabin* (1852), partly about a fugitive slave, Eliza.

More than nine hundred fugitive slaves were returned under the Fugitive Slave Act between 1850 and 1862, but Southerners estimated that as many as ten thousand slaves escaped during that period. In 1864, one year after President Abraham Lincoln (1809–1865) issued the Emancipation Proclamation freeing all slaves in the South, Congress repealed the 1793 and the 1850 fugitive slave laws.

Fuller, Charles Henry Jr.

PLAYWRIGHT
March 5, 1939–

Born in Philadelphia, Pennsylvania, in 1939, playwright Charles Fuller attended Villanova College (Villanova, Pennsylvania) from 1956 to 1958 and then served for four years in the U.S. Army. He returned to Philadelphia, attended La Salle College from 1965 to 1968, and completed his degree. Fuller began writing steadily in the 1960s, usually at night, attending school or holding a number of jobs during the day. His early writing was mostly poetry, essays, and stories, but when he realized his stories were composed mostly of dialogue, he turned to playwriting.

Fuller's first short plays were written for the Afro-American Arts Theatre of Philadelphia, which he cofounded and codirected from 1967 through 1971. In 1970 he moved to New York City and devoted himself to writing full-time.

His first full-length play, *The Village: A Party*, about the conflicts in a racially integrated community, was produced in Princeton, New Jersey, in 1968. Fuller wrote and produced several plays throughout the 1970s, but the 1980s was the decade in which he began to be recognized as one of America's premier playwrights. In 1981 Fuller won an Obie Award for *Zooman and the Sign*, a play about inner-city violence in Philadelphia. In 1982 he became the second black playwright to win a Pulitzer Prize for drama, for *A Soldier's Play*. The play narrates the investigation of the murder of a black sergeant at a Louisiana army base during **World War II** (1939–45) and explores racial prejudice as well as self-hatred of black soldiers. It was adapted for the screen and released as *A Soldier's Story* by Columbia Pictures in 1984.

In 1987 CBS televised Fuller's adaptation of **Ernest J. Gaines**'s novel *A Gathering of Old Men;* in 1988 two related one-act plays, *Sally* and *Prince*, were produced first in Atlanta, Georgia, by the First National Black Arts Festival and then in New York by the Negro Ensemble Company. Fuller also wrote a portion for the 1998 TV movie anthology (a collection of selected works) *Talismans*.

Fuller, Meta Vaux Warrick

SCULPTOR
June 9, 1877–March 18, 1968

Meta Vaux Warrick Fuller created sculpture that spoke strongly of the African-American experience. Fuller was the youngest of three children in a prosperous family. While attending Philadelphia, Pennsylvania, public schools, Fuller took weekly courses at an industrial arts school. At eighteen she won a three-year scholarship to an art school. She graduated with honors and received prizes for her metalwork and sculpture.

From 1899 to 1903 Fuller studied in Paris, France. Among her supporters in France was the philosopher **W. E. B. Du Bois** (1868–1963), who encouraged her to depict her racial heritage. Fuller produced clay, painted-plaster, and bronze works based on Egyptian history, Greek myths, French literature, and the Bible.

In 1901 the famous sculptor Auguste Rodin praised Fuller's work. His recognition gave Fuller more public notice. She exhibited twenty-two of her sculptures at the L'Art Nouveau Gallery in 1902. Certain works of hers, including *The Wretched*, a bronze group of seven figures suffering physical and mental disabilities, earned Fuller the title "delicate sculptor of horrors" from the French press.

Upon Fuller's return to Philadelphia, she established a studio in a flourishing artistic neighborhood. Her sculptures were exhibited at the Pennsylvania Academy of Fine Arts. In 1907 Fuller was hired to create figures depicting African-American progress since 1607.

Fuller's career slowed considerably after her marriage in 1909 and a fire in 1910 that destroyed the bulk of her work in storage. By 1911 Fuller was the devoted mother of two sons, an active church member, and a frequent host. Fuller began to sculpt again in 1913, when she was hired to create a sculptor for New York State's celebration of the fiftieth anniversary of the Emancipation Proclamation abolishing slavery in the United States. Encouraged by the positive response, Fuller kept working and received numerous requests and awards from African-American and women's groups.

One of Fuller's most poignant works commemorates both the silent parade of black New Yorkers against **lynching** in 1917 and the lynching of a Georgian woman and her unborn child in 1918. Fuller never finished the piece because she believed northerners would find it too inflammatory and southerners would not accept it.

She created numerous other works that depicted African and African-American culture. She also produced portrait busts of friends, family members, and African-American abolitionists and other black leaders. Fuller participated in numerous local organizations. Additionally, she designed costumes for theatrical groups and produced "living pictures": re-creations of artistic masterpieces with actors, costumes, sets, and lighting.

In the 1940s Fuller's husband went blind and became increasingly ill. She nursed him until his death in 1953, then contracted tuberculosis and stayed at the Middlesex County Sanatorium for two years. She wrote poetry there, too frail to create more than a few small sculptures.

By 1957 Fuller was strong enough to continue her work. She produced models of ten notable African-American women. She also created a number of sculptures for her community, including several religious pieces for the church, a plaque for the hospital, and the bronze *Storytime* for the library. She received an honorary doctorate. Fuller's sculptures have been included in numerous exhibitions.

Gabriel Prosser Conspiracy

Gabriel Prosser (1775–1800) was a slave who planned one of the most elaborate slave rebellions in American history. In 1800 he secretly recruited and organized thousands of Virginia slaves to help him overthrow the government that had enslaved them. But hours before the planned attack, a hurricane struck, and the damage and delays it caused put an end to the rebellion.

Gabriel was born into slavery in 1775. His owner was tavern-keeper Thomas Prosser, for whom Gabriel worked as a blacksmith. While planning his attack, Gabriel got help from his wife and his brothers, who gathered weapons and recruits. Gabriel had thousands of followers who, according to his brother, looked to Gabriel to help them "conquer the white people and possess ourselves of their property." Although their plan was to overthrow **slavery,** they meant to spare any whites who were Methodists or Quakers or who belonged to any group that supported the end of slavery.

Gabriel and his followers intended to march on Richmond (the state capital of Virginia), set fires at warehouses, and take the governor of Virginia, James Monroe, hostage in the state capitol building. Once whites agreed to free the slaves, Gabriel planned to release Monroe. The plan had to be postponed because of the severe weather, however, and with so many followers it did not take long for word of the rebellion to reach the white community. Before Gabriel could march, Governor Monroe arrested hundreds of people, and many were executed. After escaping briefly, Gabriel was also captured, and after a brief trial at which he refused to speak, he was hanged.

Gaines, Ernest J.

WRITER
January 15, 1933–

"Don't ever think that your life is too insignificant, or the place you come from too small, to write about. That is all that is necessary if the writer uses it well. My greatest reward has been to be able to show that my plantation people were worth writing about."

(Source: Ernest J. Gaines. Acceptance speech for the National Book Critics Circle Award for *A Lesson Before Dying*, 1994. *Publishers Weekly*, March 21, 1994).

The oldest son in a large family, writer Ernest Gaines was born on the River Lake Plantation in Point Coupe Parish, Louisiana. His parents separated when he was young, and his maternal great-aunt served as an example of strength and survival under extreme adversity. Gaines grew up listening to the older people in his close-knit community tell stories about their lives and the lives of their ancestors; this rich oral tradition figures prominently in his fiction.

At the age of fifteen Gaines moved from this familiar environment to the San Franciso, California, area, where he could receive a better education. After high school he spent time in a junior college and in the military before enrolling at San Francisco State College. An English major, he wrote many stories and graduated in 1957. He committed himself to a literary career, later attending the creative writing program at Stanford University in California. In 1964 he published his first novel, *Catherine Carmier*. Through the1970s, Gaines lived and wrote in San Francisco. Since the early 1980s, he has been associated with the University of Southwestern Louisiana, although he has continued to summer in San Francisco.

As a writer, Gaines has been fascinated by the interaction of various cultures and classes: blacks, mixed-race Creoles (descendants of early French or Spanish settlers on the U.S. Gulf Coast), Cajuns (descendants of French Canadians who emigrated from Canada to the Gulf Coast), white Creoles, and Anglo whites. Each of his novels is made more complex by these different layers of southern society. Probably his best-known early work is *The Autobiography of Miss Jane Pittman* (1971), an account of a woman whose life has spanned **slavery**, **Reconstruction**, **Jim Crow** (discrimination against black people), and the **Civil Rights movement**. It was made into a movie in 1974. A more recent work is his 1993 book *A Lesson Before Dying*, which is about an uneducated black man on death row and a black teacher in a Louisiana plantation school. In 1994 *A Lesson Before Dying* won a National Book Critics Circle Award, and it became a best-seller in 1997 when television personality **Oprah Winfrey** added it to her list of books recommended to viewers. In 2000, Gaines was honored with the first-ever Louisiana Writer Award for his body of work.

Garvey, Marcus Mosiah

FOUNDER AND LEADER OF THE UNIVERSAL NEGRO IMPROVEMENT ASSOCIATION (UNIA)
August 7, 1887–June 10, 1940

Marcus Garvey founded the **Universal Negro Improvement Association (UNIA)**, the largest organized mass movement in black history. He led the Back-to-Africa movement that swept the United States after **World War I** (1914–18).

PHILOSOPHY AND OPINIONS OF MARCUS GARVEY (1923)

As part of Garvey' defense campaign in his trial for mail fraud, his second wife, Amy Jacques Garvey (1896–1973), edited and published a small volume of Garvey's sayings and speeches under the title *Philosophy and Opinions of Marcus Garvey* (1923). A second and expanded volume was published in 1925 as part of Garvey's attempt to obtain a pardon.

Garvey was born in the British colony of Jamaica, where he worked as a printer's apprentice as a teenager. He officially started the UNIA in 1914, but he felt politically isolated and moved to the United States in 1916. Garvey's relocation came during a time of political discontent for African Americans. American involvement in World War I in support of democracy contradicted the undemocratic treatment of blacks at home. In 1917 Garvey organized the first American branch of the UNIA.

Garvey's main goal was the political and economic revival of Africa. His plan included a black-owned shipping line that would raise money and supply transportation to Africa. However, his Black Star Line soon failed because of financial difficulties and poor management.

By 1920 the UNIA had hundreds of divisions and chapters operating worldwide. It published the *Negro World* and hosted annual conventions. At the first convention in 1920, Garvey was elected provisional president of **Africa.** In this position, he tried unsuccessfully to establish a colony in Liberia.

However, the UNIA movement was already weakening. Garvey was faced with opposition from black critics, conflict within the UNIA, and government harassment. He unwisely tried to reduce white opposition by meeting secretly with the head of the **Ku Klux Klan.** After the meeting was revealed, angry UNIA members formed a separate group at the 1922 convention.

Meanwhile, Garvey was charged with mail fraud in connection with the Black Star Line. Found guilty on one charge, he was given a five-year prison term. After serving thirty-three months, he was deported to Jamaica and was never allowed to return to the United States. Garvey was unable to regain control of the UNIA from Jamaica. He also sought to reform Jamaican politics, but in 1930 failed to win a seat on the colonial legislative council.

Garvey moved to England in 1935, shortly before Italy invaded Ethiopia. During the surge of pro-Ethiopian support that came from the black world, Garvey lost more supporters when he began to criticize Ethiopian emperor Haile Selassie (1892–1975).

Garvey died of a stroke in 1940. Although his last years were spent in obscurity, he continues to inspire African nationalists. In 1964 Garvey was declared Jamaica's first national hero.

Gaye, Marvin Jr.

April 2, 1939–April 1, 1984

SINGER, SONGWRITER

Famous for his **Motown** recordings of the 1960s and 1970s, Marvin Gaye is credited with perfecting "soul" music, a form of **rhythm-and-blues (R&B)**. Raised in Washington, D.C., as a youth he sang in the choir and played organ in his father's church. Marvin Gay Sr. was a Pentecostal minister. (As an adult, Gaye added the 'e' to his last name.)

In 1957 Gaye was singing with a group called the Marquees when he was noticed by a scout from Chicago's Chess Records. Briefly signed to that record label, in 1960 Gaye moved to Detroit, where music entrepreneur Berry Gordy Jr. (1929–) had just founded Motown Records. After singing backup for other Motown performers, in 1962 Gaye released his first solo album, *The Soulful Mood of Marvin Gaye*. Two years later he had two hit singles.

Gaye's most popular recording, "I Heard It Through the Grapevine" (1968), has stood the test of time. In 1971 the artist released his most successful album, *What's Going On*. In it, he turned his attention to social issues such as the problems of inner-city blacks. Gaye had one more hit album on Motown, 1973's *Let's Get It On*. The singer was dismissed from the record label in 1981.

The last ten years of Gaye's life were troubled. He divorced his first wife (Gordy's sister, Anna), remarried, moved to Europe to escape tax problems, suffered from depression, and became increasingly dependent on drugs. Winning two Grammy awards in 1983, the following year he was killed by his father in a domestic dispute. (Gay was acquitted after it was determined that a brain tumor had caused his violent behavior.)

A Selection of Marvin Gaye's Hits

"Pride and Joy,"
1963

"How Sweet It Is (to Be Loved by You),"
1964

"Ain't That Peculiar,"
1965

"It Takes Two"
(duet with Kim Weston), 1966

"Ain't No Moutain High Enough"
(duet with Tammi Terrell), 1967

"Ain't Nothing Like the Real Thing"
(duet with Terrell), 1968

"I Heard It Through the Grapevine,"
1968

"What's Going On?,"
1971

"Mercy, Mercy Me (The Ecology),"
1971

"Let's Get It On,"
1973

"Sexual Healing,"
1982

Georgia

First African-American Settlers: Georgia was founded in 1733 as a sanctuary for poor white Englishman and as a military outpost against **American Indians** and Spaniards; as such it was officially slave-free in the 1730s and 1740s.

Slave Population: Before becoming a state in 1788, Georgia officially became a slave society in 1751 and began to copy South Carolina, its rich sister colony across the Savannah River. For the next hundred years or so, Georgia relied on slave labor to produce mounting quantities of rice and cotton. The number of slaves rose from about 500 in 1750 to perhaps 15,000 by the start of the **American Revolution** (1775–83). By the time the American **Civil War** (1861–65) began, slaves accounted for more than 70 percent of the population in some counties.

Free Black Population: **Free black** Georgians, who numbered 3,500 in 1860, were concentrated in the cities of Savannah and Augusta.

Civil War: During the Civil War slaves contributed immensely to the Confederate (Southern) cause by growing the corn that fed the troops, growing the cotton that clothed them, and working on railroads and defensive works. Thousands of Georgia slaves helped bring Union (Northern) victory about, whether by withdrawing their labor from the support of the Confederacy or by joining the Union army.

Reconstruction: Already by the summer of 1865, schools for black Georgians were opening up all over the state; several universities were also founded during the postwar years. Black Georgians first voted in 1867 and sent delegates to the state constitutional convention that year. Disfranchisement (denial of the right to vote) of blacks became widespread as early as the 1870s, however, and by 1908 most black Georgians were excluded from making or administering public policy. Early in the twentieth century thousands of black Georgians were driven out of the state by sharecropping (renting land and giving part of the crop as rent), the boll weevil (an insect that destroys cotton plants), **lynching,** and disfranchisement.

The Great Depression: The **Great Depression,** the New Deal (a federal government program to bring about economic recovery and social reform during the depression years), and agricultural mechanization led to the departure of many more black farmers from the lands they had worked; between the 1910s and 1970s, Georgia blacks dropped from 12 percent of the population to 6 percent.

Civil Rights Movement: Black Georgians began to reenter politics in the mid-1900s, particularly in Atlanta following a 1962 court-ordered reapportionment that gave the city more representation. The desegregation of the University of Georgia was forced in 1961 by federal court order. Taking advantage of the Voting Rights Act of 1965, black Georgians throughout the state voted in increasing numbers and won elective office.

Current African-American Population: According to U.S. Census Bureau estimates, the total black population in Georgia was 2,181,455 (28 percent of the state population) as of July 1, 1998.

Key Figures: musician **Gertrude "Ma" Rainey** (1886–1939); civil rights activist **Martin Luther King Jr.;** rhythm-and-blues musician **Ray Charles** (1930–); **Andrew Young** (1932–), the first black candidate elected to Congress from any southern state since the 1890s; baseball great **Jackie Robinson** (1919–1972); Pulitzer Prize-winning author **Alice Walker** (1944–); **Clarence Thomas** (1948–), justice of the U.S. Supreme Court.

(SEE ALSO **EMANCIPATION; SOUTHERN CHRISTIAN LEADERSHIP CONFERENCE; SIT-INS.**)

Gibson, Althea

TENNIS PLAYER
August 25, 1927–

Althea Gibson was the first African-American woman to win major professional tennis tournaments and earn international fame. Gibson was a natural athlete who could have played professional golf as well as tennis. At the time she played (1940s and 1950s), tennis did not welcome black athletes;

Althea Gibson in action at Wimbeldon (AP/Wide World Photos. Reproduced by permission)

however, her exceptional talent left the white tennis world with no choice but to recognize her. Her heroism on the court paved the way for future blacks to enter the sport.

Born in Silver, South Carolina, Gibson moved to New York City at the age of three to live with her aunt. In 1940 she began playing tennis, and her abilities were soon recognized. After graduating from high school, Gibson went on to win the American Tennis Association championship ten years in a row (1947-56). After much resistance she was allowed to play in U.S. Lawn Tennis Association (the governing body of tennis) events in 1950. Gibson

GIBSON'S LEGACY IN WOMEN'S TENNIS

Gibson's influence on modern African-American tennis has had impressive results. Among the small group of female players dominating the sport are sisters Venus (1980–) and Serena (1981–) Williams. In 2000, Venus Williams won the women's singles championship at Wimbledon; she and her sister also won the doubles championship at Wimbledon 2000.

won the French Open (1956), Wimbledon (1957 and 1958), and the U.S. Open (1957 and 1958). After her Wimbledon victory she was honored by Queen Elizabeth II and given a ticker-tape parade when she returned to New York.

After ending her professional tennis career, Gibson became a physical education teacher at Lincoln University. She then began a singing career, which resulted in an appearance on the Ed Sullivan Show in 1958. Gibson next took up golf and immediately mastered the game. However, she decided not to pursue the sport professionally because, at the time, female golfers were not paid well. In 1986 she was appointed to New Jersey's Athletic Commission, where she began coaching and counseling young black athletes.

Gibson was elected to the International Tennis Hall of Fame in 1971. In 1997 she started the Althea Gibson Foundation, which is designed to give the same opportunities to young athletes that were given to her.

Gibson, Joshua "Josh"

BASEBALL PLAYER
December 21, 1911–January 20, 1947

Joshua "Josh" Gibson may have been the best baseball player never to have played in the major leagues. Gibson dominated the Negro League for twenty years. However, because of the racial climate at the time—and his premature death at the age of thirty-six—he was unable to play professional baseball.

Born in Buena Vista, Georgia, Gibson's family later moved to Pittsburgh, Pennsylvania, where he set his sights on becoming an electrician. He soon developed a passion for the game of **baseball** and spent the majority of his spare time playing the game on neighborhood sandlots (vacant city lots where children often gathered to play). It was not long before Gibson was spotted by a scout and began playing for the Negro League. Gibson played for the Pittsburgh Crawfords alongside such greats as **Satchel Paige** (c. 1907–1982) and **"Cool Papa" Bell** (1903–1991), helping the team win a championship in 1935.

Gibson was a gifted hitter, and his batting skill was often compared to that of major league legends such as Babe Ruth and Lou Gehrig. He led the Homestead Grays to nine consecutive Negro League pennants. Gibson was so powerful at the plate that he is believed to have hit the longest home runs in Yankee Stadium and Forbes Field; he never played for a losing team. His career batting average of .379 is the best ever among batters in the Negro League. With his legendary swing came fame and fortune as he became the second-highest-paid player in the Negro League. His fame was used to promote the league.

Gibson died prematurely at the age of thirty-six. During his short career, however, his considerable athletic abilities paved the way for the acceptance of blacks in professional baseball. In 1972 Gibson was inducted into the Baseball Hall of Fame.

Gibson, Robert "Rob"

BASEBALL PLAYER
November 9, 1935–

> *"In a world filled with hate, prejudice, and protest, I find that I too am filled with hate, prejudice and protest."*
>
> (Robert Gibson)

Robert "Rob" Gibson was one of the best pitchers in the major leagues after **World War II** (1939–1945). Gibson's specialty was striking batters out, which he accomplished with a blazing fastball and a vicious slider.

Born in Omaha, Nebraska, Gibson had several illnesses as a child. However, he fought through the illnesses and played **basketball** and **baseball** in high school and college. Gibson spent his early years playing in the minor leagues, and he also played for the **Harlem Globetrotters**. His breakout years in the majors were 1961 and 1962, during which he posted winning records with the St. Louis Cardinals. During his career (1959–75) Gibson consistently frustrated batters, and in 1968 he posted an amazing 22 wins and 9 losses with 268 strikeouts and 13 shutouts, earning him the Most Valuable Player award. In 1970 he won the Cy Young Award for best pitcher. Gibson was voted to the All-Star team eight times and was elected to the Baseball Hall of Fame in 1981.

Gibson retired in 1975 and began a career as a radio announcer for the Cardinals. He also began coaching with the New York Mets and later with the Atlanta Braves. In 2000 Gibson hosted his third annual celebrity golf tournament in Omaha, Nebraska, which raises funds for charities.

Gillespie, John Birks "Dizzy"

JAZZ TRUMPETER, COMPOSER
October 21, 1917–January 6, 1993

One of the founders of modern **jazz**, Dizzy Gillespie was known for his exuberant playing, as well as for his sense of humor and his generous spirit. Gillespie was born in Cheraw, South Carolina. Although his family was Methodist, young Gillespie secretly attended the free-form services at the Sanctified Church. He later said it was there he learned the meaning of rhythm. He began playing the trumpet at age thirteen. Largely self-taught,

GILLESPIE'S LANDMARK OVERSEAS TOUR

In 1956 Dizzy Gillespie organized a jazz ensemble that, sponsored by the U.S. State Department, toured first in the Middle East and Europe and later in Latin America. Always an outspoken opponent of segregation, Gillespie made sure the band included black and white members alike. It was the first time that the United States sent jazz musicians as cultural representatives to other countries. Since jazz was still viewed by many Americans as a renegade form of music, the highly successful tours helped give the music the seal of approval.

Dizzy Gillespie in performance with his trademark "bent" trumpet and puffed out cheeks (AP/Wide World Photos. Reproduced by permission)

he secured a music (and athletic) scholarship to North Carolina's Laurinburg Institute. But when his family moved to Philadelphia, Pennsylvania, in 1935, he went with them. He gained his first true band experience in Philadelphia, earning the nickname "Dizzy" for his clowning—both on stage and off.

In 1937 Gillespie moved to New York, where, into the 1940s, he played with various big bands, including those of music greats **Cab Calloway** (1907–1994) and **Earl "Fatha" Hines** (1903–1983). He soon began leading small ensembles. In 1945 he joined with saxophonist **Charlie "Bird" Parker** (1920–1955) to lead the All Star Quintet, a group that ushered in the modern jazz era. Their 1945 recordings, including the tunes "Shaw 'Nuff" and "Salt Peanuts," are considered the first true examples of bebop, a form of jazz characterized by speed, adventurous harmonies, and surprising turns of phrase. During the 1940s, a time of great creativity for him, Gillespie wrote many songs that became jazz standards.

By this time Gillespie had developed a unique style of trumpet playing. An early technical mistake of puffing out his cheeks had become his trademark. Still, he managed to push the limits of the brass instrument, making astonishing runs (blowing out notes continuously) and leaping into the trumpet's highest registers. After 1953 he played the trumpet with an upturned bell. Though he joked that the instrument was bent when someone sat on it, in truth it was specially built with an elbow joint so the sound was smooth.

Gillespie's flare, sometimes criticized by serious jazz fans, was one of his greatest assets. Continuing to record and perform prolifically during the 1960s and 1970s, he enjoyed a wide audience. He also taught and nurtured young, and even rival, talents. Credited with opening jazz to more musicians, he was widely recognized for his efforts. For example, in 1975 he was the subject of a tribute concert. He was also the recipient of numerous honors, including Grammy awards.

By the 1980s Gillespie was considered jazz's unofficial "ambassador." He made television appearances on popular shows such as *Sesame Street* and *The Cosby Show*, introducing young audiences to the form of music he helped found four decades earlier. He continued giving hundreds of concert each year until his death at age seventy-four.

Gilliam, Sam

ARTIST
November 30, 1933–

Born in Tupelo, Mississippi, Sam Gilliam began painting at an early age and received bachelor's and master's degrees from the University of Louisville (Kentucky). Gilliam's paintings have earned him many prizes, including a 1966 National Endowment for the Humanities fellowship.

Gilliam has exhibited his work in one-man shows at the Washington Gallery of Modern Art, the Museum of Modern Art in New York, and the Whitney Museum of American Art. His works have been shown in many group exhibitions, among them the first World Festival of Negro Arts (1966) in Dakar, Senegal, in West Africa. His work is found in the permanent collections of more than forty-five U.S. museums.

In 1980 Gilliam and thirteen other artists were commissioned to design an artwork for the Atlanta, Georgia, airport terminal. This was the first contemporary artwork created for public viewing at any American airport.

Gilpin, Charles Sidney

ACTOR, SINGER
November 20, 1878–May 6, 1930

Born and raised in Richmond, Virgina, Charles Gilpin worked as a print shop apprentice before becoming one of the most highly regarded actors of the 1920s. Gilpin first appeared onstage as a singer when he was only twelve. In 1896 he joined a minstrel show (a show featuring songs and jokes), thus beginning the life of a traveling performer, which he would lead for many years. Between engagements in restaurants, variety theaters, and fairs, he worked at various odd jobs.

In 1915 Gilpin joined the Anita Bush Stock Company, one of the first black stock (theatrical) companies in New York City, as its star performer. He accompanied the troupe when it moved from the Lincoln Theater in Harlem to the neighboring Lafayette Theatre, where the company became known as the Lafayette Players and eventually launched the careers of many famous black performers.

The famous playwright Eugene O'Neill saw Gilpin perform and recommended him for the lead role in his new play *The Emperor Jones.* The play opened in 1920 in New York's Greenwich Village and, following favorable reviews, moved to the Princess Theatre on Broadway. Gilpin, having beaten out numerous white actors for the part, became famous overnight. He played the title role for four years, to great critical and popular acclaim. The play marked O'Neill's first great success, and it greatly advanced the case for the public acceptance of black performers in serious **drama.**

In 1921 Gilpin's work in the play was honored by the Drama League of New York, which named Gilpin as one of the ten people who had done the most for the American theater. Gilpin was the first African American so honored. In 1921 the **National Association for the Advancement of Colored People (NAACP)** awarded Gilpin its highest award, the Spingarn Medal, for his achievement, and he was received at the White House in a private audience by President Warren G. Harding (1865–1923). Although he never again achieved such success, Gilpin continued to perform. He died of pneumonia in 1930 in Eldridge Park, New Jersey.

Giovanni, Yolanda Cornelia "Nikki"

POET
June 7, 1943–

Poet Nikki Giovanni was born in Knoxville, Tennesee, into a close-knit family. Giovanni felt a special bond with her grandmother, Louvenia Terrell Watson, who instilled in the young poet a fierce pride in her African–American heritage. After graduating from **Fisk University** in 1967,

Giovanni was swept up by the black power and **Black Arts movement**s. Between 1968 and 1970 Giovanni published three books of poetry reflecting her focus on revolutionary politics: *Black Judgment* (1968), *Black Feeling, Black Talk* (1970), and *Re: Creation* (1970).

In 1969 Giovanni gave birth to a son. The experience, she said, caused her to reconsider her priorities. Her work through the middle 1970s concentrated less on politics and confrontation and more on personal issues such as love and loneliness. During this time she began writing poetry for children. *Spin a Soft Black Song: Poems for Children* appeared in 1971, *Ego-Tripping and Other Poems for Young People* in 1973, and *Vacation Time: Poems for Children* in 1980.

Between 1971 and 1978 Giovanni also made a series of six records, speaking her poetry to an accompaniment of gospel music. She published essays and two books of conversations with major **African-American** literary figures **James Baldwin** and **Margaret Walker**. Giovanni is a popular reader and lecturer and performs across the Unites States. She has produced numerous books of poetry—for both children and adults—including *My House* (1972), *Cotton Candy on a Rainy Day* (1978), *Those Who Ride the Night Winds* (1983), *Racism 101* (1993), and *The Sun Is So Quiet* (1996). In 1999 Giovanni published her first volume of all-new verses in nearly fifteen years, *Blues: For All the Changes*.

Glover, Danny

ACTOR
July 22, 1947–

One of the foremost modern African-American actors, Danny Glover was a student activist in the 1960s. After graduation from college he worked as an economic planner in San Francisco, California. He began taking acting classes in the 1960s at the Black Actors' Workshop in Oakland, California. In the 1970s Glover acted with playwright and actor Sam Shepard's Magic Theater, the San Francisco Eureka Theater, and the Los Angeles Theater and also made several guest appearances on television. In 1982 he appeared in the Broadway play *Master Harold . . . and the Boys*, where he was seen by writer and director Robert Benton, who cast him as a sharecropper in the motion picture *Places in the Heart* (1984).

In 1985 Glover appeared in three films: *Witness, Silverado*, and *The Color Purple*. *The Color Purple* is Steven Spielberg's adaptation of Alice Walker's novel of the same name. Glover played the role of the cruel "Mister," opposite **Whoopi Goldberg**. In 1987 Glover starred as a Los Angeles detective who is partners with Mel Gibson in *Lethal Weapon*. The action-adventure movie was a major commercial success and led to three sequels.

In 1990 Glover produced and starred in **Charles Burnett**'s *To Sleep with Anger*, a film about middle-class black life in south-central Los Angeles. That same year, he was inducted into the Black Filmmakers Hall of Fame. In 1994 Glover starred in the popular film *Angels in the Outfield*, and in 1998 he won critical praise for his featured role in *Beloved*, based on **Toni Morrison**'s novel. Glover lives in San Francisco, where he is involved in many community activities. He is also engaged in international activism

after becoming a goodwill ambassador for the United Nations Development Program.

Goldberg, Whoopi

ACTRESS
November 13, 1950–

Whoopi Goldberg was born Caryn Johnson in New York City and raised in a housing project by her mother. She went on to become one of the most popular actresses on the screen today.

In the mid-1960s Goldberg dropped out of high school and worked on Broadway as a chorus member in the musicals *Hair*, *Jesus Christ Superstar*, and *Pippin*. In 1974 she moved to Los Angeles, California, to continue her career and adopted the name Whoopi Goldberg.

Goldberg wrote and performed comedy sketches with characters such as a surfer girl, a showbiz actor-turned-beggar, and a Jamaican maid. Goldberg's style earned her both critical acclaim and a large audience. She opened on Broadway in 1984 in a new version of her comedy sketches, *Whoopi Goldberg*.

The following year, Goldberg starred as Celie in the film *The Color Purple*, and she received an Academy Award nomination for her performance. She also appeared in a continuing role on the television series *Star Trek: The Next Generation* from 1988 through 1993. In 1990 she received an Academy Award for best supporting actress for her role as a psychic in *Ghost*. Goldberg became the second black woman in history—the first since **Hattie McDaniel** (*Gone With the Wind*) in 1939—to win an Oscar in a major category.

In 1992 Goldberg cofounded the annual comedy benefit "Comic Relief" on the cable television network Home Box Office to raise money for the homeless. In 1994 Goldberg hosted the Oscar Awards. Her film appearances during this period include *The Player* (1995), *Boys on the Side* (1996), and *The Ghosts of Mississippi* (1998). In 1997 she returned to Broadway in *A Funny Thing Happened on the Way to the Forum*. In 1998 she revived the television quiz show *Hollywood Squares* with great success.

An African-American FIRST

In 1994 Whoopi Goldberg was the first African American and first woman to be the solo host of the Academy Awards. Goldberg served as host again in 1996. Critics and viewers alike enjoyed Goldberg's performances.

Golf

Golf has historically been considered a white man's game. It has probably been the most difficult sport for blacks to penetrate. Although more blacks are taking up the sport, according to a 1990 survey only a small percentage of the golfing population (2.5 percent) was black.

In 1896 John Shippen became one of the first American-born professional golfers. However, it took nearly a century before blacks became generally accepted in the sport. African Americans developed an interest in golf through caddying (carrying the clubs of other golfers). The economic surge of the 1920s resulted in a greater number of people taking up the sport, which resulted in an increase in demand for caddies. Caddies were allowed to play one day per week, which gave teenage blacks an opportunity to play.

According to the 1934 Constitution of the Professional Golf Association (PGA), blacks were specifically prohibited from playing in PGA tournaments. This guideline all but locked blacks out of professional golf competition. However, exclusion from the PGA did not prevent blacks from opening clubs on their own and establishing an all-black golf association. In 1921 the Shady Rest Golf Club was created, which is generally considered to be the first black country club. In 1926 Robert Hawkins invited blacks to participate in a tournament, and by 1928 the group had established the Unified Golfers Association. Among the prominent black golfers to play in

THE LEGAL BATTLE FOR THE RIGHT TO PLAY GOLF.

During the **Civil Rights movement** many social advances were made in the United States. In 1947 P.O. Sweeny sued the Parks Department of Louisville, Kentucky for the right to play golf on public courses, from which blacks had traditionally been excluded. Although he was denied, several later cases eventually led to a change in policy. In 1955 the Supreme Court finally declared that it was illegal to prevent blacks from playing on public golf courses. Despite the ruling, it took several years before public golf courses actually began to open their doors to blacks.

the UGA were Robert "Pat" Ball and John Dendy. Black women also began to take up the sport and soon developed the Chicago Women's Club. Among the early black female standouts in the sport were Lucy Williams and Laura Osgood.

Although blacks could play in the military and at some universities, they were still excluded from public courses until 1955. It was not until 1948, after blacks threatened to sue, that the PGA began to open its doors to blacks. However, the PGA still refused to withdraw its "Caucasian clause" (or whites-only rule). An event in 1952 brought national attention to the problem of racism on the golf course. African-American boxing champion **Joe Louis** was invited to play at a PGA tournament. Louis was an amateur golfer invited to play by Chevrolet, which was a sponsor of the tournament. The PGA tried to prohibit Louis from playing but had to rethink its decision because of its own rules. The PGA constitution indicated that professional blacks were banned, not amateurs. Louis was permitted to play; however, it was not until 1961 that the PGA withdrew its ban on blacks.

From the 1950s until the 1990s there were very few well-known black golfers. Charles Shiffer became the first black to win a "white" event in 1957. Perhaps the first black golfer to open the door for blacks professionally was Lee Elder. In 1975 Elder became the first black to compete in the Masters (perhaps the most prestigious professional golf tournament). Until the 1990s the most successful black golfer had been Calvin Pete. In 1982 Pete won four professional tournaments and finished third in the PGA Championship. It took even longer for women to break into the sport. It was not until 1967 that a black female began to play regularly in Ladies Professional Golf Association (LPGA) tournaments.

In 1997 a golfer by the name of **Tiger Woods** stunned the golfing world by becoming the first black to win the Masters and also achieving two record scores during the tournament. Woods went on to win several major tournaments, including the U.S. Open, the PGA Championship, and the British Open (2000). Woods has nearly single-handedly shattered decades of racial discrimination and exclusionary policies on courses throughout the United States. Not only has he encouraged more blacks to take up the sport by becoming a role model with his brilliant play, he has also become a highly respected spokesman for the game. Although black participation in golf is

still low in relation to whites, Woods offers the promise of inclusion and harmony in an arena that has historically been off-limits to blacks.

Gospel Music

Gospel music, a distinctively American religious music associated with evangelism (preaching "the gospel," or trying to win converts to Christianity), was popular among African-American slaves, who often sang songs of sorrow, religious joy, suffering, and hope while working on plantations in the South. After slavery ended, gospel music, which is based on simple melodies of folk music combined with elements of spirituals and **jazz,** continued to thrive among African Americans, who still suffered overwhelming discrimination and racism despite their liberty. During the twentieth century, gospel music influenced other musical styles, including jazz, **the blues,** soul, country music, and even hip-hop.

The Founding Years

Although much gospel music can be traced to African song traditions, early gospel music was influenced mainly by nineteenth-century British hymns. These songs relied on a "call-and-response" style, which means that singers called out to the audience and the audience responded in song. Early African-American churches, such as the **African Methodist Episocopal (AME) Church,** used hymns that had been specially composed for use in black churches. In addition to their call-and-response style, these gospel hymns had powerful rhythms and were less solemn than traditional Christian hymns of the time.

Throughout the nineteenth century, gospel music gained popularity in both white and black churches. Some Christians, both African-American and white, began to believe that spiritual progress required a closer, more emotional relationship with God. The singing of gospel hymns was part of that emotional religious experience.

Gospel music continued to gain popularity among black and white congregations in the early twentieth century. Congregations looking for a more direct relationship with God sprang up all over the South, particularly in poor communities. In less than a decade, gospel music was being sung in Baptist and Methodist congregations throughout the South. Early forms of gospel music, such as singing sermons and stories, were used alongside prayers. Members of a congregation would repeat a phrase from the sermon and, on the spur of the moment, compose a simple melody to accompany it. Other church members would join in, and soon the whole congregation would be singing the new melody and words.

Gospel Quartets

During the 1920s and 1930s gospel music continued to exert a strong appeal. In 1921 the **National Baptist Convention,** the largest organization of black Christians in the world, published a collection of gospel hymns. That hymnal contained songs written by the composer **Thomas Andrew**

Dorsey (1899–1993), who came to be known as "the father of gospel music."

Gospel music reached its largest audiences by word of mouth, however. In the South workers in coal mines and factories used their lunch hours to organize quartets (singing groups of four men) to sing these religious songs. The most famous gospel quartets of this time were the Foster Singers, the Birmingham Jubilee Singers, and the Soul Stirrers. These groups performed all over the country, singing at churches and community gatherings throughout the South and the North. By the late 1930s larger gospel groups, with both men and women, also became popular.

The Golden Age of Gospel Music

By 1945 gospel music was no longer reserved for churches and religious gatherings. It had become popular entertainment. This period became known as gospel's golden age. Gospel composers created new, exciting songs that drew upon other musical styles and included complicated rhythms and singing techniques. Just as early gospel singers traveled from church to church to sing their songs, the gospel singers of the 1940s also took their music on the road. By 1945 singers such as **Mahalia Jackson** had quit their regular jobs to join the growing number of professional gospel singers performing in churches, schools, and stadiums. These singers were the first generation of gospel singers able to support themselves with their singing, and some, like Jackson, were very successful.

After **World War II** (1939–45), radio also played a large part in the growing popularity of gospel music. Record companies recruited gospel singers, and the popularity of many records led to gospel radio programs. In cities like New York, Baltimore, Chicago, and New Orleans, gospel radio shows and gospel disc jockeys became very successful. The most famous gospel singer of this era was **Sam Cooke**, who joined the Soul Stirrers in 1950 and had several gospel hits before becoming famous as a pop singer in 1956.

By the end of the 1950s, gospel music had become an important part of American culture. In 1961 a gospel category was added to the Grammy Awards, with Mahalia Jackson as the first winner. During the 1960s gospel choirs began to appear on Broadway, at New York's Carnegie Hall, and in Las Vegas, Nevada, as well as on television shows. In addition to Sam Cooke, many singers trained in the gospel tradition used gospel rhythms in popular music. Singers such as **Ray Charles**, **Aretha Franklin**, **James Brown**, **Little Richard**, and **Stevie Wonder** used gospel singing techniques to gain international fame as rock-and-roll, soul, and **rhythm-and-blues (R&B)** singers.

Gospel Music and the Civil Rights Movement

Gospel music also played an important role in the **Civil Rights movement** of the 1960s. Black leaders throughout the South, including **Martin Luther King Jr.**, protested racist laws by marching peacefully and singing gospel music. In addition, singers such as Mahalia Jackson and **Fannie Lou Hamer** appeared at marches, rallies, and meetings. During this time gospel songs originally written for religious purposes were used in the political struggles of blacks. Popular songs like "We Shall Overcome" and "Eyes on the Prize" helped civil rights leaders recruit and inspire activists.

The Contemporary Sound and Beyond

During the closing decades of the twentieth century, gospel music continued to thrive and artists kept on creating new gospel sounds and rhythms. In 1976 the widely acclaimed gospel musical, "Your Arms Too Short to Box with God," made a successful run on Broadway. During the 1980s and 1990s contemporary gospel continued to attract large audiences. Groups such as the Sextet 6, who combined gospel sounds with jazz rhythms, achieved huge popular success. Many gospel groups began to use modern synthesizers and drum machines in their music, combining these new sounds with more traditional gospel instruments.

In 1993 one of the greatest gospelers ever, Marion Williams, became the first gospel singer to win a MacArthur "Genius" Award—an honor granted to a very select few Americans—and the first gospel singer to receive honors from the Kennedy Center for the Performing Arts, a government-sponsored staging ground for the nation's finest performing artists.

While gospel music continues to be one of the most dominant forms of African-American and American music (there are now six Grammy categories for gospel music), in the late twentieth century many African-American Christians began to revive an old argument from the onset of gospel's golden age: gospel music, they claimed, had always been for the church and should be kept off the airwaves. But the rhythms and emotional power of gospel music could not be kept from influencing other emerging forms. For example, in the 1990s some artists of the now-established urban hip-hop music, a form that often makes use of profanity and violent imagery, began to borrow melodies, rhythms, and Christian messages of redemption for their songs. While some church leaders may be unhappy with the emergence of "gospel rap," it is another example of gospel music's power to penetrate many aspects of African-American life.

Grace, Charles Emmanuel "Sweet Daddy"

January 25, 1881–January 12, 1960

Charles Emmanuel Grace, better known as Sweet Daddy, was born in the Cape Verde Islands, of mixed African and Portuguese descent. Around 1908 he immigrated to New Bedford, Massachusetts, where he worked several jobs, including cranberry picking. A journey to the Holy Land inspired him to found a church in Massachusetts around 1919. Daddy Grace gathered several thousand followers at religious revivals in North Carolina. In 1926 he formed the United House of Prayer for All People of the Church on the Rock of the Apostolic Faith.

A flamboyant and charismatic leader, Grace wore his hair and fingernails long. His nails were painted red, white, and blue. He baptized converts with fire hoses and sold his followers specially blessed products such as soap, coffee, eggs, and ice cream. He specialized in buying expensive real estate, such

as mansions and hotels, but he also supported church members with housing, funds, and burial plans. At his death in Los Angeles, Califrnia, in 1960, he was worth some $25 million, but it was unclear what was owned by the church and what were his personal assets.

Sweet Daddy never took the credit for the divinity his followers gave him. "I never said I was God," he once noted, "but you cannot prove to me I'm not." At Daddy's death in 1960, Bishop Walter T. McCullogh took over the House of Prayer following a successful lawsuit against rival James Walton.

Granville, Evelyn Boyd

MATHEMATICIAN, EDUCATOR, AUTHOR
May 1, 1924–

Evelyn Boyd Granville was born in Washington, D.C., and was reared primarily by her mother and aunt. She won a partial scholarship to study at Smith College in Massachusetts. She excelled in mathematics, and in 1945 she graduated summa cum laude (with highest honors) from Smith. She won several grants and entered a graduate program at Yale University, from which she earned a Ph.D. degree in 1949. She was one of the first two black females to receive a doctorate (Ph.D.) in mathematics. In 1950 she was appointed to the mathematics faculty of **Fisk University** in Nashville, Tennessee. She remained on the faculty for two years and inspired at least two young women to pursue a Ph.D. in mathematics. She left Fisk and spent sixteen years working in government and private industry.

In 1967 Granville was appointed to the faculty at California State University in Los Angeles. While there, she cowrote a book with Jason Frand, *Theory and Application of Mathematics for Teachers* (1975). She accepted a position in 1985 at Texas College in Tyler, where she had purchased a farm with her husband. Granville left Texas College in 1988 and in 1990 was appointed to the Sam A. Lindsey Chair at the University of Texas in Tyler. In addition to teaching at the university level, Granville has taught in secondary school programs in the California and Texas public school systems.

Graphic Arts

The graphic arts include all forms of expression in which tools (paper, ink, or even computers) are used to print or make multiple copies. All forms of printmaking, including engraving, etching, and lithography, are considered graphic arts.

Early Black Printmakers

African traditions of printed arts (such as textile printing) did not survive in colonial America. Instead, black printmakers were trained by white artisans. Perhaps the earliest known black American graphic artist was Scipio Moorhead (flourished c. 1773), a Massachusetts slave. Moorhead learned

FINE ART PRINTS

Painter **Henry Ossawa Tanner** (1859–1937) is generally regarded as the first African American to create fine art prints. While many black printers had been working commercially, Tanner employed graphic arts (in this case etching and lithography) for their own sake, printing landscapes, seascapes, and portraits.

During the heightened period of creativity known as the Harlem Renaissance, black graphic artists began using African designs in their prints

printmaking from his master's wife, artist Sarah Moorhead. One of his engravings appeared as the frontispiece to a 1773 edition of poems by Senegalese-born **Phillis Wheatley** (c. 1753–1784).

As the **abolition** movement gained strength, more white people in the North were willing to do business with black merchants and artisans, including printmakers. Some, such as Cincinnati, Ohio, lithographer **James Presley Ball** (1825–1905), enjoyed thriving businesses. (Lithography is a printing process that uses a smooth stone or metal plate and ink to reproduce images.) Ball was further recognized for staging an antislavery photography display, which was accompanied by a pamphlet he designed and printed.

African Styles Emerge

During the heightened period of creativity known as the **Harlem Renaissance** (1917–35), black graphic artists began using African designs in their prints. For example, artist **Aaron Douglas** (1899–1979) made a series of prints to illustrate American playwright Eugene O'Neill's *The Emperor Jones* (1921). Douglas rendered people in much the same way as in traditional African art. The figures are highly stylized, meaning they are represented according to a pattern, rather than according to nature.

During the severe economic downturn of the **Great Depression** (1929–39), the government began the Federal Arts Project (FAP; 1935) as a way to put Americans to work. But the program achieved much more. It created art in public spaces, developed community art centers, and set up artists' workshops. In cities throughout the country, significant numbers of African-American artists participated in these projects. FAP-sponsored artist Dox Thrash (c. 1892–1975) developed a new printmaking process.

Artists Express Social Concerns

Beginning in the mid-1940s, the work of African-American printmakers became varied. While **Elizabeth Catlett** (1919–) made prints that commented on racial inequalities (for example, a 1946 work was titled *I Have Special Reservations*), others focused on black ambitions and racial pride.

By the 1960s, when the **Civil Rights movement** was at its peak, black graphic artists increasingly represented social themes in their works and used styles that echoed African tradition. In the later decades of the 1900s, black graphic artists experimented with new approaches as they worked to represent cultural issues in their prints.

Gray, William Herbert III

CONGRESSMAN

August 20, 1941–

William Herbert Gray III has dedicated his life to the economic and social development of blacks. Gray did important work in the U.S. Congress (1978-1991) for African Americans as well as for blacks in Africa and has promoted higher education through the United Negro College Fund. (UNCF).

Born in Baton Rouge, Louisiana, Gray was the child of parents who both valued education. His father was the president of a university and his mother was a teacher. Gray earned a bachelor's degree from Franklin and Marshall College (1963) and a master's degree from Princeton (1970). He became a pastor in 1964 and led a politically active church that helped low-income families find homes.

Gray was elected as a Democrat to the House of Representatives in 1978 and worked on important committees such as Appropriations (which determines which projects get funded) and Foreign Affairs. Gray focused his efforts in Congress on the economic development of blacks. He also helped pass laws designed to bring an end to the racist system of apartheid in South Africa. Gray's efforts in Congress were rewarded by his party in 1989 when he was elected to the highest position ever held by an African American, majority whip. (Party "whips" are in charge of communicating their party's position.) Gray retired from Congress in 1991 to become the president of the United Negro College Fund (UNCF). He has focused his attention on fund-raising for the UNCF. Under his leadership the UNCF has broken fund-raising records, including a drive that generated $280 million in 1995.

Great Depression and New Deal

The Great Depression (1929–39) was a period of such difficult economic times that all Americans, both rich and poor, experienced hardships. African Americans, whose political and economic status was already low, felt the effects of the depression earlier than other groups. Because so many blacks worked in agriculture, falling prices for cotton and other crops brought devastating results. By 1926 the **National Urban League,** a prominent African-American organization, was advising southern black workers not to move to northern cities unless they were certain they had a job. White workers who had lost higher-paying jobs were taking jobs that had traditionally belonged to African Americans. Unemployment increased rapidly during the 1930s, but the percentage of unemployed black workers was estimated to be twice that of U.S. workers as a whole.

When Franklin D. Roosevelt (1882–1945) was elected president in 1932, he moved swiftly to create laws and programs that would put Americans back to work and provide relief for the many poor. His plan was known as the New Deal. But many of Roosevelt's programs did not help African Americans. They were often excluded from work programs because employers would hire few blacks, because of segregation policies and because of local rules against admitting blacks to labor unions (workers' organizations formed to protect workers' interests). When wages were set by a government agency, jobs with mostly black workers paid less, and wages determined by geographic area were lowest in the Southeast, where a majority of African Americans lived.

African-American organizations protested this discrimination and tried to eliminate it. The Joint Committee on National Recovery, made up of twenty-two national African-American fraternal, civic, and church groups, watched job codes and pay rates in industries and areas with a large number of black workers. The National Urban League and the **National Association for the Advancement of Colored People (NAACP)** pressured the American Federation of Labor (AFL) to abolish discrimination but these practices continued.

Programs That Helped Blacks

The National Youth Administration (NYA), established in 1935 to help young men and women who were living at home, proved fairly successful for black youths. This was largely due to the influence of African-American educator **Mary McLeod Bethune** (1875–1955), who served as the head of the Negro Affairs section of the NYA and was able to get funding for programs. The NYA helped young people who were not attending school to receive job training and helped those in school to continue their education.

The Works Progress Administration (WPA), established in 1935, coordinated agencies that provided work to more than 3.5 million people. The WPA had good qualities, such as federal administration (it was run by the federal government, rather than by the states), an emphasis on work rather than welfare, jobs for professionals as well as for laborers and factory workers, set wage rates, and a system for giving jobs to those most in need of financial help. But it also had policies that were disturbing to blacks, such as wage rates that were lower than private-sector jobs, with different geographic-area pay rates.

The WPA built or improved hospitals, schools, roads, playgrounds, and landing strips. African-American professionals were put to work in office jobs. African-American actors, writers, and artists found work through the Federal Theatre Project, the Federal Writers' Project, and the Federal Arts Project. But as private-sector jobs increased, the WPA cut back on jobs, and by 1940 more than eight million people were unemployed and were forced to return to government welfare.

In addition to creating temporary programs to help relieve the nation's economic troubles, the New Deal produced some permanent, significant social welfare laws, like the Social Security Act, passed in 1935. This act had a lasting and major effect on African Americans because it created a social welfare system on two tiers (levels). One is a plan to which workers or their employers contribute a portion of earnings to be used for old-age and survivors' insurance and for unemployment insurance. The second is a system of public assistance programs, such as aid to the elderly poor, the blind, and dependent children. But the Social Security bill did not include domestic and agricultural workers in the first tier, excluding two-thirds of black workers from receiving these benefits. The NAACP and the National Urban

League worked to change these aspects of the bill, saying that welfare was no substitute for earning a living through work.

Black Leadership

The Roosevelt administration was the first to include a fairly large number of African Americans, with several black leaders serving as advisers for Negro Affairs in presidential cabinet departments. This group was known as "the black cabinet" or "the black brain trust." Some prominent blacks appointed to these positions were **Robert Clifton Weaver,** Mary McLeod Bethune, **William Henry Hastie,** and Forrester Washington. Although the black cabinet had little power in policy making, its presence was a positive force for African Americans.

However, the leadership that was most helpful to African Americans came from black organizations such as the National Urban League and the NAACP. Their members watched the development of New Deal legislation and programs, testified in favor of certain policies, kept the African-American population informed about programs, and helped them take advantage of the programs. But the organizations had little political power and were unsuccessful at persuading Congress to support policies that would have been more helpful to African Americans.

An Imperfect Solution

Throughout the Great Depression, New Deal legislation had to keep the support of the southern states. This proved harmful to African-American workers because legislation was passed with policies that limited their access to programs and benefits. By 1940 a large portion of the black population remained unemployed and on welfare, and no real change had been made in employment practices that discriminated against blacks. The New Deal was not the cure-all that the African-American population had hoped it would be.

Greaves, William

ACTOR, FILM DIRECTOR, WRITER, TV PRODUCER
October 8, 1926–

Born and raised in New York City, William Greaves briefly studied engineering before first working in radio, television, theater, and film during the 1940s. He has since gone on to produce major motion pictures, television programs, and numerous documentary (based on "documented" facts) films.

In 1950 Greaves began taking film classes at the City College of New York. In 1952 he went to work in Canada's film industry, where he gained technical experience but felt restrained artistically. In 1963 he moved back to New York. He was soon working for the United States Information Agency (USIA), documenting The First World Festival of Negro Arts (1966), a historic meeting of African and African-descent artists and intellectuals in Dakar, Senegal, in West Africa.

In 1967 Greaves made a documentary film entitled *Still a Brother: Inside the Negro Middle Class* for National Educational Television (NET). Greaves also became a cohost and later the executive producer of *Black Journal*, a new NET magazine-type program focusing on national black issues.

Greaves's first independent feature-length film was the experimental *Symbipsycotaxiplasm: Take One* (1967), a movie within a movie. The film was not commercially released until the early 1990s and was praised by critics.

In 1970 Greaves left *Black Journal* to give more time to filmmaking. In 1971 he made the commercially successful *Ali the Fighter*. Greaves's 1974 documentary about the early 1900s period of cultural achievement known as the **Harlem Renaissance,** *From These Roots* (1974), won twenty-two awards. In 1981 Greaves was executive producer for the **Richard Pryor** comedy *Bustin' Loose.*

In all, Greaves has been involved in the production of more than three hundred documentary films. In 1998 he produced ***Ralph Bunche***: *An American Odyssey*, a four-part documentary series for public television.

Green, Al

SINGER, SONGWRITER
April 13, 1946–

Al Green's musical career included both soul and **gospel music.** He was born in Arkansas and began singing in a family gospel quartet at age nine. A gospel quartet includes four people singing harmony in religious songs. For six years the group toured in the American South and the Midwest, and then the family relocated to Michigan.

Green formed his own pop group, Al Green and the Creations, in 1964 after his father removed him from the gospel quartet for listening to what he called the "profane" music of singer **Jackie Wilson** (1934–1984). The group changed their name in 1967 to Al Green and the Soulmates. That year, Green made his first record, with the single "Back Up Train," which went to number five on the national soul charts in 1968. However, there were no follow-up successes, and Green was plunged back into obscurity, playing small clubs again.

While touring, Green met Willie Mitchell, vice president of Hi Records in Memphis, Tennessee. Mitchell produced Green's version of "I Can't Get Next to You," which went to number one on the national soul charts in 1971. Continuing to work with Mitchell and drummer Al Jackson Jr., Green went on to record a string of million-selling singles and LPs throughout the early 1970s. Combining sensuous vocals with strings, horns, and hard-driving backbeats, Green helped define the sound of soul music in the 1970s.

At the height of his career, Green shifted back toward gospel music. A turning point was an incident in 1974 in which his girlfriend scalded him with a pot of boiling grits before killing herself with his gun. When Green recovered from his burns, he became a minister, and in 1976 he purchased a church in Memphis and was ordained pastor. He did not immediately give up pop music, but his attempts to mix gospel themes with nonreligious music did not succeed.

In 1979 Green decided to sing only gospel music, and the next year he released his first gospel album. The lines between gospel music and love songs remained blurred for Green. During his shows he would lose himself in religious ecstasy one moment and toss roses into the audience the next. Throughout the 1980s and early 1990s, Green continued to record gospel records and pastor the Full Gospel Tabernacle.

Greer, William Alexander "Sonny"

JAZZ DRUMMER
December 13, 1895–March 23, 1982

Sonny Greer's music career spanned six decades and was highlighted by a thirty-year association with swing and **jazz** great **Duke Ellington** (1899–1974). Born in Long Branch, New Jersey, Greer played drums as a child. By 1919 he was playing professionally.

Greer met pianist Duke Ellington, then just starting out, and in 1920 became the first drummer for Ellington's band, the five-piece Washingtonians. Though he was known as a true showman, Greer had a subtle touch on the drums, which many jazz lovers viewed as the perfect fit for the band's sound. He stayed with the band after Ellington added orchestra members to create the **Cotton Club** (in 1927).

But Greer's personal life put a strain on his relationship with the bandleader. The drummer had a reputation for drinking, playing pool, and occasionally needing to buy back his drum set from pawn shops, where he sold them when money was tight. When Ellington hired a different drummer to tour with his band in 1950, he and Greer parted ways. Greer worked with various artists through the 1950s, 1960s, and 1970s, including a group of musicians who played a program of tributes to Ellington.

Gregory, Richard Claxton "Dick"

COMEDIAN, ACTIVIST, RIGHTS ADVOCATE
October 12, 1932–

Dick Gregory has had a long and varied career as a **comedian,** activist, and nutrition consultant. Gregory was born and raised in a slum in St. Louis, Missouri. With the aid of an athletic scholarship, he attended college, where he became a track star and dreamed of becoming a comedian.

Gregory traveled to Chicago, Illinois, to pursue his goal of becoming a comedian. In the late 1950s he worked in small black clubs and struggled to gain popular recognition. Gregory's breakthrough occurred in January 1961, when the Playboy Club in Chicago hired him. Gregory's bold, cool, and detached humor completely charmed his audience. After this success, his contract was extended from several weeks to three years. By 1962 he had become a national celebrity and the first black comic superstar in the modern era. He also became an author, publishing *From the Back of the Bus* (1962) and, with Robert Lipsyte, *Nigger: An Autobiography* (1964).

Gregory emerged as an outspoken political activist during the 1960s. As a supporter of the **Civil Rights movement,** he participated in voter registration drives, marched in parades and demonstrations, and was arrested numerous times. He also began to entertain at prisons and for civil rights organizations, using his humor as a powerful tool to highlight racism and inequality in the United States.

Gregory found numerous ways to dramatize his chosen causes. He fasted to demonstrate his commitment to civil rights and to protest the **Vietnam War** (1959–75), the abuse of narcotics, and world hunger. By the late 1960s Gregory was increasingly devoting his attention to the youth of America, lecturing at hundreds of college campuses each year and making fewer and fewer nightclub appearances; he released his last comedy album, *Caught in the Act*, in 1973.

After moving to a farm in Massachusetts in 1973, he became a well-known advocate of vegetarianism. Often limiting himself to a diet of fruit and juices, he became a nutritional consultant, often appearing on talk shows in his new role, and wrote (with Alvenia Fulton) *Dick Gregory's Natural Diet for Folks Who Eat, Cookin' with Mother Nature* (1974). He also wrote *Up from Nigger*, with James R. McGraw, the second installment of his autobiography (1976).

In 1984 Gregory founded Health Enterprises, a successful marketing venture for various weight-loss products, and expanded his financial holdings to hotels and other properties. In 1992 he returned to his home town of St. Louis to organize the Campaign for Human Dignity, whose stated purpose was to reclaim predominantly African-American neighborhoods from drug dealers. During the mid-1990s he also returned to performing, notably in an Off-Broadway show, *Dick Gregory Live*, in October 1995. Gregory continues to perform and is a tireless supporter fo the political causes he believes in.

Griffith-Joyner, Florence Delorez

ATHLETE
December 21, 1959–September 28, 1998

Florence Delorez Griffith-Joyner was one of the world's fastest women runners. Griffith-Joyner not only ran fast, she ran with style, wearing colorful one-legged running outfits in combination with long black hair and long painted fingernails. Sadly, she will be remembered as much for her premature death as for her unique athleticism.

Born in Los Angeles, California, Griffith-Joyner began running at the age of seven and started winning races at the age of fourteen. In high school she joined the track team where she set two records before graduating in 1978. She began her college studies in 1979, but she had to drop out because she could not afford it. Determined to get a college education, Griffith-Joyner then earned a scholarship to attend the University of California at Los Angeles (UCLA) in 1981. While earning a degree in psychology, she won the National Collegiate Athletic Association (NCAA) championship for the two hundred meter (1982) and four hundred meter competitions (1983).

In 1984 Griffith-Joyner participated in the Olympics where she won a silver medal in the two hundred meter event. She then dropped out of competition for a while and worked two jobs before deciding to get more serious about her athletic career. She trained vigorously for the 1988 Olympics and flew past her competitors winning three gold medals, one silver medal, and setting an Olympic record for the one hundred meter run and a world record in the two hundred meter run. Griffith-Joyner was honored in 1988 with the **Jesse Owens** Award and Sullivan Award. After the Olympics she began an acting career and developed a line of sportswear. In 1993 President Bill Clinton named her chair of the President's Council of Physical Fitness and Sports. On September 21, 1998 Griffith-Joyner died tragically of an apparent seizure. There was speculation that her doctors had given her the wrong type of medicine.

Griggs, Sutton Elbert

NOVELIST, PREACHER
1872–1933

Novelist and preacher Sutton E. Griggs was born in Chatfield, Texas, and was raised in Dallas. Following the path of his father, the Reverend Allen R. Griggs, he studied for the Baptist ministry at the Richmond Theological Seminary (later part of Virginia Union University) and was ordained (became a minister) in 1893. He went on to serve more than thirty years as a Baptist minister in Nashville and Memphis, Tennessee.

Griggs was also an author of novels, political essays, and religious pamphlets. In response to the wave of segregation and antiblack violence in the South after **Reconstruction** (1865-77), Griggs and other African-American writers created works that portrayed black Americans in a positive light and demanded civil rights.

Griggs wrote more than thirty books, most of which he published himself and promoted during preaching tours. His five novels investigate African-American life in the South and explore interracial marriage, racial violence, and civil rights. Griggs called for social equality for blacks, but he also argued against radical militancy (violence, fighting) in the quest for civil rights.

Griggs's best-known work is *Imperium in Imperio* (1899), one of the first African-American political novels. The book centers around a character named Belton Piedmont, who is an integrationist, someone who believes that whites and blacks should live peacefully together. During this time there was a movement to create separate regions of the United States where blacks could form their own society. In Griggs's *Imperium*, Belton Piedmont chooses to die rather than support a plot to seize Texas and Louisiana from the United States as a haven for African Americans.

Similar themes appear in Griggs's political works, most notably *Wisdom's Call* (1909), which comments on civil rights in the South, **lynching**, the right to vote, and the rights of black women. *Guide to Racial Greatness; or, The Science of Collective Efficiency* (1923), which was published along with a volume of biblical verses, *Kingdom Builders' Manual* (1924), offers a plan for the political organization of the African-American southern population, stressing education, religious discipline, employment, and land ownership.

At the end of his life, Griggs returned to Texas to take over his father's position as pastor of the Hopewell Baptist Church in Denison. He eventually moved to Houston, and at the time of his death Griggs was trying to establish a national African-American religious institute there. (*See also* **Baptists**.)

Grimké, Angelina Weld

WRITER
February 27, 1880–June 10, 1958

Born in Boston, Angelina Grimké attended integrated schools in wealthy Hyde Park, Massachussetts, and graduated in 1902 from the Boston Normal School of Gymnastics, later part of Wellesley College. After graduation Grimké worked as a teacher in Washington, D.C., until her retirement in 1926. In 1930 she moved to Brooklyn, New York, where she lived for the rest of her life.

Grimké's best-known work is a short play entitled *Rachel,* which was first presented in 1916. The play portrays a young African-American woman who, despite her love of children, resolves not to bring any of her own into the world. With its tragic view of race relations, *Rachel* was staged several times by the **National Association for the Advancement of Colored People (NAACP)** as a response to white director D. W. Griffith's racist 1915 film *The Birth of a Nation.*

Grimké's best work, although less well known, is her poetry. As her work matured in the early twentieth century, she began to experiment with forms and themes. She even discussed sexual themes in her poetry with an openness uncommon among African-American poets of her time. Although she only occasionally addressed racial issues in her poems, she did so with strength and conviction.

Grimké, Charlotte L. Forten

ABOLITIONIST, TEACHER, WRITER
August 7, 1837–July 22, 1914

Charlotte Forten was born into one of Philadelphia's leading African-American families with a tradition of fighting for **abolition,** or ending slavery. Charlotte Forten continued her family's traditions.

As a teenager, Forten joined a community of radical abolitionists in Massachusetts, where she attended school. She also entered enthusiastically into the literary and intellectual life of nearby Boston and began writing. Some of her earliest poetry was published in antislavery journals during her student years. She kept a diary, published almost a century later, which remains one of the most valuable accounts of that era.

Forten became a teacher in Salem, Massachusetts, and later in Philadelphia. Unfortunately, she suffered from ill health, which would plague her for the rest of her life. She continued to write and remained involved in antislavery activity. During the **Civil War** (1861–65), she joined other abolitionists on the liberated islands off the South Carolina coast to teach and work with the newly emancipated slaves.

On the Sea Islands (islands off the coast of South Carolina and Georgia), she also kept a diary, later published. This diary, and two essays for the *Atlantic Monthly,* are among the most vivid accounts of the abolitionist experiment. Forten worked with dedication to teach and to prove the value of freedom. After the war she continued her work for the freed people.

She also continued writing and translated a French novel. In 1872 Forten moved to Washington, D.C., where she met the Reverend Francis Grimké, thirteen years her junior. At the end of 1878, they married. The marriage was long and happy, despite the death in infancy of their only child. The Grimkés lived in Washington, D.C., and made their Washington home a center for the capital's social and intellectual life. Although Charlotte Grimké continued to suffer from poor health, she was active as a member of the school board and participated in organizations like the National Association of Colored Women. She did a small amount of writing, although little of it was published. After 1909 her failing health led her to retire from active life.

Guillory, Ida Lewis "Queen Ida"

ZYDECO SINGER, ACCORDIONIST
January 15, 1929–

Queen Ida: Selected Works

Zydeco
(album, 1976)

On Tour
(album, 1982)

Cookin' with Queen Ida
(album, 1989)

Cookin' with Queen Ida
(cookbook, 1990)

Ida Lewis became a famous **zydeco** musician relatively late in her life. She was raised in Louisiana and studied music with two of her uncles, who were musicians playing the popular Gulf Coast dance style known as zydeco. Zydeco music developed in southwest Louisiana and usually features fast vocals and accordion. When Lewis was seventeen, her family moved to San Francisco, California, where she learned to play the accordion. She married Ray Guillory in 1949; for most of the next twenty years she was a housewife, occasionally working as a bus driver.

In the early 1970s she began to perform at private functions. In 1975, while attending a Mardi Gras dance, she was called onstage to perform as "the queen of zydeco." That appearance started her career as Queen Ida. She has become one of the most famous and successful zydeco musicians, touring the world and recording many releases. While she is an energetic and exciting singer, she is better known for playing the thirty-one-key accordion, an instrument that allows her greater musical freedom than the button or piano accordion. Guillory has most often performed with the Bon Temps Band, an ensemble including her son and two of her brothers.

Gullah

The Gullah are a community of African Americans who have lived along the Atlantic coastal plain and on the Sea Islands off the coast of South Carolina and Georgia since the late seventeenth century. They are descendants of West and Central Africans who were brought to the region as slaves to work on rice, indigo, and cotton plantations.

Gullah farming and fishing communities continue to exist in the twenty-first century even though the Sea Islands have been heavily developed and populated by whites and many Gullah have left the islands. Efforts began in about 1950 to increase public awareness of the Gullah and to preserve their remaining speech patterns and culture.

The Early Gullah

During the mid-1700s South Carolina and Georgia rice growers moved their plantations from the inland swamps to the Atlantic coastal mainland. This move, along with the production of indigo and, later, cotton, caused the demand for slave labor to soar. Plantation owners began to request more slaves from **Africa**'s Windward Coast (present-day Sierra Leone, Senegal, and Gambia) and Rice Coast (part of present-day Liberia) because they were familiar with rice and indigo production. These slaves brought skills and knowledge of rice planting that transformed southern rice-production methods.

Few whites settled in the coastal plain and the Sea Islands because the land was isolated and the hot, swampy climate contributed to disease. Because the large African slave population was rarely in contact with whites, the slaves were able to preserve many native African speech patterns and cultural traditions. Until the end of the eighteenth century, new slaves were constantly coming from Africa, providing a vital link to native customs and traditions.

The American **Civil War** (1861–65) and the end of **slavery**, along with a declining market for rice as more was produced in western states, drove white plantation owners off the land, but the Gullah stayed on, farming and fishing to survive.

Gullah Culture and Religion

Gullah handicrafts, such as basketry and woodcarving, show African roots. Wooden mortars and pestles, rice "fanners" used in harvesting, and palm leaf brooms used to maintain grass-free dirt yards all reflect African customs. The Gullah diet is based on rice, eaten with gumbos and stews similar to West African dishes.

Gullah proverbs and animal trickster folktales such as those about Brer Rabbit, made famous by white folklorist Joel Chandler Harris (1848–1908), are important forms of entertainment for the Gullah people. They reflect the African tradition of storytelling and speaking in parables (short stories that illustrate a moral or religious principle). In 1888 author Charles C. Jones Jr. published *Gullah Folktales of the Georgia Coast*, the first collection of its kind. These were tales he heard Gullah servants tell on his family's plantation.

The church, called the Praise House, played an all-important role within the Gullah slave community and into the twentieth century. Everyone was expected to obey the Praise House customs and rules and live by certain standards of behavior and trust. The Gullah mixed African religious traditions with their Christian beliefs. For example, they maintained their belief in witchcraft (called wudu, wanga, joso, or juju) and continued to visit "root doctors" for protection and healing.

Gullah spirituals, or religious songs, used the West African pattern of call-and-response singing to accompany a spiritual dance called the "ring shout," in which church members sang, clapped, and shuffled their heels to dance in a circle. This was based on an African dance linked to natural and supernatural forces.

THE GULLAH LANGUAGE

The Gullah speak an English-based creole, a language that has evolved from a "pidgin" language (a simplified form of communication between people with different languages). This language is called Gullah, or Geechee by people of the Georgia Sea Islands. The origins of the names Gullah and Geechee are uncertain, but scholars believe they are shortened forms of West or Central African names, because most South Carolina and Georgia slaves were brought from that region.

Gullah grew from the West African–English pidgin language that developed along the African coast during the peak of the slave trade. It was used to help Africans communicate with British slave traders.

Slaves brought to America used this language to communicate with one another. Over time their language mixed with that of the white South Carolina and Georgia planters and took on a new form. The creole language that developed was Gullah. Gullah changed over the years, and by the twentieth century it had more words in common with standard English. Some Gullah words used in English, especially in the southeastern United States, are buckra (a white person), goober (peanut), and juke (disorderly).

In 1979 the Summer Institute of Linguistics and the Wycliffe Bible Translators began a program on St. Helena Island, South Carolina, to translate the Bible into Gullah, to develop a written system for recording the Gullah language, and to produce teaching aids for use in schools. Translation of the New Testament was scheduled to be completed by 1996 and translation of the Old Testament by 2001.

The Gullah in the Twentieth Century

When bridges were built between the Sea Islands and the mainland during the 1920s, the Gullah communities began to break up as members moved away for new economic opportunities. Beginning in the 1950s, wealthy developers began buying land on Hilton Head and other Sea Islands to build vacation resorts and homes. These provided a few low-paying service jobs for the Gullah.

During the 1940s Esau Jenkins, of Johns Island, South Carolina, led a movement to register voters and helped to establish the South's first Citizenship School in 1957. These efforts began to break down the isolation of the Gullah and involve them in the nationwide struggle for civil rights.

In 1948 the Penn Center on St. Helena Island, South Carolina, was converted to a community resource center and began teaching the Gullah language to schoolchildren. In 1985 Beaufort, South Carolina, began an annual Gullah Festival to celebrate the rich Gullah culture. In 1989 a dance-theater piece about Gullah culture on Johns Island, called "In Living Color," opened in New York City.

The 1991 film *Daughters of the Dust*, written and directed by **Julie Dash,** whose father was raised in the Sea Islands, provided national recognition for the Gullah. In 1994 the children's television network Nickelodeon began work on a new animated series called *Gullah Gullah Island*, about a black

couple who explore the culture of the Sea Islands. In 2000 the University of Georgia Press reprinted Jones's *Gullah Folktales of the Georgia Coast* (1888). These and other efforts have helped to protect the Gullah community from further breakdown of its culture.

Guy, Rosa Cuthbert

AUTHOR
September 1, 1925–

Born in Trinidad, author Rosa Cuthbert moved to New York City as a young girl. Shortly before **World War II** (1914–18), Cuthbert married Warner Guy. While he served in the army, she cared for their son, worked in a factory, and became involved in the American Negro Theater. Disappointed by the roles available to black actresses, she turned to writing drama and, later, fiction. In the late 1940s Guy and **John Oliver Killens** founded the Harlem Writers Guild, a much-needed forum for young black writers. The end of her marriage forced Guy to work at a variety of jobs, but she managed to continue writing.

In 1966 Guy published her first book, *Bird at My Window*, about a black family that has fled the South only to be destroyed by racism in New York. The success of this novel allowed her to concentrate on writing, and she steadily published work for the next two decades. Of her many books, Guy received perhaps her widest acclaim for *A Measure of Time* (1983), the story a young maid who flees Alabama and after a series of humiliations and misadventures becomes a millionaire with a tavern business in New York. A later work by Guy, *My Love, My Love; or, The Peasant Girl* (1985), was the basis for *Once on This Island* (1990), a successful Broadway musical. The musical was revived in a 1999 production by The Cab Calloway School of Performing Arts in Wilmington, Delaware.

In recognition of her lifelong commitment to young people and their aspirations, the Young Men's Christian Association (YMCA) selected Guy to give a nationwide series of readings at art centers traditionally underserved by the literary community.

Gymnastics

African Americans have not had a significant presence in the world of gymnastics. This is primarily because gymnastics requires professional training, costly equipment, and leisure time in order to compete at a high level. The public schools that blacks attended at the time gymnastics began to grow as a sport were not granted the funding necessary to promote gymnastics training.

The first black gymnast to earn national acclaim was Mike Carter, who helped the men's gymnastics team at Louisiana State University win several college competitions (1973–75). In the 1970s Ron Galimore became the first black gymnast to win individual titles at National Collegiate Athletic Association (NCAA) championship events. Although Galimore was named to the 1980 Olympic team, the event was boycotted because of political tension between the United States and the former Soviet Union.

The first female black gymnast to earn national fame was Diane Durham. Durham was a favorite to win a gold medal at the 1984 Olympics; however, an injury prevented her from competing. There were three African Americans on the 1992 U.S. Olympic team (Betty Okino, Dominique Davis, and Charles Lakes). Although none of the blacks won an Olympic medal, their presence suggests that a greater number of blacks are participating in gymnastics.

Hagler, Marvelous Marvin

BOXER
May 24, 1954–

Marvelous Marvin Hagler was a middleweight boxing champion who packed a powerful left hook. He was so confident in his abilities that he crowned himself "Marvelous" Marvin in the early 1980s. The nickname was appropriate because Hagler seldom left his opponents standing at the end of a match.

Born in Newark, New Jersey, Hagler and his family moved to Brockton, Massachusetts, when he was seventeen. He was an exceptional amateur boxer, winning fifty-seven fights, including the Amateur Athletic Union middleweight championship (1973). Hagler turned professional boxer shortly afterward and soon became a dominant force in the middleweight division, winning his first twenty-six matches. In 1980 Hagler fought for the title against world champion Vito Antuofermo and knocked him out in three rounds.

Hagler successfully defended his title for six years, defeating middleweight powerhouses such as Mustafa Hamsho, William "Caveman" Lee, and Thomas "Hit Man" Hearns. However, his most famous match came in 1987 when "Sugar Ray Leonard" came out of retirement to face Hagler. The two fought a grueling twelve-round match won by Leonard. The highly publicized match brought Hagler's career to a distinguished end as he took home $12 million in the highest-paid boxing event in history at the time. Hagler retired from boxing with an impressive sixty-one wins (fifty-one by knockout) and a mere three losses.

After boxing, Hagler appeared in television commercials and began a television announcing career. He moved to Milan, Italy, in the 1990s and began working full-time on an acting career.

Hale, Clara McBride "Mother"

SOCIAL ACTIVIST
April 1, 1905–December 18, 1992

Clara Hale became known as "Mother" Hale because of the work she did caring for children, including those with drug-addicted mothers. Born Clara McBride in Philadelphia, Pennsylvania, she moved to New York City

after marrying Thomas Hale, who died when she was just twenty-seven. At first, she supported her three children by doing cleaning work, which left them alone all day. She chose instead to care for other people's children in her home, as well as to take in foster children. Over the next two decades, she raised forty children.

Hale retired in 1968, but the following year began helping a young heroin-addicted mother and baby. She agreed to care for the baby while the mother sought help for her addiction. Within two months she was caring for twenty-two such children, with only the financial support of her own family.

In the early 1970s Hale received funding that allowed her to renovate a building in New York's Harlem area, which became the Hale House Center for the Promotion of Human Potential. By 1992 Hale House had cared for one thousand children, and most of these were returned to their mothers once they had gone through drug withdrawal and their mothers were able to care for them.

Clara Hale brought attention to the lack of services available to the poor and the drug addicted. Among many tributes to Hale, President Ronald Reagan honored her as "a true American hero" in his 1985 State of the Union Address. After Clara Hale's death in 1992, Hale House continued operating under the direction of her daughter, Lorraine Hale.

Clara Hale with film director Spike Lee and some of the children of Hale House (AP/Wide World Photos. Reproduced by permission)

Roots author Alex Haley autographing one of his books (AP/Wide World Photos. Reproduced by permission)

Haley, Alexander Palmer "Alex"

JOURNALIST, NOVELIST
August 11, 1921–February 10, 1992

Alex Haley was born in Ithaca, New York, and raised in Henning, Tennessee. He left college at age seventeen and enlisted in the U.S. Coast Guard, where he eventually served as an editor. After leaving the Coast Guard, Haley became a freelance writer. He first received widespread attention for *The Autobiography of Malcolm X* (1965), a writing partnership with the black nationalist **Malcolm X.** The book quickly achieved international success and was translated into many different languages.

Haley is best known, however, for his historic novel *Roots: The Saga of an American Family* (1976). Based on Haley's family history as told to him by his grandmother, *Roots* traces Haley's ancestry to Kunta Kinte, an African youth who was kidnapped from his homeland and forced into **slavery.** Combining fact with fiction, *Roots* shows the African-American struggle from its beginnings in **Africa,** through slavery and **emancipation,** and up to the continuing modern-day fight for equality. The novel was an immediate best-seller, and two years after its publication had won 271 awards, including a special Pulitzer Prize. Presented as a television miniseries in 1977, *Roots* reached the homes of millions.

Haley's book was controversial, however. After it was released—and even after his death—evidence came to light suggesting that Haley had distorted historical facts in his book, and had even committed plagiarism (using the work of others without giving credit). In one case, Haley admitted that several passages from another author's book had been used in *Roots*, and he was forced to pay a financial settlement.

A television sequel to the *Roots* miniseries was produced in 1979, and Haley produced several films and records, including advice on how to research family histories. In the 1980s Haley helped produce a television series loosely based on his childhood, made numerous public appearances around the world, and wrote for popular magazines. In his last years Haley concentrated on writing the story of his ancestry through his father, *Queen: The Story of an American Family*. The book was published and adapted for television the year following his death in 1992 in Seattle, Washington.

Hall, Prince

CIVIC LEADER
c. 1735–December 4, 1807

Civic leader Prince Hall was a slave owned by William Hall, a Boston craftsman. He became a free man in 1770, and in 1775 asked to join the St. John's Lodge of Freemasons (a major male fraternal organization, or "brotherhood") but was turned down. Hall and fourteen other free African-American men were then accepted by a lodge connected with an Irish regiment of the British army. As an independent group, they participated in limited lodge activities throughout the American Revolution (1775–83).

Hall worked as a leather crafter in his shop, the Golden Fleece, and as a caterer. He supplied leather drumheads to the rebel army and may have served in combat. Hall signed petitions asking that African Americans be allowed to fight in the war, and in January 1777 he joined others asking the Massachusetts legislature to outlaw **slavery.**

In 1784 Hall headed an unofficial African Lodge and applied for membership from the London Grand Lodge. African Lodge 459 finally received official status in 1787. Hall remained "grand master" until his death, and soon thereafter the lodge took his name. It later became the largest African-American fraternal order, the Prince Hall Masons.

Acting as a spokesperson for the masons and the African-American community, Hall protested the seizure of three free blacks (one a mason) in Boston by slave traders, and in February 1788 he successfully petitioned the Massachusetts government for their return. He also denounced the **slave trade,** which contributed to the March 26, 1788, decision banning the trade in Massachusetts.

Hamer, Fannie Lou

CIVIL RIGHTS ACTIVIST
October 6, 1917–March 14, 1977

Fannie Lou Hamer was one of the greatest civil rights leaders in American history. She withstood poverty, beatings, and a lifetime of racial inequality throughout her crusade for political and social change. Hamer's famous words, "I am sick and tired of being sick and tired," stand as a historical slogan for the widespread frustration regarding racial injustice that led to revolutionary changes in American society.

Hamer was born in Montgomery County, Mississippi. Her original name was Fannie Lou Townsend. Hamer spent the majority of her childhood in the cotton fields helping her family, which allowed her to receive only six years of schooling. Although Hamer knew nothing but poverty and a racist society, she had a glowing optimism that things would get better.

Hamer married Perry Hamer in 1944 and began working on a plantation in Ruleville, Mississippi. She rose to the position of record keeper and developed a reputation for creating better working conditions for share-croppers. **Sharecropping** was an often abusive farming arrangement whereby plantation owners rented out their land to workers, who received a portion of the proceeds from the harvest (usually 50 percent) for their work. Frustrated by the way blacks were treated, Hamer decided to involve herself in politics. In 1962 she participated in a black voter registration drive. At the time, although blacks were given the right to vote, literacy tests and poll taxes prevented blacks from casting their ballots.

Hamer's awareness of the unfair voting condition for blacks prompted her to join the **Student Nonviolent Coordinating Committee (SNCC)** in 1963. By 1964, at the peak of the **Civil Rights movement,** Hamer had fully committed herself to promoting racial equality. She became vice-chairperson of the Mississippi Freedom Democratic Party (MFDP), which, unlike

the Mississippi Democratic Party, did not discriminate against blacks. Hamer led a fight to change the voting conditions in the South, beginning with a television appearance in which she described the reality of voting conditions for blacks.

In addition to helping empower African-American political participation in the South, Hamer helped develop the Head Start Program (which helped poor children receive a quality education) and the Freedom Farm Cooperative (which helped poor blacks become more self-sufficient and helped to feed over five thousand families). Well-respected learning institutions such as **Morehouse College** and **Howard University** have honored Fannie Lou Hamer by granting doctoral degrees in her name.

Hammon, Jupiter

POET, PREACHER

1711–c. 1806

Jupiter Hammon produced a number of literary works, including poetry. Some were inspired by religion. He was born in New York and raised in slavery. Little is known about his personal life; he may have attended school and had access to his master's library. He is known to have purchased a Bible from his master in 1773. A favored slave in the household, he worked as a servant, farmhand, and artisan.

In early 1761 Hammon published the first poem by a black person to appear in British North America. When British troops invaded Long Island, New York, Hammon fled with the family to Hartford, Connecticut, where he remained for the duration of the **Revolutionary War** (1775–83). Hammon returned to Long Island in 1782.

Hammon spoke to members of the African Society in New York on September 24, 1786. The text of that speech, "An Address to the Negroes of the State of New York," was printed in New York early in 1787.

Hammon's poems follow a strict mechanical rhyme scheme and meter, and, like his sermons, warn the reader to seek salvation by obeying the will of God. Due to his religious beliefs, he refused to speak out in public against **slavery.** However, even as he urged African Americans to "obey our masters," he questioned whether slavery was "right, and lawful, in the sight of God." "I do not wish to be free," he said at age seventy-five, "yet I should be glad, if others, especially the young negroes were to be free." The exact date of his death, and the place of his burial, are not known.

Jupiter Hammon: Selected Works

An Evening Thought. Salvation by Christ with Penitential Cries: Composed by Jupiter Hammon, a Negro belonging to Mr. Lloyd of Queen's Village, on Long Island, the 25th of December, 1760
(poem, 1760)

An Address to Miss Phillis Wheatly [sic], Ethiopian Poetess, in Boston, who came from Africa at eight years of age, and soon became acquainted with the gospel of Jesus Christ
(poem, 1778)

An Essay on Ten Virgins
(1779)

A Winter Piece: Being a Serious Exhortation, with a Call to the Unconverted; and a Short Contemplation on the Death of Jesus Christ
(sermon, 1782)

Poem for Children, with Thoughts on Death
(poem, 1782)

An Evening's Improvement, Shewing the Necessity of Beholding the Lamb of God
(prose, 1786)

Hammons, David

ARTIST

1943–

Born in Springfield, Illinois, artist David Hammons moved to Los Angeles, California, to study graphic design and fine arts in 1964. In the late

1960s and early 1970s, he produced prints with repeating themes of self-portraiture, the American flag, and the spade shape. Hammons next began making assembled sculptures, combining spades (shovels), chains, barbecue bones, and African-American hair.

In 1975 Hammons moved to New York City, where he sometimes displayed his work on the streets of Harlem and the East Village. Within the art community he was known for never having a telephone and for his sense of drama. For example, his work *Higher Goals* (1983) is a series of six-story-tall basketball hoop sculptures. In a 1997 seven-minute video, *Phat Free*, Hammons featured himself kicking an empty pail through Manhattan.

In the early 1990s Hammons reluctantly accepted international attention with shows at the Museum of Modern Art in New York and at the Documenta exhibition in Kassel, Germany. He also won a MacArthur Award, including a large cash prize.

Hampton, Lionel Leo

JAZZ VIBRAPHONIST, BANDLEADER
April 12, 1908–

A masterful musician, Lionel Hampton introduced the vibraphones to jazz music in the 1930s. During his long career he made "the vibes" (a percussion instrument similar to the xylophone) an important part of the jazz tradition.

Hampton spent most of his childhood in Birmingham, Alabama, where he learned to play drums and performed in the black church. While in his teens, his family moved to Chicago, Illinois, where the young drummer played regularly with local musicians. In the mid-1920s Hampton settled in Los Angeles, California, where he gained his first recording experience and began playing the vibraphones. He also met his future wife, Gladys Riddle, who became his business partner.

In 1936 Hampton was invited by clarinetist Benny Goodman (1909–1986) to join his band. Though Goodman had a national audience, **jazz** was still not accepted by many Americans as a legitimate form of music. That attitude began to change after a 1938 performance of the Benny Goodman Quartet at New York's Carnegie Hall. The highly celebrated concert made music history.

LIONEL HAMPTON'S INFLUENCE

Many jazz musicians got their start playing in Hampton's band. Among the fresh talents the vibraphonist influenced were:saxophonist-trumpeter Benny Carter (1907–) bass player **Charles Mingus** (1922–1979) singer **Dinah Washington** (1924–1963) trumpeter Art Farmer (1928–1999) singer **Betty Carter** (1929–1998) composer and trumpeter **Quincy Jones** (1933–)

Lionel Hampton (AP/Wide World Photos.
Reproduced by permission)

By 1940 Hampton's career was in full swing. With his own big band, he performed and recorded regularly for the next forty-five years. A popular musician in the United States and abroad, he also became known for nurturing new musicians. His band was described as a "university" for young talent. Remaining active through the 1990s, Hampton is admired by audiences for his energetic and stylish onstage presence as well as for his own brand of highly rhythmic jazz music.

Hampton University

Founded: Hampton University was established in 1868 by Samuel Chapman Armstrong (1839–1893) as a school where young African-American men and women could be trained as teachers.

History Highlights:

- 1868: Hampton Normal and Agricultural Institute is founded. At first, students are provided an industrial education, meaning they work in the school's farms and trade shops and the only "book learning" they receive focuses on writing, botany, and simple arithmetic. Because it is a boarding school, students are instructed in social skills when not in the classroom. Armstrong's educational philosophy with its emphasis on a "practical" education is known as the Hampton Idea and spreads throughout the South. The system is so popular among whites that the school receives much funding and develops into one of the largest and wealthiest black schools in the United States.

- 1903: Armstrong's philosophy is not supported by black leaders who believe that the school should place greater emphasis on academics. Editor and writer **W. E. B. Du Bois** (1868–1963) publishes his first major attack on industrial education.

- 1927: After **World War I** (1914–18), there is a reform movement in the United States to ensure that teachers are better educated. When these standards are enforced, many Hampton graduates fail to meet the requirements. Hampton students demand that the college raise its quality of teaching and that more African Americans be hired to the staff. Hampton is forced to make changes to its academic program, and by 1927 over 40 percent of Hampton students are enrolled in the new collegiate program.

- 1930: Hampton Normal and Agricultural Institute becomes Hampton Institute, and the college will no longer accept students who have not already completed high school.

- 1984: Hampton Institute develops into a prominent liberal arts and teachers' college and changes its name to Hampton University.

Location: Hampton, Virginia

Number of Students (1999–2000): 5,670

Grade Average of Incoming Freshman: 3.0

Admission Requirements: ACT or SAT scores; four years of English, three years of math, two years of science, two years of history; personal essay.

Mailing Address:
Hampton University
Office of Admission
Hampton, Virginia 23368

Telephone: (800) 624-3328

E-mail: admit@hamptonu.edu

URL: http://www.hamptonu.edu

Campus: Hampton's 204-acre campus is located within forty miles of Jamestown, Yorktown, and Williamsburg, Virginia. Buildings include art galleries, a laboratory elementary school, and African, Native American, and oceanic museums. The library houses more than 200,000 documents.

Extracurricular Activities: Student government; student newspaper, the *Hampton Script*; literary magazine; student radio; six fraternities and six sororities; over eighty organizations, including honor societies, Fellowship of Christian Athletes, the Hampton band, and the University Players (drama club); athletics (men's basketball, cheerleading, cross-country, football, golf, tennis, track-and-field; women's basketball, cheerleading, cross-country, golf, softball, tennis, track-and-field, volleyball).

Hampton Alumni: Booker T. Washington (c. 1856–1915), educator and founder of Tuskegee Institute; Susan La Flesche, the first American Indian woman to receive the degree of doctor of medicine.

(SEE ALSO **COLLEGES AND UNIVERSITIES**.)

Hancock, Gordon Blaine

SOCIOLOGIST, MINISTER
June 23, 1884–July 24, 1970

Gordon Hancock was an early scholar in the field of race relations. Born in Greenwood County, South Carolina, he earned bachelor's degrees in the arts and divinity before entering Harvard University (Cambridge, Massachusetts) to do graduate studies in sociology. He also became an ordained **Baptist** minister in 1911.

After earning a master's degree in 1921, Hancock became a professor at Virginia Union University in Richmond, where he organized one of the first courses on race relations at any black college. In 1931 he founded the university's Torrance School of Race Relations.

Hancock also wrote a weekly column that appeared in 114 black newspapers. During the **Great Depression** of the 1930s, his "Double Duty Dollar" campaign encouraged blacks to spend their money in black-owned businesses. He also had a "Hold Your Job" campaign, stressing the importance of a solid black working class.

Alarmed by growing racial tension in the South, Hancock brought together fifty-two black leaders at the Southern Conference on Race Relations in 1942. They produced the Durham Manifesto, containing carefully worded demands for improvements in the position of African Americans in the South. The black leaders soon met with white representatives who agreed to form the Southern Regional Council.

In 1952 Hancock retired from teaching. In 1963 he left his pastorship of Richmond's Moore Street Baptist Church, a position he had held since 1925. He spent his later years collecting black spirituals and composing and publishing his own songs.

Hancock, Herbert Jeffrey "Herbie"

JAZZ PIANIST, COMPOSER
April 12, 1940–

Herbie Hancock has written and played jazz in many forms, even pioneering the form of "fusion." He was the first jazz musician to have a video featured regularly on MTV, and he continues his creative journey today.

Born and raised in Chicago, Hancock was a child prodigy. Beginning formal piano lessons at age seven, he performed with the world-renowned Chicago Symphony Orchestra when he was eleven. Forming his own jazz ensemble in high school, he went on to study engineering at Grinnell College (Iowa). Graduating in 1960, he played as a sideman in Chicago for saxophonist **Coleman Hawkins** (1904–1969).

After moving to New York in 1962, Hancock joined jazz trumpeter **Miles Davis'** (1926–1991) ensemble. The quintet released several celebrated recordings, including *Maiden Voyage* and *Empyrean Isles*, both in 1964. All of the songs on both albums were written by Hancock.

In the 1970s Davis began infusing jazz with electric instruments to create a form of jazz called fusion. Hancock was at the front of the movement. The form got its name for fusing (mixing) jazz with elements of funk music and rock and roll. Though disliked by many jazz purists, fusion found a wide audience and gave Hancock his first hit single—1973's "Chameleon." Ten years later, he had his second hit single with "Rockit." Influenced by rap music, the song appealed to a young audience, and its video was played on MTV.

Hancock has composed music for film, including *Round Midnight* (1986), for which he won an Academy Award. He continues to play in many forms today.

Handy, William Christopher "W. C."

ANTHOLOGIST, COMPOSER
November 16, 1873–March 28, 1958

Because of his role in popularizing blues music, W. C. Handy is known as "the father of the blues." As a teenager in Alabama, he played cornet in a traveling minstrel show. He also worked as a teacher, factory worker, and college bandmaster before settling into the music-publishing business.

In 1908, Handy cofounded the Pace and Handy Music Company with Harry Pace. The business moved from Memphis, Tennessee, to New York in 1918 and became the leading publisher of music by African Americans. In 1920 the partners agreed to start separate businesses. Handy opened Handy Brothers and the short-lived Handy Record Company.

Handy also continued playing, composing, arranging, touring, and recording. He appeared with popular groups at theaters, dance halls, and concert venues as an instrumentalist and bandleader.

Handy's first published blues music, "Memphis Blues" (1912), was immediately popular. By 1914 he had published the song for which he is best known, "St. Louis Blues." Later he published "Beale Street Blues," which is the third Handy "standard" in American blues music (his third song that has become a basic part of blues music).

Jazz historians agree that some of Handy's compositions copy the work of others. He is most respected for collecting, publishing, and popularizing **the blues.** His transcribing and arranging of blues and spirituals led to his books *Blues: An Anthology* (1926; reprinted as *Treasury of the Blues*, 1930) and *Book of Negro Spirituals* (1938).

Handy's productivity declined after he was accidentally blinded in 1943, and he died in 1958. In 1998 Handy Brothers Music Publishing Company marked its eightieth anniversary as the oldest black-owned music publishing company.

Hansberry, Lorraine

PLAYWRIGHT
May 19, 1930–January 12, 1965

Playwright Lorraine Hansberry was the youngest child of a very well known African-American family. Guests who frequently visited the Hansberry home included actor **Paul Robeson** and jazz great **Duke Ellington.** Hansberry became interested in theater while in high school and in 1948 began studying drama and stage design at the University of Wisconsin. She moved to New York without completing college and worked odd jobs and wrote.

In 1959 her first play, *A Raisin in the Sun,* was produced. It won praise from critics and was also a commercial success, winning the New York Drama Critics Circle Award and breaking the record for longest-running play by a black author. Hansberry was the first African American and the youngest person ever to win that award.

Based on an incident in the author's life, *A Raisin in the Sun* tells the story of a black family that attempts to move into a white neighborhood in Chicago, Illinois. Critics praised Hansberry's ability to deal with a racial issue and at the same time explore the American dream of freedom and the search for a better life. The play was turned into a film in 1961 and later adapted as a musical, *Raisin,* which won a Tony Award in 1974.

Hansberry died of cancer in 1965. Her former husband, Robert B. Nemiroff, edited her writings and plays, including *To Be Young, Gifted and Black* (1969), which became the longest-running Off-Broadway play of the 1968-69 season.

Harlem Boycotts

During the 1930s African Americans in several cities organized boycotts of stores (refused to shop in them) in black neighborhoods that refused to hire blacks. In New York City's Harlem neighborhood, a major center of black life in the United States, several boycotts were held.

In 1934 members of St. Martin's Protestant Episcopal Church complained to their minister, Rev. John H. Johnson, about the absence of black salespeople at Blumstein's department store, the largest store on Harlem's 125th Street. Johnson approached the owner of the store, William Blumstein, and requested that he hire black salespeople, since the majority of his customers were black. When the owner refused, Johnson appealed to the Harlem community to protest Blumstein's hiring practices. The newspaper *New York Age* actively took up the cause, and as a result, the Citizen's League for Fair Play was established. The league, whose members included sixty-two of Harlem's social, religious, and business groups, was committed to ending job discrimination and obtaining jobs for blacks.

A boycott began in June 1934. It became known as the Jobs-for-Negroes-Campaign, borrowing the slogan that had been used in a Chicago boycott. After the store was picketed (volunteers carrying signs walked or stood in front of the store, discouraging people from entering) for six weeks, an agreement was reached in which Blumstein agreed to hire blacks as sales clerks. After the success of the boycott, other stores along 125th Street, such as Koch's, also began to employ blacks in clerical positions.

In 1935 the Communist Party (a political party active in workers' causes) started its own boycott of the Empire Cafeteria. Party activists, who favored interracial labor organization, had participated in the Blumstein's boycott, carrying signs that also demanded that no white workers be fired (replaced by blacks). Their success in securing jobs for four black countermen at Empire, without any other workers losing jobs, made the party a power in boycott organizing.

The next large boycott was not organized until 1938, when two of Harlem's influential ministers, Rev. **Adam Clayton Powell Jr.** and Rev. Lloyd Imes, helped form the Greater New York Coordinating Committee for Employment (GNYCC).

The GNYCC was committed to fighting discriminatory practices throughout the city, including those of the utility companies. Eventually, under pressure from GNYCC, Consolidated Edison Electric Company agreed to hire a few trainees. In 1939 a GNYCC boycott of the New York World's Fair resulted in the hiring of seven hundred blacks.

The last major boycott of the era was that of the Fifth Avenue Coach Company and the Omnibus Corporation, which began in 1941. Powell led the United Negro Bus Strike Committee. After months of active boycotting and intermittent violent confrontations with white unionists, Powell announced victory. The bus companies agreed to hire thirty-two black trainees immediately and set a black employment quota.

The boycotts' results were mixed. They did help break discriminatory hiring practices that either kept blacks in menial jobs or excluded them from jobs completely. However, the boycotts had mostly aided middle-class blacks. During the Depression the long-term effect of boycotts on poor blacks was simply to increase competition with displaced white workers, which meant that wages dropped and blacks working in white areas would be fired. Perhaps the most important legacy of the boycotts was that, by the 1940s, blacks could be seen working in white-collar positions all over the city.

Harlem Globetrotters

BASKETBALL PLAYERS

The Harlem Globetrotters are a basketball team that travels across the country and entertains crowds with delightful basketball tricks. They originally began as a competitive **basketball** team, but they are best known for their fun-loving basketball routines.

The Harlem Globetrotters (Archive Photos. Reproduced by permission)

Founded in 1926 by Abe Saperstein in Chicago, Illinois, the Globetrotters were a well-trained group of black players who challenged any team, regardless of color, to beat them. At the time, blacks were not allowed to play professional basketball because of racism. Their talent on the court and their popularity made the case that blacks should be admitted into professional leagues. The Globetrotters became popular through competitions with their archrivals, the New York Rens, and through entertaining audiences by drop-kicking the ball and bouncing it off of each other's heads.

In 1943 the Globetrotters traveled to Mexico City, where they won the International Cup Tournament. In the late 1940s the team went on a fifty-two game winning streak and competed against professional teams such as the Minneapolis Lakers.

When blacks were admitted into the National Basketball Association (NBA) in the late 1940s and early 1950s, the Globetrotters changed their style dramatically. Famous Globetrotters such as Reece "Goose" Tatum, Meadowlark Lemon, and Fred "Curly" Neal added trick shots and comedy to the routine. In the 1950s the team split up into East and West Coast squads and played to audiences in America. In the 1960s the team began making international tours, playing to enormous crowds.

Although some blacks criticized the Globetrotters for making light of the game of basketball and not taking a stance during the **Civil Rights movement**, they have been adored by the majority of blacks and whites alike. In 1985 the first female Globetrotter, Lynette Woodward, joined the team. Although their popularity decreased in the 1980s and 1990s, their talented play helped bring blacks into professional basketball, and, true to their name, they entertained millions of people across the globe. In 2000 they were inducted into the Basketball Hall of Fame.

"How do I know when we played a good 'game'? When I look up at the crowd and I see all those people laughing their heads off. It's a hard world and if we can lighten it up a little, we've done our job."

Curly Johnson

Harlem, New York

A section of New York City, Harlem during the twentieth century became the most famous African-American community in the United States, the home of the literary and artistic flowering known as the Harlem Renaissance.

Harlem Beginnings

Prior to 1900, Harlem had been primarily a white neighborhood. In the 1870s it evolved from an isolated, impoverished village in the northern reaches of Manhattan into a wealthy residential suburb with the growth of commuter rail service. With the opening of the Lenox Avenue subway line in the early years of the twentieth century, a flurry of real estate speculation contributed to a substantial increase in building. In 1904 Philip A. Payton, Jr., a black realtor, founded the Afro-American Realty Company with the intention of leasing vacant white-owned buildings and then renting them to African Americans. Although the Realty Company survived for only four years, due to Payton's unwise financial investments, it played an important role in opening up the Harlem community to African Americans. Coupled with this development, black migration from the South during the early years of the new century dramatically altered Harlem's composition, until by 1930 it had become a largely all-black area.

The Early Twentieth Century

As early as 1915 Harlem had become the entertainment capital of black America. Performers gravitated to Harlem and New York City's entertainment industry. The birthplace of the early jazz piano style known as the Harlem Stride around the time of **World War I** (1914–18), Harlem later also saw the creation of be-bop jazz. Harlem also became a major center of tap and popular dance. Tap dancer **Bill "Bojangles" Robinson** carried the honorary title of "The Mayor of Harlem." Theatrical life was also vibrant in Harlem. The Lafayette Theater became a home of serious drama, due to the success of such actors as **Paul Robeson** and others. Harlem was also a center of nightclubs. The best known included the black-owned Smalls Paradise, the **Cotton Club**, and the mobster-connected and racially exclusive Connie's Inn. Harlem's cultural vitality was celebrated in plays by Wallace Thurman, Langston Hughes, and others.

From a social perspective, Harlem was labeled a "city within a city," because it contained the normal range of classes, businesses, and cultural and recreational institutions traditionally identified with urban living. By the 1920s, moreover, Harlem's place in American intellectual and political history had progressed significantly. This transition was fueled on the cultural scene by the literary and artistic activity which is called the Harlem Renaissance. Emerging after the promise of racial equality in return for black military service in World War I had been squelched by renewed racism and a series of race riots during the summer of 1919, the Renaissance reflected the evolution of a "**New Negro**" spirit and determination. As one of its acknowledged leaders, **Alain Locke**, explained, self-respect and self-dependence became characteristics of the New Negro

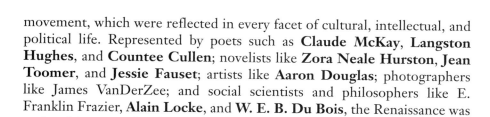

movement, which were reflected in every facet of cultural, intellectual, and political life. Represented by poets such as **Claude McKay**, **Langston Hughes**, and **Countee Cullen**; novelists like **Zora Neale Hurston**, **Jean Toomer**, and **Jessie Fauset**; artists like **Aaron Douglas**; photographers like James VanDerZee; and social scientists and philosophers like E. Franklin Frazier, **Alain Locke**, and **W. E. B. Du Bois**, the Renaissance was national in scope, but it came to be identified with the emerging African-American cultural capital, Harlem.

Also fostering Harlem's growth in the 1920s were a series of political developments. Both the **National Association for the Advancement of Colored People (NAACP)** and the National Urban League established offices in the area. Moreover, by 1920 two major New York black newspapers, *The New York Age* and *The New York Amsterdam News*, moved to Harlem. Nothing, however, caught the attention of Harlemites as quickly as the arrival in 1916 of **Marcus Garvey**, who established the headquarters of the **Universal Negro Improvement Association (UNIA)** in the district. Garvey's emphasis on race pride, the creation of black businesses and factories, and his appeal to the masses awakened and unified the Harlem community.

As Harlem became a political and cultural center of black America, the community's black churches became more influential as well. The Abyssinian Baptist Church became the most famous. The Rev. Adam Clayton Powell, Sr. moved the church from West 40th Street in midtown Manhattan to West 138th Street in Harlem in 1923. He combated prostitution, organized classes in home economics, built a home for the elderly, and organized soup kitchens and employment networks during the **Great Depression**. He was followed as senior pastor in 1937 by his son, **Adam Clayton Powell, Jr.,** who expanded the scope of the Abyssinian church's community activism. Many of Harlem's scores of storefront churches imitated Abyssinian's community aid efforts on a smaller scale.

The 1930s were a period of stagnation and decline in Harlem, as they were throughout the nation. Civil rights protest increased during the decade, and much of it originated in Harlem. In response to white businessmen's unwillingness to hire black workers for white-collar jobs in their Harlem stores, a series of "Don't Buy Where You Can't Work" boycott campaigns commenced in 1933 and became an effective method of protesting against racial bigotry throughout the decade. In 1935 a riot, fueled by anger toward white businesses and the police, left three dead, and caused over 200 million dollars in damage. New York City Mayor Fiorello LaGuardia later assigned his Mayor's Commission on Conditions in Harlem to study this uprising; the commission revealed a great number of underlying problems that were giving rise to racial tensions in Harlem. In 1943 Harlem experienced another major race riot, which left five dead. This second riot was fueled by race discrimination in war-related industries and continuing distrust between white police officers and Harlem's black citizens.

The Civil Rights Era

By the end of **World War II** (1939–45), Harlem experienced another transition. The migration of middle-class blacks to richer neighborhoods upset the class balance of earlier decades. Many of the remaining businesses were owned not by black residents but by whites who lived far removed from the ghetto. At the same time, most of the artists associated with the Renaissance had left the district. However, Harlem's literary life was preserved by a number of dedicated authors, such as **Ralph Ellison** (whose 1952 novel *Invisible Man* was centered in Harlem) and Harlem native **James Baldwin**. The Harlem Writers Guild was founded in 1950 by **John Killens, Maya Angelou,** John Henrik Clarke, and others, and has for over four decades offered writers in the community a forum for the reading and discussion of their works. Photographers such as Austin Hansen and **Gordon Parks, Sr.** continued to capture and celebrate Harlem's community on film.

For most of those who remained in Harlem after the war, however, a sense of powerlessness set in, aggravated by poverty and a lack of control over their community. The quality of Harlem housing continued to be an acute problem. Paradoxically, as the quality of Harlem's inadequately heated, rat-infested buildings continued to deteriorate, and as housing health ordinances were increasingly ignored, the rents on those units continued to rise. People were evicted for being unable to keep up with the costs, but having no other place to go, many either entered community shelters or joined the swelling ranks of the homeless.

It was in this period of decay that another charismatic organization emerged in the community, the **Nation of Islam** (NOI). **Malcolm X,** the head of Harlem's mosque, blended the intellectual insight of the writers of the 1920s with the political sophistication and charisma of Garvey. Malcolm X rekindled in the masses a sense of black pride and self-determination, appealing to their sense of disgruntlement with a message that was far angrier than that offered by other major civil rights leaders. He was assassinated on February 21, 1965, in the Audubon Ballroom in Upper Manhattan.

By the late 1960s, Harlem precisely fit the conclusion reached by the 1968 National Commission of Civil Disorders report. It was a ghetto, created, maintained, and condoned by white society. Literary works of the postwar era, from **Ann L. Petry**'s *The Street* (1946) to **Claude Brown**'s *Manchild in the Promised Land* (1965), reflected this progressively deteriorating state of affairs as well.

Harlem Today

Harlem since the 1960s has been severely affected by the same forces that plagued many other American urban centers. As the mainstay of the United States economy underwent a transition from heavy manufacturing to service and information technologies, large-scale industry left urban areas. Large numbers of the Harlem population followed this departure from the community, settling in suburban areas in Queens, the Bronx, and other boroughs. The resulting unemployment among those who remained further devastated Harlem. The community had long lost its position as the population center of black New York to the Bedford-Stuyvesant area of Brooklyn.

Residents made efforts to reassert control over their community in the 1990s, as the Harlem Chamber of Commerce led efforts to revitalize

Harlem's businesses and reclaim the community's buildings. A plan to spend over 170 million dollars to build permanent housing for the poor and homeless began early in the decade, and such landmark structures as the Astor Row houses on West 130th Street were rehabilitated as well.

Harlem was marked by a series of crises revolving around race and economics in the mid-1990s. In 1994, following complaints by local merchants, police forcibly removed street peddlers selling African artifacts and other wares from 125th Street. In 1995, after the Jewish landlord of a space in a building owned by an African-American church announced plans to terminate the sublease of a popular African-American clothing store, violent protests broke out, and an arsonist shot himself and four others before setting fire to the store. In 1998 national attention was again fixed on Harlem when former Nation of Islam activist Khalid Abdul Muhammad announced plans for a Million Youth March. New York Mayor Rudolph Giuliani refused a permit on the pretext that the city could not afford police protection. Organizers ultimately won a court order authorizing the march, which drew only an estimated 40,000 people. At the same time, however, there remains in Harlem, as there has been in every decade of its existence, an inner energy and spirit.

(SEE ALSO HARLEM RENAISSANCE; THE COTTON CLUB; DANCE THEATRE OF HARLEM; HARLEM BOYCOTTS; THE NATION OF ISLAM; MAYA ANGELOU; JAMES BALDWIN.)

Harlem Renaissance

The Harlem Renaissance was a period of great cultural creativity by African-American artists and writers that began around 1925 and lasted until about 1935. Many of the people involved in these cultural activities lived and worked in Harlem, a neighborhood in New York City where many African Americans lived.

Many of the works created during the Harlem Renaissance focused on African-American culture and experience and on black pride. It was the first time that many white people gave serious attention to African-American artists and writers.

The Harlem Renaissance was also a period when African-American music styles, such as **jazz** and **the blues**, became more widely heard and appreciated.

During the Harlem Renaissance, African Americans produced twenty-six novels, ten volumes of poetry, five Broadway plays, and countless essays and short stories. Three ballets were created and performed and hundreds of paintings and sculptures were presented to the public.

The economic hardships of the **Great Depression** caused many Harlem Renaissance writers and artists to move from New York to find work. Many became involved in social issues and became active in political work. By the time the Harlem Renaissance's great surge of creativity had ended, African-American culture had become part of the culture of the United States.

Selected Artists of the Harlem Renaissance

Jelly Roll Morton
(musician)

Countee Cullen
(writer, poet)

Langston Hughes
(writer)

Jean Toomer
(writer)

Jessie Fauset
(writer)

Claude McKay
(writer)

William Grant Still
(composer)

Paul Robeson
(actor, singer)

Aaron Douglas
(artist)

IOLA LEROY; OR, SHADOWS UPLIFTED, A NOVEL BY FRANCES WATKINS HARPER

Though she published many books of poetry and wrote a number of moving speeches, Frances Harper is probably best known for her novel *Iola Leroy; or, Shadows Uplifted* (1892). It is the story of a young octoroon (one-eighth black) woman who is sold into slavery when her African-American heritage is revealed. In the book, Harper addresses the complex relations between blacks and whites, the women's movement, and the development of African-American intellectual communities.

Harper, Frances Ellen Watkins

WRITER, REFORMER
September 24, 1825–February 20, 1911

An avid writer, Frances Harper was also active in the antislavery movement. Born Frances Ellen Watkins in Baltimore, Maryland, she was raised in the city's free black community. After her parents died when she was very young, her uncle, a minister, was her guardian. She received a strict education at the Academy for Negro Youth, where she studied the Bible, Greek, and Latin. In her early teens she left school to take a job as a household servant.

Watkins published her first poetry collection in 1845. Called *Forest Leaves*, there are no existing copies of it today. During the early 1850s she held teaching jobs at black schools in Ohio and Pennsylvania.

By 1854 Watkins was part of Philadelphia's abolitionist society, which included black and white reformers, and whose members helped run the **Underground Railroad.** Her first work to receive widespread acclaim was *Poems on Miscellaneous Subjects* (1854). The collection included poems about the horrors of **slavery.** She published four more books of poetry by 1895.

Watkins was also an active and powerful speaker for the antislavery movement. Though there were relatively few women speakers and few African-American speakers at the time, she toured widely on the lecture circuit. In 1860 Watkins married Fenton Harper, and the couple later had a daughter.

After her husband's death in 1864 and the abolition of slavery in 1865, Frances Harper turned her activism to other social issues, including making it legal for women to vote (also called **suffrage**) and outlawing the sale of alcohol, which was the goal of the temperance movement. She was a member of many influential groups, including the American Woman Suffrage Association and the National Association of Colored Women. Harper continued her public career to about 1900, a decade before her death.

Harper, Michael Steven

POET, PROFESSOR, EDITOR
March 18, 1938–

Michael Harper has been called a poet "of kinship—of 'race and soul,' blood and experience—[who] holds his kin close. . .in his poems." Born in Brooklyn, New York, in 1951, Harper moved to Los Angeles, California, in the 1960s. "I wouldn't have become a poet had I not moved from Brooklyn to Los Angeles," he remembers. "At thirteen the world was both collapsing and full of possibilities."

Harper received degrees from California State University and the University of Iowa. At California State he was encouraged to write one-act plays about jazz musicians. In Iowa City he began to write poetry that had the unique sound and rhythm of **jazz.** Meanwhile, he worked a number of jobs ranging from paperboy to school tutor. Harper moved to San Francisco in 1964 and married Shirley Anne Buffington. They had three children.

Harper was a visiting assistant professor at Lewis and Clark and Reed Colleges in Portland, Oregon, from 1968 to 1969; during this time he finished his first volume of poems. Back in California in 1969, he was appointed associate professor of English at California State. He later spent a year at the Center for Advanced Study at the University of Illinois before moving to Brown University, where he was appointed professor in 1990. Harper was awarded the George Kent Poetry Award in 1996 and the Claiborne Pell Award for excellence in the Arts in 1997.

Michael Harper: Selected Poetry

Dear John, Dear Coltrane
(1968–69)

History Is Your Own Heartbeat
(1969)

Song: I Want a Witness
(1972)

Debridement
(1973)

Nightmare Begins Responsibility
(1975)

Images of Kin: New and Selected Poems
(1977)

Healing Song for the Inner Ear
(1985)

Harrington, Oliver Wendell "Ollie"

February 14, 1912–November 2, 1995

"Krazy Kat" comic-strip creator Ollie Harrington was raised in the South Bronx (New York City), the first child of an African-American man and his Hungarian wife. After graduating from high school in 1929, he studied drawing and painting at the National Academy of Design in Harlem. Harrington earned a bachelor's degree from the Yale University School of Fine Arts in 1940.

In 1932 Harrington began contributing comic strips to several black newspapers. For the *New York Amsterdam News*, he created the character Bootsie in a cartoon called "Dark Laughter." The Bootsie cartoons made honest fun of life in Harlem's black community, and Harrington would continue drawing the feature until the 1960s.

Harrington became the art director for *The People's Voice*, a weekly newspaper started in 1942. Beginning in 1943, he produced an adventure comic strip about a black aviator named Jive Gray. Near the end of **World War II** (1939–45), he served as a war correspondent (reporter) in Italy and France.

Harrington worked as a journalist and book illustrator following the war. In 1951 he moved to Paris, France, to pursue painting and became friends with African-American novelist **Richard Wright.** After Wright's death in 1960, Harrington moved to East Berlin, Germany, where he met his future wife, Helma Richter. He lived in East Berlin for the rest of his life, contributing political cartoons to several German publications.

Beginning in 1968, Harrington's political cartoons appeared in the *New York Daily World.* These cartoons criticized American racism and foreign policy. His use of caricature (exaggerated features, such as a huge nose), combined with gritty realism (showing the harsher aspects of life), made Harrington's political cartoons powerful statements about world affairs and race relations.

Hastie, William Henry

LAWYER, EDUCATOR
November 17, 1904–April 14, 1976

Born and raised in Knoxville, Tennessee, William Hastie was one of the best legal minds of the twentieth century. His father was a government office clerk and his mother was a teacher. In 1916 the family moved to Washington, D.C., where Hastie excelled in the classroom and in athletics at Dunbar High School, nationally known for its academic achievement. Graduating as valedictorian in 1921, he enrolled at Amherst College, Massachusetts. He graduated the head of his class in 1925.

After teaching math and science for two years, Hastie studied law at Harvard University (Massachusetts). An outstanding student, he was named to the editorial board of the *Harvard Law Review*, only the second African American to earn that honor. In 1933 he received his doctoral degree in law. That year, he was one of the first lawyers to argue against the practice of racial discrimination in American graduate schools. The case set the course for later trials won by the **NAACP (National Association for the Advancement of Colored People)**. Those court victories were important milestones in the struggle for civil rights.

From 1933 to 1937 Hastie was a lawyer for the U.S. Department of the Interior. In 1937 he became the first African American to be appointed a federal judge; he worked in the U.S. District Court for the Virgin Islands. In 1939 he returned to Washington, D.C., where he became a professor and dean at **Howard University** Law School. In 1940 he also took on a job in the office of the U.S. secretary of war. In that role Hastie fought discrimination in the armed services.

Hastie remained at Howard University until 1946, when he returned to the U.S. Virgin Islands as the first black governor of the territory. After three years he left the islands and became a judge in the U.S. Third Circuit Court of Appeals. In more than twenty years on the bench, his decisions were never overturned by other courts, and many of his rulings set legal precedents (examples for how justice is carried out).

Hastie was named chief justice of the circuit court three years before retiring in 1971. During his long career he was recognized with many honors, including the NAACP's prestigious Spingarn Medal (1943).

HIGH PRAISE FOR WILLIAM HASTIE

With his cousin, lawyer Charles Hamilton Houston (1895–1950), Hastie is credited with transforming Howard University's Law School into a first-class institution. Black economist **Robert C. Weaver** (1907–1997), who was the first head of the U.S. Department of Housing and Urban Development, said, "the Houston-Hastie team became the principal mentors of [U.S. Supreme Court justice] **Thurgood Marshall** [1908–1993], as well as symbols for, and teachers of, scores of black lawyers, many of whom played a significant role in Civil Rights litigation."

Havens, Richard Pierce "Richie"

FOLKSINGER
January 21, 1941–

Richie Havens's music appealed to young African Americans as well as the hippies of the 1960s. Born in New York, he sang in church choirs and street-corner boys' groups. While in high school, he formed the McCrea Gospel Singers and performed locally. A self-taught guitarist, Havens began working professionally in 1962, singing in Greenwich Village coffeehouses. He first recorded in 1963 and came to national attention through an appearance on *The Tonight Show* in 1967 and his performance at the Woodstock music festival in New York State in 1969. He continued to record and tour through the 1970s, as well as sing in musicals.

Known for his straightforward, simplified guitar playing and hoarse, bluesy voice, Havens expressed the concerns of a young generation. Although he was brought up in a volatile African-American ghetto in Brooklyn, Havens considered all humans to be equal. He once claimed, "I didn't choose to be a Negro. I'm all mankind. I'm balanced, a peaceful man." This attitude allowed the hippie movement of the 1960s to easily identify with his style. In the 1980s and 1990s Havens appeared in television and film and worked with Songwriters for the Earth.

Richie Havens: Selected Works

Peter and the Wolf
(musical, 1969)

Tommy
(1972)

Mixed Bag
(album)

Somethin' Else Again
(album)

Richard Havens 1983
(album)

Hawaii

First African-American Settlers: The earliest settlers of African ancestry arrived in Hawaii, then called the Sandwich Islands, well before the missionaries' arrival in 1821. Black "beachcombers" serving on whaling and other vessels jumped ship and remained on the islands.

Slave Population: Although no established slave population existed in Hawaii, black settlement was discouraged by King Kamehameha III (1813–1854) because he feared the extension of black **slavery** and segregation to Hawaii. Despite repeated attempts by white Americans to import black labor, there was not a significant number of black immigrants until after Hawaii became a U.S. territory in 1900. Hawaii did not become a state until 1959.

Free Black Population: Many early black settlers were active in business matters; records exist of bakers, boardinghouse keepers, barbers, and tailors.

Reconstruction: In 1874 U.S. Secretary of War William Belknap (1829–1890) suggested that the rich soil and climate of Hawaii would be ideal for the "discontented colored people" of the South. After repeated refusals by Hawaii to import black laborers, it took the 1898 U.S. annexation (incorporation as a territory) of Hawaii to end legal barriers to black settlement. The 1900 census, the first in Hawaii after annexation, listed 233 black Hawaiians. Forty years later there were only 255.

The Great Depression: During **World War II** (1939–45) there was much friction between white and African-American soldiers, and so the army, navy, and marines usually maintained segregated living quarters. After the war most blacks returned to the mainland and conditions became less racially strained.

Civil Rights Movement: In the years since 1959, when Hawaii became a state, African-American residents served as **military** personnel, businesspeople, educators, and politicians. Under the influence of the **Civil Rights** movement and a growing black population living in Hawaii, African Americans grew more interested in their black identity and in creating black institutions.

Current African-American Population: According to U.S. Census Bureau estimates, the total black population in Hawaii was 34,993 (nearly 3 percent of the state population) as of July 1, 1998.

Key Figures: Lawyer and politician Thomas Stewart (1854–1923); Dorie Miller (1918–1943), navy seaman who earned the Naval Cross during World War II after shooting down four enemy planes during the Japanese attack on Pearl Harbor.

(SEE ALSO **GOSPEL MUSIC**.)

Hawkins, Coleman Randolph

JAZZ SAXOPHONIST
November 21, 1904–May 19, 1969

A major figure in the development of **jazz**, Coleman Hawkins was born and raised in St. Joseph, Missouri. His mother, a schoolteacher and organist, introduced him to music. By age nine, he had studied piano, cello, and tenor saxophone. By age fourteen, he was playing at dances in Kansas City. In 1921 Hawkins quit his studies of music theory to tour with a jazz band.

Moving to New York in 1923, Hawkins was hired by bandleader **Fletcher Henderson** (1897–1952). He also worked with a group led by saxophonist Benny Carter (1907–) and other ensembles, but it was his eleven-year association with Henderson's orchestra that made Hawkins a star.

Leaving Henderson's group in 1934, Hawkins performed to wide acclaim across Europe. With **World War II** (1939–45) threatening, he returned to the United States in 1939, where he soon reestablished his reputation as a masterful jazz saxophonist. In October he recorded "Body and Soul," considered one of the great landmarks of twentieth-century music. It remains his best-known recording and showcases his mature style, described as relaxed and warm.

Though his playing was firmly rooted in the traditions of swing, Hawkins was open to new developments in jazz. In 1940 he organized his own big band, which was the first to record bebop, a new style of jazz. During the next decade he performed with other musicians who were developing the form, such as **Thelonious Monk** (1917–1982), **Miles Davis** (1926–1991), and **Dizzy Gillespie** (1917–1993).

In the late 1940s and 1950s Hawkins recorded often and toured the United States and Europe. By the 1960s he was considered an elder statesman of jazz. Hawkins continued to perform at music festivals and in New York clubs the rest of his life.

Hayden, Robert Earl

POET
August 4, 1913–February 25, 1980

Born in Detroit, Michigan, Robert Hayden often used his childhood and his family as the subjects of his poems. His love of literature won him a scholarship to Detroit's Wayne City College (later Wayne State University). The **Great Depression** of the 1930s, however, forced him to leave college just before completing his studies. He joined the Federal Writers' Project, a government program to aid Depression-era writers, and researched local history and black **folklore.** Enrolling at the University of Michigan in 1938, he went on to work for the Federal Historical Records Survey, studying the letters of several abolitionists (antislavery activists). His historical research is evident in much of his work as a poet, including such noteworthy poems as "The Ballad of Nat Turner," "Frederick Douglass," "The Dream (1863)," and "John Brown." In many of his poems, African-American history seemed to give Hayden something to focus on while allowing him the freedom to discover his own identity.

In 1941 Hayden and his wife, Erma, moved to Ann Arbor, where he studied English at the University of Michigan. After receiving a master's degree in 1944, Hayden moved to Nashville, Tennessee, in 1946 to teach at **Fisk University,** where he remained for twenty-two years before returning to the University of Michigan as a professor of English. Although Hayden wrote three small books of poetry in the 1940s and 1950s, his first mature work did not appear until 1962, with the publication of *A Ballad of Remembrance. Angle of Ascent*, his best-known volume, was published in 1975; his *Collected Poems* was published five years after his death, in 1985. In all, Hayden wrote nine volumes of poetry. In 1966 he received the grand prize for poetry in English at the First World Festival of Negro Arts, and he became a member of the American Academy of Poets in 1975.

Hayes, Isaac

SINGER, MUSICIAN, COMPOSER, RECORD PRODUCER
August 20, 1942–

Isaac Hayes was born in Covington, Tennessee and attended Memphis public schools. He played saxophone in his high school band, sang in church choirs, and began playing saxophone and piano in local clubs as early as the 1950s, completing his first solo recording in 1962. From 1962 to 1965, he played with a variety of small groups that played in the Memphis area R&B club circuit, including Sir Isaac and the Doo-Dads. He soon formed a songwriting and producing partnership with his friend, David Porter. The team

worked together for several years at Stax Records in Memphis, and was very instrumental in establishing "the Memphis Sound."

Hayes and Porter together wrote and produced numerous recordings, and Hayes personally worked as arranger, pianist, organist, and producer, with major Stax artists such as Otis Redding and Carla Thomas. Their hit songs of the period 1965–68 included "Soul Man," and "Hold On, I'm Coming," followed by the *Hot Buttered Soul* album, which reached Top Ten status and then went Platinum, in 1969. Perhaps the crowning achievement of this period was Hayes's 1971 score for the film *Shaft*, an instant hit for both the film and the subsequent record releases. *Shaft*, earned Hayes an Academy Award, two Grammys, and a Golden Globe award. Next came *Black Moses*, another Grammy winner, in 1972. His creative work continues, and an extensive list of his compositions is included in the International Dictionary of Black Composers's article covering Hayes's creative output through the 1990s.

As a composer, Hayes features a performing style that blends rhythm and blues with jazz elements, including sampling and a liberal use of synthesizers and overdubbing. He fits his music to his artists (including himself), and the result often crosses over between various performing styles (blues, jazz, gospel, etc.). The remake of the movie *Shaft* (2000), follows in this vein, and Hayes's artistic efforts continue.

Hayes, Robert Lee

TRACK-AND-FIELD ATHLETE, FOOTBALL PLAYER
December 20, 1942–

Robert Lee Hayes was a gifted athlete with lightning speed. His quickness earned him an Olympic gold medal and a career in the National Football League. However, Hayes had a secret that he kept from the world—he was a drug user. Fortunately, Hayes learned a difficult lesson about drug abuse in time to turn his life around and lead others to the path of recovery.

Born and raised in Jacksonville, Florida, Hayes was athletically gifted and starred in **baseball**, **basketball**, **football**, and **track-and-field**. Hayes attended Florida A&M University, a historically black college, where he excelled in track and football. In 1963 Hayes participated in the Amateur Athletic Union (AAU) events and set a world record in the 100-yard dash (9.1 seconds). The following year, he won a gold medal in the Olympic Games for the same event.

In 1965 Hayes was drafted by the Dallas Cowboys, where he quickly became a star pass receiver. Hayes's speed enabled him to catch a club record of receptions (sixty-four) and forced defenses to adopt a different strategy (called zone coverage). Hayes played for the Cowboys until 1975 and retired from football in 1976. After football, Hayes began a computerized marketing company. However, in 1979 he was convicted of selling cocaine and sentenced to five years in jail. In the 1980s Hayes quit using drugs and alcohol and began lecturing on the dangers of substance abuse. In the 1990s he began operating a drug rehabilitation center in Dallas. In 1999 the National

Football League decided not to admit Hayes into the Hall of Fame because of his past, which sparked controversy among Hayes's supporters.

Haywood, Harry

COMMUNIST ACTIVIST, THEORETICIAN
February 4, 1898–1985

Harry Haywood was a political activist who believed in Communism and that blacks should form their own nation. (Communism is a political system calling for a classless society and community ownership of all property, doing away with private party.) The youngest child of former slaves, Haywood dropped out of school at fifteen and took a string of jobs, including shoe shiner, barbershop helper, and bellhop (a hotel employee who escorts guests to their rooms). During **World War I** (1914–18) he fought in France with the 370th Infantry. After the war Haywood settled in Chicago, Illinois, and in 1923 he was recruited into the African Blood Brotherhood, a secret black nationalist organization associated with the Communist Party of the U.S.A. Two years later he became a full-time party worker.

Haywood, along with other young African Americans from his organization, traveled to the Soviet Union in 1926 and studied there until 1930, when he returned to the United States. While in the Soviet Union, Haywood was strongly influenced by the revolutionaries who were his fellow students.

In 1931 Haywood was chosen to head the Communist Party's Negro Department. He helped lead the party's campaign to defend the Scottsboro boys, eight black teenagers convicted and sentenced to death for allegedly attacking two white women in Alabama. In 1934 Haywood became national secretary of the party's civil rights organization, the League of Struggle for Negro Rights.

Haywood continued to promote his theory that the black population in the United States represented a people who should organize as a nation before being integrated into American society. In the 1960s Haywood supported various black nationalist movements, such as the **Nation of Islam (NOI)** under the leadership of **Malcolm X**, the Revolutionary Action Movement, and the League of Revolutionary Black Workers. Throughout his later years Haywood remained critical of the politics of civil rights leaders such as Rev. Dr. **Martin Luther King Jr.** and Rev. **Jesse Jackson.** (*See also* **Black Nationalism**.)

Hearns, Thomas

BOXER
October 18, 1958–

Thomas Hearns was a world champion boxer who made up for his lanky build (six feet one inch and 145 pounds) with a powerful right punch. He is perhaps best known for becoming champion in three different weight classes: lightweight, middleweight, and light heavyweight.

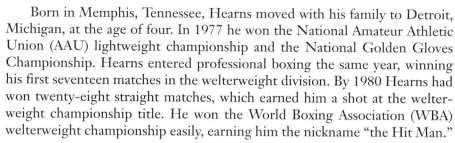

Born in Memphis, Tennessee, Hearns moved with his family to Detroit, Michigan, at the age of four. In 1977 he won the National Amateur Athletic Union (AAU) lightweight championship and the National Golden Gloves Championship. Hearns entered professional boxing the same year, winning his first seventeen matches in the welterweight division. By 1980 Hearns had won twenty-eight straight matches, which earned him a shot at the welterweight championship title. He won the World Boxing Association (WBA) welterweight championship easily, earning him the nickname "the Hit Man."

Hearns took on **Sugar Ray Leonard** in 1981 but lost in a fourteen-round battle that ended in a technical knockout. In 1983 Hearns switched to the middleweight division and won the WBA championship. In 1985 Hearns attempted to move up another weight class but met "Marvelous" Marvin Hagler, who knocked him out in a punishing match that lasted three rounds. However, Hearns was not discouraged by the loss, and in 1987 he became the WBA light heavyweight champion. Hearns picked up the gloves again in the 1990s, and at the age of forty-one he won the International Boxing Organization's title for the cruiserweight division. Hearns finished his stellar boxing career with sixty wins (forty-six by knockout) and four losses.

Height, Dorothy

ACTIVIST
March 24, 1912–

Born in Richmond, Virginia, Dorothy Height has devoted her life to improving conditions for working African-American women. When she was four, her family moved to a Pennsylvania mining town, where she was active in her church and community.

Height attended New York University, earning her master's degree in educational psychology in 1933. During college she also worked part-time at restaurants, laundries, factories, and newspapers, including **Marcus Garvey**'s (1887–1940) *Negro World.*

After working at a Brooklyn community center, Height was employed as a caseworker for the New York City Department of Welfare until 1937, when she took a job at the Harlem YWCA. As assistant director of the YWCA's Emma Ransom House, she gained firsthand experience in addressing the problems faced by women. After two years she became executive secretary of the Washington, D.C., YWCA. Throughout the 1930s she traveled widely, attending Christian youth conferences and other programs.

By 1944 Height's outstanding work for the YWCA earned her a position on the organization's national board. In that role, she led a movement to integrate the group's programs. In addition to her work with the YWCA, she was actively involved in Sigma Delta Theta. As president (1947–56), Height encouraged the black sorority to expand its community work at home and abroad.

A recognized leader, in 1957 she became president of the National Council of Negro Women (NCNW), which took a leading role in the civil rights struggle. Height continued to work on behalf of women into the 1990s.

Hemings, Sally

1773–1836

Born a slave, Sally Hemings was the sixth child of John Wayles of Bermuda Hundred, Virginia, and his slave, Elizabeth Hemings. Wayles died the year Hemings was born, and Hemings and her five brothers and sisters were inherited by her white half-sister Martha Wayles Jefferson, wife of Thomas Jefferson, who would later become third president of the United States. Martha died in 1782, and two years later Thomas Jefferson left for France as ambassador, taking his oldest daughter, also named Martha. In 1787 he sent for his youngest daughter, Maria, and Hemings accompanied her as her nurse. During her stay in France, where she was legally free, Hemings allegedly became Jefferson's girlfriend. In 1789 she returned with him to Virginia, thereby becoming a slave again. She remained at Monticello, Jefferson's estate near Charlottesville, Virginia, for the rest of her life. Between 1790 and 1808 she gave birth to seven children.

In 1802 the journalist James T. Callender published the story in the *Richmond Recorder.* This article created an international political scandal. Jefferson never said that the story was untrue and did not send Hemings or her children away from Monticello; the children were allowed to run away and "pass" for white at twenty-one. Jefferson died in 1826, and his daughter Martha later freed Hemings.

Henderson, Fletcher Hamilton Jr.

JAZZ BANDLEADER, COMPOSER
December 18, 1897–December 28, 1952

A pioneer of the big band sound, Fletcher Henderson began playing piano at age six in his hometown of Cuthbert, Georgia. He studied chemistry and math at **Atlanta University.** Graduating in 1920, he moved to New York to continue his education. But he soon became involved in the music business. By 1922 he had formed his own ensemble.

In 1924 Henderson added trumpeter **Louis Armstrong** (1901–1971) to his fledgling band. Henderson's compositions, featuring Armstrong's brilliant solos, ushered in the big-band sound. They made a series of recordings ("Copenhagen," "Houston Blues," and "Shanghai Shuffle," all in 1924) that are considered defining works of the jazz era.

Tenor saxophonist **Coleman Hawkins** (1904–1969) also joined Henderson's band. Hawkins's innovative playing further developed the solo "voice" in big-band jazz. Composer Don Redman (1900–1964) arranged songs for the group, which played regularly at New York's famed Roseland Ballroom.

In the 1920s and into the early 1930s Henderson's ensemble was the most prominent black jazz band in the nation. It helped launch great talents, including saxophonist Benny Carter (1907–), trumpeter Roy Eldridge (1911–1989), and singer **Billie Holiday** (1915–1959). Henderson also worked with other orchestras, including that of clarinetist Benny Goodman (1909–1986), with whom he had a long-standing association.

Henderson continued composing, arranging, and leading bands until 1950, when he suffered a stroke.

Hendrix, James Marshall "Jimi"

ROCK GUITARIST, SINGER, SONGWRITER
November 27, 1942–September 18, 1970

Jimi Hendrix, one of rock music's most inventive and influential guitarists, was born in Seattle, Washington, where he played with local rock groups as a teenager. He left school at sixteen and a year later joined the U.S.

Army as a paratrooper, but his career was cut short when he was injured on a practice jump. Once out of the army, he played backup guitar for several popular **rhythm-and-blues (R&B)** artists, including **Wilson Pickett,** Ike and **Tina Turner**, and **James Brown**. During this period (1962–1964), Hendrix began inventing his trademark crowd-pleasers—playing guitar with his teeth, behind his back, and between his legs. Early in his career, Hendrix played with either hand, but he eventually settled on a right-handed guitar, restrung upside down and played left-handed. With the tone and volume controls, he created unique effects and sounds.

In 1964 Hendrix moved to New York and, using the name Jimmy James, led his own band, the Blue Flames. In 1967 Hendrix left for London, England, mainly to meet the guitarist Eric Clapton. Within just three weeks of his arrival in England, Hendrix had formed a group named the Jimi Hendrix Experience. "Hey Joe," their first single, went all the way to number 6 on the British charts in 1967. An appearance on British television attracted wide attention when Hendrix played their new single, "Purple Haze." That same year, Hendrix's outstanding performance at the Monterey Pop Festival, in California, ended with his setting his guitar on fire—and afterward the twenty-four-year-old was a rock superstar. His debut album, *Are You Experienced?*, was called "revolutionary" by *Guitar Player* magazine.

In 1968 Hendrix released his second album, *Axis: Bold As Love*, and a third album, titled *Electric Ladyland,* was released just nine months later. In 1969 Hendrix performed at the Woodstock Festival in rural New York State, the only black performer of his time to enter the largely white world of hard and psychedelic rock. He was pressured by black groups to take a more political stance, but Hendrix took no part in formal politics. His celebrated electric version of the "Star-Spangled Banner," played at Woodstock, was considered in itself a political statement.

Hendrix's career was tragically cut short in London in 1970 after complications resulting from drug use. Although his period as a headline performer lasted only three years, his influence on popular music—and even jazz, to an extent—has been immeasurable.

Herndon, Angelo Braxton

POLITICAL ACTIVIST
May 6, 1913–

Angelo Braxton Herndon spent the majority of his life trying to improve the conditions of the working class through his membership in the Communist Party. Born in Wyoming, Ohio, Herndon traveled to Kentucky and Alabama to work. In 1930 he joined the Communist Party (which advocates community ownership of property and champions working-class interests) while living in Alabama. He began working for the Unemployment Council and was arrested for attempting to organize a union for mine workers in Tennessee. Although the charges were dropped, the experience added

to his mistrust of the capitalist system (private ownership of property). He also did not trust leaders of the African-American community at the time.

In the summer of 1932 Herndon led a group of blacks and whites on a hunger march. He was arrested on the grounds that he had broken an 1861 law (which was designed to prevent slaves from revolting). Although the law was outdated, he lost his appeal to the Supreme Court. In 1937 his attorneys made another appeal after he wrote an **autobiography** called *Let Me Live*, which resulted in his release. Herndon then moved to Harlem, New York, where he engaged in other political activities and wrote a journal with the famous author **Ralph Ellison.** He dropped out of the Communist Party during World War II (1939–45) and retired from public life. Herndon moved to the Midwest and refused to ever discuss his former participation in the Communist Party. In the late 1990s a play based on *Let Me Live* was performed in Chicago, Illinois.

Herriman, George

CARTOONIST
August 22, 1880–April 24, 1944

The creator of the comic strip *Krazy Kat*, George Herriman was born in New Orleans. While his birth certificate listed him as "Colored," his death certificate identified him as "Caucasian" (white). Herriman supposedly admitted to having some "Negro blood." It is likely that his parents were African Americans who passed for white after they left Louisiana for California.

Growing up in Los Angeles, Herriman demonstrated a talent for drawing and contributed sketches to local newspapers. After 1900 he moved to New York and published cartoons in *Life* and other magazines. His first successful comic strip was *The Family Upstairs*, a domestic comedy about the Dingbats and their noisy neighbors. The artist later began to include characters that would evolve into Krazy Kat and Ignatz Mouse, who had their own separate strip after 1911.

The story and jokes in *Krazy Kat* are about unrequited love. Ignatz is the object of Krazy's love, to which he responds by hitting the cat alongside the head with a brick. The cat accepts this act as sign of affection. The black cat is seen by some as a symbol of the harsh experience of blacks in America, to which they have responded with a forgiving heart.

Hill, Peter

July 19, 1767–December 1820

CLOCKMAKER

Clockmaker Peter Hill was born a slave in Burlington Township, New Jersey, in 1767. Trained in the craft by his master, Joseph Hollinshead Jr., Hill worked as Hollinshead's assistant until 1794. At age twenty-seven, Hill was released from slavery. With the help of his former master, he established

Anita Hill being sworn in during the Hill-Thomas Hearings (AP/Wide World Photos. Reproduced by permission)

himself as a maker of clocks and watches, becoming the first African American in his trade.

Hill married a slave from the same household in which he had served and arranged to make scheduled payments for both his own freedom and his wife's. He continued to live in Burlington for the next twenty-three years, and was a successful businessman. However, at the time of his death in 1820, his debts greatly exceeded the worth of his property and possessions.

At least five tall case clocks made by Peter Hill still exist. They have in common an eight-day movement (they need to be wound every eight days) with painted iron dials and mahogany and walnut cases made by a cabinet-maker named George Deacon.

Hill-Thomas Hearings

In September 1991, U.S. District Judge Clarence Thomas, nominated to the U.S. Supreme Court by President George Bush, began his confirmation hearing by the Senate Judiciary Committee (the Senate must confirm, or approve, all Supreme Court nominees.) On October 6, 1991, National Public Radio aired a story about Anita Hill, a law professor at the University of Oklahoma. Hill, who had been a staff attorney under Clarence Thomas at the Department of Education and the Equal Employment Opportunity Commission (EEOC) in the early 1980s, had told FBI investigators that Thomas had "harassed" her, making inappropriate and unwanted romantic advances toward her at work. Thomas strongly denied any such conduct. On October 8, following a long debate in the Senate, the vote on Thomas's confirmation was delayed. Senate Judiciary Committee chairman Joseph R. Biden scheduled further hearings in order to provide Hill and Thomas an opportunity to testify publicly on the issue.

On October 11, 1991, before a nationwide television audience, the hearings on Thomas's conduct began. Hill described Thomas's harassing comments and actions. When asked why, if Thomas had harassed her, Hill had accepted a position under him at the EEOC, she explained that the harassment had stopped for a period, and she feared she would be unable to find another job without his recommendation. Thomas's testimony flatly contradicted Hill's. Thomas denied any wrongdoing and repeatedly refused to discuss his private life.

During the following days, as the Senate debated the hearings, Senate Republicans launched a furious assault on Hill's character and truthfulness in order to discredit her. At the same time, many observers felt the Senate committee had not investigated Thomas very thoroughly. Nationwide argument raged over whether Thomas or Hill was telling the truth.

On October 15, the Senate confirmed Thomas, 52 to 48, the second-narrowest winning margin in history. Public opinion polls published at the time showed the majority of Americans believed Thomas and suspected Hill's story was not true. Within a year after the hearings, however, new opinion polls suggested that a majority of Americans believed Anita Hill had told the truth.

Himes, Chester

NOVELIST, SHORT STORY WRITER
July 29, 1909–November 12, 1984

Born in Jefferson City, Missouri, the youngest of three sons, Chester Himes spent his childhood in Arkansas. His parents, both of whom were children of former slaves, had achieved a measure of success, and both appear as thinly disguised characters in Himes's autobiographical novel *The Third Generation* (1954).

After graduating from high school in 1926, Himes worked as a busboy at a hotel in Cleveland, Ohio. In September 1926 he enrolled at Ohio State University, but was soon expelled for failing grades and improper behavior. He then drifted into a life of crime, and in 1927 he was sentenced to twenty years in the Ohio State Penitentiary for armed robbery.

While in prison, Himes began a lifelong career writing fiction; in 1934 he reached a national audience in *Esquire* magazine for "To What Red Hell," an essay describing a 1930 fire at the penitentiary that killed more than 330 inmates. He was paroled in 1936, and within a year married Jean Lucinda Johnson, a longtime friend. He departed for California in 1940 in hopes of writing for Hollywood, but repeated rejections forced him to seek work at racially tense California shipyards. These experiences are reflected in two bitter novels, *If He Hollers Let Him Go* (1946) and *Lonely Crusade* (1947).

From 1945 to 1953 Himes lived mainly in New York and New England, but he sailed for France soon after the publication of his prison novel, *Cast the First Stone* (1952). For the rest of his life he lived mainly in France and Spain, making only occasional visits to the United States. Among his books written during this period were seven Harlem police thrillers; the novel *The Primitive* (1955), depicting a troubled relationship between a black man and a white woman in post–World War II (1939–45) New York; and *A Case of Rape* (1985), his only published novel with a non-American setting.

Toward the end of his life, Himes came to view his writings as being in the "absurdist" tradition: racism, he said, made blacks and whites behave absurdly. He saw organized violence as the only means of ending racial oppression in America. Himes's literary reputation was never as high in the United States as it was in Europe, but American interest in his writings was renewed in the 1970s. Upon his death in Spain, he left a number of unfinished projects.

Hines, Earl "Fatha"

JAZZ PIANIST, COMPOSER, VOCALIST
December 28, 1903–April 22, 1983

Called "the father of modern jazz piano," Earl "Fatha" Hines influenced the style of countless musicians. He has been credited with playing an important role in the early careers of **jazz** greats **Charlie Parker** (1920–1955), **Dizzy Gillespie** (1917–1993), **Billy Eckstine** (1914–1993), and **Sarah Vaughan** (1924–1990).

Trained in classical music in his youth, he moved to Chicago, Illinois, in 1925. For the next four years he played with jazz groups and made his first recordings. Those he did with the great jazz trumpeter **Louis Armstrong** (1901–1971) are among the most celebrated in jazz.

After forming his own band in 1928, Hines played Chicago's Grand Terrace Ballroom for the next twelve years. Leading his own band until 1947, the next year he joined Louis Armstrong's All-Stars, touring with them until 1951. Spending the rest of the 1950s on the West Coast, Hines toured Europe and recorded extensively during the following two decades. He made his last public performance the week before his death.

Hines, Gregory

TAP DANCER, ACTOR
February 14, 1946–

Tap dancer Gregory Hines has also built a varied career as a musician and actor. Born in New York City, he began dancing at age three and turned professional when he was five. For fifteen years he performed with his older brother Maurice as "The Hines Kids." They were successful in vaudeville acts (a form of entertainment that included song and dance and was popular in the early 1900s) and in nightclubs. His father joined the act as a drummer in 1964, changing the act's name to "Hines, Hines & Dad."

The Hineses learned their technique from older tap masters, becoming the direct inheritors of the great black **tap dance** traditions. Tappers like Howard "Sandman" Sims (c. 1925–) would tutor them between shows; these men became their heroes and mentors.

In the early 1970s Hines decided to leave the family tap team and moved to California, where he turned his attention to guitar and formed the jazz-rock ensemble Severance in 1973. He released a record album of original songs, then returned to the New York stage to tap dance in the late 1970s. His stage performances earned him three Tony nominations. He received Emmy Awards for his performances in television specials.

Such fame has made Hines an especially important influence on the younger generation of male tap dancers. Like a jazz musician who ornaments a melody with improvisation, Hines improvises within the frame of the dance. His style combines the phrasing of music, the rhythms of a drummer, and the lines of a dancer. Hines, like experimental jazz artists, purposely breaks free of the regular rhythms of musical phrasing. He also updates tap by performing on a special acoustic stage where his taps are highly amplified. The leading tap dancer of his generation, Hines is a generous artist and teacher. Hines continued to appear in film, stage, and television throughout the 1990s.

Hinton, Milton John "Milt"

MUSICIAN
June 23, 1910–

Born in Vicksburg, Mississippi, in 1910, Milton John Hinton began taking piano lessons from his mother, a church organist, after the family moved to Chicago. He received more formal training in violin, string bass, and tuba in high school and first performed professionally in the late 1920s on bass, in groups led by saxophonist and violinist Boyd Atkins, and pianist Tiny Parham. Later he played at Chicago's Showboat Cabaret in bands led by trumpeter Jabbo Smith and pianist Cassino Simpson. In the 1930s he played for violinist Eddie South, drummer Zutty Singleton, and singer **Cab Calloway.**

Hinton (who was nicknamed "The Judge" by his lifelong friend and former Calloway band member Ben Webster) played a supporting role in the development of bebop, offering his highly skilled playing at jam sessions at Minton's Playhouse in Harlem in the late 1930s and early 1940s. After leaving Calloway in 1951, Hinton performed in New York City with **Billie Holiday,** Joe Bushkin, and Jackie Gleason, and toured with **Count Basie, Louis Armstrong**'s All-Stars, and other performers. In the 1960s Hinton continued to record and perform, most notably with **Harry Belafonte** in support of the **Student Nonviolent Coordinating Committee**. Starting in the 1970s Hinton began teaching music at Hunter College in New York, the City University of New York, and at Yale University. In the 1970s he also toured with **Pearl Bailey** and Bing Crosby, and recorded *Here Swings the Judge* (1975). In the 1980s and 1990s Hinton remained active, performing with saxophonist Branford Marsalis, recording, and exhibiting his photographs of jazz musicians. In 1988 Hinton, who has lived for many years in Queens, New York, published a volume of memoirs and photographs, *Bass Line: The Stories and Photographs of Milt Hinton*. In 1993 he was awarded an American Jazz Master Fellowship from the National Endowment for the Arts and in 1996 he received a New York State Governor's Arts Award. (*See also* **Jazz.**)

Hodges, John Cornelius "Johnny" ▪▪▪

MUSICIAN
July 25, 1907–May 10, 1970

Born in Cambridge, Massachusetts, Johnny Hodges resisted the piano lessons offered by his parents, and started out on drums made from household items before trying his hand at a real trap kit (a name often used to describe a drum set). The family moved to Boston, where Hodges started playing the soprano saxophone. From the beginning he played in the broad-toned "singing" style that characterized the reed players of Boston. From the larger world of **jazz**, Hodges modeled his approach to music after that of **Louis Armstrong**, jazz's first great soloist, and **Sidney Bechet,** the clarinet and soprano sax player who, like Armstrong, was a master of the jazz styles associated with **New Orleans**. When Bechet came through Boston on tour, the thirteen-year-old Hodges met him and began an informal apprenticeship. During the 1920s Hodges played sax and sometimes piano at house parties and public dances in Boston; he spent weekends in New York, where he played with Bechet, Chick Webb, and other well-known musicians.

When one of **Duke Ellington**'s original reed players, Otto Hardwick, left the band temporarily, Ellington convinced Hodges to quit the Chick Webb Orchestra and join the Ellingtonians. With apparent ease, Hodges

Jazz saxophone legend Johnny Hodges performing with Duke Ellington's band (Archive Photos. Reproduced by permission)

covered the coolly lyrical parts that Ellington had prepared for Hardwick; he also could perform snarls and growls in the Bechet style that jazz players of the day praised as "playing dirty." He could play fast and "hot"; he could shout the blues; he could present ballads with lyrical grace. By the early 1930s Hodges was widely regarded as Ellington's most eloquent soloist. Aside from the hundreds of records Hodges made with the full band, beginning in 1937 he also made a series of records with small groups drawn from the Ellington orchestra. These included such masterworks as "Jeep's Blues," "Hodge Podge," and "The Jeep Is Jumpin'," all composed by Hodges and Ellington.

From 1951 to 1955 Hodges left Ellington to form his own small band. Along with other former Ellington players, Hodges produced a hit record, *Castle Rock* (1951), and dozens of other records that featured the Ellingtonians playing informally arranged ballads, blues, jump numbers, and blue-mood pieces, many of them associated with Duke. The period after Hodges's return to Ellington was marked by soaring success. *Ellington at*

Newport 1956, featuring a stunning remake of "Jeep's Blues," became a hit album. Hodges stayed with Ellington for the rest of his life, and died only days before he was scheduled to play a piece Ellington had written especially for him: *Portrait of Sidney Bechet* (1970).

Johnny Hodges was one of the first great soloists on the alto saxophone. Some would argue that he was the music's very greatest alto. His tone, with its expressive vibrato, and his elegant and yet soulful phrasing, had a significant impact on the playing of many other saxophonists. By the mid-1930s, everyone playing saxophone seemed to owe something to Hodges. **Charlie Parker** admired him, referring to him as "the Poet." **John Coltrane**, who played in one of Hodges's bands in the 1950s, listed him as one of his favorites. In the 1980s and 1990s, many young players showed the Hodges touch; some dedicated pieces and albums to his memory.

Holder, Geoffrey

DANCER, CHOREOGRAPHER, PAINTER
August 20, 1930–

Born in Port-of-Spain, Trinidad, an island in the West Indies off the northeastern coast of Venezuela, Geoffrey Holder received lessons in painting and dancing from his older brother Boscoe. When Holder was seven, he made his first performance with his brother's dance troupe, the Holder Dance Company.

A decade later, Geoffrey began directing the company, and in 1952 was invited to audition in New York City. To pay for the trip, he sold twenty of his paintings. Although the audition did not result in a job offer, Holder stayed in New York City, teaching dance classes.

Holder's impressive height (six feet six inches) and formal attire at a dance recital persuaded a producer to put him in the 1954 Broadway musical *House of Flowers*. During the musical's run, Holder met dancer **Carmen DeLavallade**, and the two married in 1955.

Holder went on to appear as principal dancer with the New York Metropolitan Opera Ballet and performed with his troupe, Geoffrey Holder and Company, through 1960. During this time, Holder continued to paint and was awarded a 1957 Guggenheim Fellowship.

In 1957 Holder began acting on the stage, and in 1961 he had his first film role in *All Night Long*. He was later cast in Woody Allen's *Everything You Always Wanted to Know About Sex* (1972), as Punjab in *Annie* (1982), and with Eddie Murphy in *Boomerang* (1992).

Holder has also been active as a director. His work on the Broadway musical *The Wiz*, (1975) an all-black retelling of *The Wizard of Oz*, earned him Tony Awards for best director and best costume design. In 1978 he directed and choreographed the lavish Broadway musical *Timbuktu!*

Holder's many interests, however, have not taken him away from his oldest passions. During the 1990s he was still active as a choreographer and painter. In 1998 he redesigned sets and costumes for a new production of his piece *Prodigal Prince* by the **Alvin Ailey** American Dance Theater.

Holiday, Billie Eleanora Fagan

SINGER
April 7, 1915–July 17, 1959

Born Eleanora Fagan in Philadelphia, the daughter of Sadie Fagan and **jazz** guitarist Clarence Holiday, Billie Holiday grew up in Baltimore and suffered a childhood of poverty and abuse. As a teenager, she changed her name (after screen star Billie Dove) and came to New York, where she began singing in speakeasies (illegal bars that operated during Prohibition). Her singing, she said, was influenced, by **Louis Armstrong** and **Bessie Smith**. In 1933 she was spotted performing in Harlem by critic and record producer John Hammond, who brought her to Columbia Records, where she recorded classic sessions with such jazz greats as pianist Teddy Wilson and tenor saxophonist **Lester Young**.

Following grueling tours with the big bands of **Count Basie** and Artie Shaw, Holiday became a solo act in 1938, achieving success with appearances at Cafe Society in Greenwich Village, and with her 1939 recording of the dramatic antilynching song "Strange Fruit." Performing regularly at clubs along New York's Fifty-second Street, she gained a sizable income and a reputation as a singer of torch songs. A heroin addict, she was arrested for narcotics possession in 1947 and spent ten months in prison, which afterward made it illegal for her to work in New York clubs. Yet despite such hardships and her worsening health and voice, she continued to perform and make memorable recordings on the Decca, Verve, and Columbia labels until her death in 1959.

Although riddled with flaws, Holiday's 1956 **autobiography**, *Lady Sings the Blues*, remains a fascinating account of her changeable personality. A 1972 film of the same title, starring pop singer **Diana Ross**, further distorted her life but introduced her to a new generation of listeners. Holiday was one of America's finest and most influential jazz singers. Her voice was light, with a limited range, but her phrasing, in the manner of a jazz instrumentalist, places her among the most skillful of jazz musicians. She was distinguished by her flawless timing, her ability to transform song melodies through improvisation, and her ability to sing lyrics with complete conviction. While she was not a blues singer, her performances were infused with the same stark depth of feeling that characterizes the blues.

Hooker, John Lee

BLUES SINGER, GUITARIST
August 22, 1917–

John Lee Hooker began his career playing **blues** in nightclubs in Memphis, Tennessee. He moved to Detroit, Michigan, in the 1940s and began recording in 1948, achieving great success with "Boogie Chillun." Between 1949 and 1953 Hooker recorded under different names on about seventy recordings. He began to use a full band in the 1950s to back up his guitar and deep voice.

Blues legend John Lee Hooker ((c)Jack Vartoogian. Reproduced by permission)

A 1964 remake of his song "Boom Boom" by the British band the Animals introduced Hooker to a bigger audience, and he toured widely through the 1970s and 1980s. In 1991 Hooker was inducted into the Rock and Roll Hall of Fame. In 1994, at the age of seventy-seven, he announced his retirement from touring; he released a retrospective album (one featuring songs spanning his career), *Don't Look Back*, in 1997.

Hooks, Benjamin Lawrence

LAWYER, MINISTER, CIVIC LEADER
January 31, 1925–

Benjamin Lawrence Hooks has devoted his life to improving the social and economic conditions of blacks. He is one of the most prominent leaders of the African-American community in modern times, having taken on the fight for racial equality from a variety of platforms.

Born in Memphis, Tennessee, Hooks earned a bachelor's degree from **Howard University** (Washington, D.C.) in 1944 and a law degree from De Paul University. After he finished his studies, Hooks returned to Memphis and practiced law with the goal of ending segregation. He began civil rights activism in the 1950s. Hooks was ordained as a minister in 1956 and became pastor of a Memphis church. In 1961 he became the first black judge in the state of Tennessee. Nominated by Richard Nixon in 1972, Hooks became the first black to serve on the Federal Communications Commission (FCC). At the FCC Hooks helped improve employment opportunities for blacks and insisted that blacks be shown in a more positive fashion in electronic media.

In 1977 Hooks took on the important position of executive director of the **National Association for the Advancement of Colored People (NAACP).** At the time the NAACP was suffering financially and membership was declining because many blacks believed that the organization had grown too conservative. Hooks helped turn the organization around by broadening the NAACP's political ties and forging new relationships with businesses. Hooks resigned his post in 1992, however, under criticism that the organization had become less effective. After he resigned, Hooks continued his fight against racial inequality as chairman of the Leadership Conference on Civil Rights (LCCR). He later moved back to Memphis to devote more time to the ministry and help develop a civil rights museum in Memphis. In 1998 the National Civil Rights Museum honored Hooks with the Freedom Award for promoting civil and human rights for more than half a century.

Hope, John

EDUCATOR, CIVIL RIGHTS ACTIVIST
June 2, 1868–February 20, 1936

John Hope entered the field of **education** at a time when **Booker T. Washington** was encouraging job training for African Americans. Hope disagreed with Washington, insisting that black people must pursue higher learning if they were to make a case for social equality. Hope turned down an offer to teach at Washington's **Tuskegee Institute.** Instead, from 1894 to 1898 he taught Greek, Latin, and the natural sciences at Roger Williams College in Nashville, Tennessee. He went on to teach classics at Atlanta Baptist College (which became **Morehouse College** in 1913). In 1906 Hope became the college's first black president.

As president of Atlanta Baptist College, Hope faced many obstacles. Just before school was set to begin in September 1906, an antiblack riot swept through Atlanta; Hope demonstrated his leadership by ensuring that classes went on as scheduled. Over the years, he proved extraordinarily successful in increasing enrollment, raising money, and attracting leading black scholars.

Hope did not limit his activities to the university setting. He traveled to France during World War I (1914–18), where he insisted that the Young Men's Christian Association (YMCA) adopt new policies to ensure equal treatment for black soldiers. Hope served as president of the National Association of Teachers in Colored Schools, and he acted as honorary president of the Association for the Study of Negro Life and History. In addition, he was a member of both the **National Association for the Advancement of Colored People's (NAACP)** Advisory Board and the Urban League of New York's Executive Committee. In 1920 he joined the Commission on Interracial Cooperation, a group of Atlanta civic leaders; he was elected president of the commission in 1932.

In the late 1920s and early 1930s, through his considerable organizational connections, Hope traveled widely in Europe, the Soviet Union, the Middle East, Latin America, and the Caribbean. Until his death, Hope remained committed to the idea of education as a tool for gaining equality.

Lena Horne takes a bow during a live performance (AP/Wide World Photos. Reproduced by permission)

Horne, Lena

SINGER, ACTRESS
June 30, 1917–

Lena Horne's throaty singing voice and beautiful stage presence have enchanted audiences for decades. Horne began her career at the age of sixteen as a dancer in the chorus line at the **Cotton Club** in New York's Harlem neighborhood. She also became a favorite at Harlem's Apollo Theatre and was among the first African-American entertainers to perform in "high-class" nightclubs.

Horne made her first recording in 1936 and recorded extensively as a soloist and with others. She toured widely in the United States and Europe. In 1941 she became the first black performer to sign a contract with a major motion picture studio—Metro Goldwyn Mayer (MGM). Her first film role was in *Panama Hattie* (1942), which led to roles in *Cabin in the Sky* (1942), *Stormy Weather* (1943), *Ziegfeld Follies* of 1945 and 1946, and *The Wiz* (1978). Her Broadway musicals include 1939's *Blackbirds*, *Jamaica* (1957), and the highly successful one-woman Broadway show *Lena Horne: The Lady and Her Music* (1981). The record album of the latter musical won her a Grammy Award as best female pop vocalist in 1981.

Horne's spectacular beauty and unique voice helped to make her the first nationally celebrated black female vocalist. In 1984 she was a recipient of the Kennedy Center honors for lifetime achievement in the arts. She published two autobiographies: *In Person: Lena Horne* (1950) and *Lena* (1965).

Horne remained active through the 1990s. She recorded a live performance at New York's Carnegie Hall, *An Evening with Lena Horne* (1997), and a jazz album, *Being Myself* (1998).

Horse Racing

During the early years of horse racing in the United States, from approximately 1747 to 1894, blacks dominated the sport. The first jockey to win the Kentucky Derby was black (1866), and black jockeys won fifteen out of the first twenty-eight Kentucky Derby races. However, the presence of blacks in horse racing came to an abrupt end in 1894. The participation of African Americans in professional horse racing never recovered after they were virtually exiled from the sport.

In colonial America wealthy whites used black slaves to train and race horses. Not only was horse racing popular among the upper classes, many poor whites and freed slaves made a wild social event out of the sport. At one point a law was created that prevented horse racing from taking place near Quaker meetings (Quakers were social and religious conservatives).

After several black jockeys and trainers began to dominate the sport in the late 1800s, a wave of discrimination dramatically changed the face of horse racing. Whites began to envy the successes of blacks and decided to ban them from the sport. In 1894 the Jockey Club was established, which made licensing a requirement for horse racing. Blacks were continually denied access to the sport and found the environment too hostile to remain. Many blacks therefore turned to steeplechase racing (horse racing over a course with obstacles such as hedges and walls). Steeplechase racing was open to blacks because there was a high demand for skilled jockeys and trainers at the time.

THE GOLDEN AGE OF HORSE RACING FOR BLACKS.

The late 1800s was the golden age of African-American horse racing. In 1877 William "Billy" Walker won the Kentucky Derby and the Dixie Handicap (two of the most prestigious horse-racing events). **Isaac Murphy,** who was born a slave, won an incredible 44 percent of his races, including three Kentucky Derbies. Murphy was widely considered the best jockey of the time and may have been the most widely known black athlete of the nineteenth century. Willie Simms and James "Soup" Perkins were two other famous black jockeys at the time; Simms earned more than $300,000 in his lifetime racing horses.

Although a handful of blacks have managed to become successful jockeys and trainers, the level of black participation has never recovered since 1894. Since the 1960s horse racing has been dominated by whites and Latinos. However, in the 1980s and 1990s a few wealthy African Americans, such as Barry White and Berry Gordy Jr., began investing in racehorses. It remains to be seen whether this will result in greater black participation in a sport they originally dominated.

Hosier, Harry "Black Harry"

PREACHER

c. 1750–1806

Harry Hosier, who was frequently referred to as "Black Harry," was born into slavery in North Carolina. After being freed, he converted to Methodism and became the first African-American Methodist preacher. He served as the traveling companion, servant, guide, and co-preacher of the white Methodist Bishop Francis Asbury. Known to his colleagues for his intelligence and his inspired preaching, Hosier halted his own education for fear that his growing ability to read and write interfered with the Lord's speaking through him. Audiences applauded Hosier's gift for preaching. Prominent preachers of the day knew that if Hosier took the pulpit with them, they would draw a larger crowd.

In 1784 Hosier accompanied English religious reformer John Wesley's representative, Bishop Thomas Coke, on a tour around Pennsylvania, Delaware, and Maryland. After their journey, Coke wrote that Hosier was one of the "best preachers in the world." Hosier participated in the founding of the Methodist Episcopal Church in America.

From 1789 to 1790 Hosier traveled and preached north along the Hudson River. He then continued on to speak throughout New England. In 1803 Asbury assigned Hosier to the Trenton (New Jersey) Circuit. In his later years, Hosier had bouts with alcoholism, though this resulted in only a short leave from his preaching duties. He died of natural causes in Philadelphia, Pennsylvania, in May 1806.

Hospitals, Black

Before the **Civil Rights movement** of the 1960s, hospitals either denied African Americans admission or placed them in segregated (separated by race) wards, often in unheated attics and damp basements. This practice occurred in both the northern and the southern United States. The first all-black hospital was the Georgia Infirmary, established in Savannah, Georgia, in 1832. By the end of the nineteenth century, several others had been founded, including St. Agnes Hospital in Raleigh, North Carolina, and MacVicar Infirmary in Atlanta, Georgia. Some white founders of black hospitals wanted to supply health care to black people and offer training opportunities for black doctors and nurses. They also wanted to prevent the spread of disease from African-American to white communities.

African Americans also began founding hospitals to meet the needs of their communities. The first, Provident Hospital, opened its doors in Chicago, Illinois, in 1891. (Black doctors and nurses were barred from white Chicago hospitals and nursing schools.) Other black-controlled hospitals to open during the 1890s were the Tuskegee Institute and Nurse Training School at **Tuskegee Institute,** Alabama, and the **Frederick Douglass** Memorial Hospital and Training School in Philadelphia, Pennsylvania. These hospitals improved the health status of African Americans and helped develop a black professional class.

By 1919 about 118 segregated and black-controlled hospitals existed, 75 percent of them in the South. Most were small and poorly equipped and lacked clinical training programs, so they were not prepared to survive the changes in medicine and hospital technology that took place at the turn of the twentieth century. A black medical society, the National Medical Association (NMA), and a black hospital organization, the National Hospital Association (NHA), launched a movement for change during the 1920s that would help black hospitals survive. They feared that the growing importance of hospital and medical standards would lead to the closing of black hospitals, the only place for most African-American doctors to train and practice medicine.

The NMA and the NHA worked to raise funds to improve black hospitals, but funds were scarce for all hospitals during the severe economic downturn known as the **Great Depression** (1929–39). Three organizations—the Julius Rosenwald Fund, the General Education Board, and the Duke Endowment—responded to the needs of black hospitals and provided crucial financial support.

Although their help produced some improvements in black hospitals, by the mid-1940s the number of hospitals approved by the American Medical Association (AMA) and the American College of Surgeons was decreasing. The AMA admitted that a number of these hospitals would not have been approved except for the need to have some internship hospitals for black physicians.

During the **Civil Rights movement,** the NMA and **National Association for the Advancement of Colored People (NAACP)** led the campaign for medical civil rights, saying a segregated health care system resulted in inferior medical care for blacks. They called for the integration (inclusion of both blacks and whites) of existing hospitals and the building of interracial hospitals.

These activists initiated court cases against hospital segregation. The U.S. Supreme Court ruled segregation policies unconstitutional in 1963 and provided for integration of public and private hospitals. The 1964 Civil Rights Act prohibited racial discrimination in any programs that received money from the federal government. This applied to most hospitals after the passing of Medicare and Medicaid health insurance laws in 1965.

The main role of historically black hospitals before 1965 had been to provide medical care and medical training for African Americans within a segregated society. After civil rights legislation gave blacks access to previously white hospitals, the number of black hospitals sharply declined. In 1944 there were 124 black hospitals; by 1990 the number had decreased to eight. A majority of their patients are the poor, who are uninsured or receive government medical assistance. Historically black hospitals have evolved from a source of pride and achievement for a segregated black society to a fading institution.

Houston, Charles Hamilton

LAWYER

1895–1948

Charles Houston (Corbis Corporation. Reproduced by permission)

Born in the District of Columbia the son of William L. Houston, a lawyer, and Mary Hamilton Houston, a teacher, Charles Hamilton Houston attended Washington's M Street High School, and then went to Amherst College in Amherst, Massachusetts. He graduated in 1915, then taught English for two years at **Howard University.** In 1917 Houston joined the Army and served as a second lieutenant in a segregated unit of the American Expeditionary Forces during **World War I** (1914–18). Following his discharge, he decided on a career in law and entered Harvard Law School, where he earned two law degrees. While at Harvard Houston became the first African-American editor of the *Harvard Law Review.* In 1924 Houston entered law practice with his father at the law firm of Houston & Houston in Washington, D.C. He remained with the firm until his death.

Throughout his career, Houston served on many committees and in many organizations. He also wrote columns on racial and international issues for the ***Crisis*** and the *Baltimore Afro-American.* In 1927 and 1928, after receiving a grant from the Rockefeller Foundation, Houston wrote an important report, "The Negro and His Contact with the Administration of Law." The next year he was appointed vice dean at **Howard University**, where he served as professor of law and as head of the law school. Houston mentored such students as **Thurgood Marshall**, William Bryant, and Oliver Hill. Under his direction, Howard Law School became a unique training ground for African-American lawyers to challenge segregation through the legal system.

In 1935 Houston took a leave of absence from Howard to become the first full-time, salaried special counsel of the **National Association for the Advancement of Colored People** (NAACP). As special counsel, Houston argued civil rights cases and traveled to many different areas of the United States, sometimes under difficult conditions, in order to defend blacks who stood accused of crimes. He won two important Supreme Court cases, *Hollins v. Oklahoma* (1935) and *Hale v. Kentucky* (1938), which overturned death sentences given by juries from which blacks had been excluded because of their race. Houston persuaded the NAACP and the American Fund for Public Service to support an ongoing legal struggle against segregation, with public education as the main area of challenge. In 1896 the U.S. Supreme Court had ruled in ***Plessy v. Ferguson*** that "separate but equal" segregated facilities were constitutional. Houston realized that a direct attack on the decision would fail, and he designed a strategy of trying test cases, and slow buildup of successful precedents based on inequality within segregation. He focused on combating discrimination in graduate education, a less controversial area than discrimination in primary schools, as the first step in his battle in the courts.

University of Maryland v. Murray was Houston's first victory, and an important psychological triumph. As a result of this case the Maryland Supreme Court ordered Donald Murray, an African American, admitted to the University of Maryland Law School, since there were no law schools for blacks in the state. In 1938, suffering from tuberculosis and heart problems, Houston resigned as chief counsel, and two years later he left the NAACP. However, he remained an important adviser over the next decade through his membership on the NAACP Legal Committee. His position as special counsel was taken over by his former student and deputy **Thurgood Marshall**, who formed the **NAACP Legal Defense** and Education Fund, Inc. (LDF) to continue the struggle Houston had begun. Their endeavor resulted in the famous 1954 Supreme Court decision ***Brown v. Board of Education of Topeka, Kansas***, which overturned school segregation.

During his career Houston was involved in many other legal cases, involving unfair labor practices, housing discrimination, and other forms of segregation. In 1948 Houston suffered a heart attack, and he died of heart problems two years later. After his death he was awarded the NAACP's Spingarn Medal in 1950. In 1958 Howard University named its new main law school building in his honor.

Howard University

Founded: Howard University was established in 1867 with the mission of educating youth in the liberal arts and sciences.

History Highlights:

- 1866: The idea of establishing a school to train ministers and educators to work among newly freed slaves is proposed. Among those who support the plan are Gen. Oliver Otis Howard, head of the Freedmen's Bureau, and several other Civil War generals and U.S. congressmen. (The Freedmen's Bureau was a government agency formed after the **Civil War** (1860–65) to protect the rights of former slaves.)

- 1867: Howard University is founded with substantial funding from the federal government.

- 1868: Howard's medical department is established.

- 1869: Howard's law department enrolls its first students.

- 1870: The first students graduate from Howard's normal school (teacher-training school); the four or five young women are white. Howard's theology department opens; it does not use federal funds, but rather relies on contributions from the American Missionary Association.

- 1871: The first five students (two blacks and three whites) graduate from Howard's medical department. The first ten students graduate from Howard's law department.

- 1872: The first three students (two blacks and one white) graduate from Howard's collegiate department.

- 1900: By 1900 Howard University has more than 700 students and is considered one of the most prominent black academic colleges in the United States. Among the African Americans who serve on the board of trustees are abolitionist **Frederick Douglass** (1818–1895) and educator **Booker T. Washington** (c. 1856–1915).

- 1922: Lucy Slowe Diggs becomes the first dean of women at Howard.

- 1926: Baptist minister Mordecai W. Johnson (1890–1976) becomes Howard's first African-American president; he serves until 1960.

- 1969: Howard's African-American Studies program is established.

- 1990s: Although Howard continues to receive approximately 40 percent of its budget from the federal government, it launches the Howard 2000 program to make sure its budget remains sound and that it can continue to draw the top African-American students in the nation.

Location: Washington, D.C.

Known For: Since its beginnings, Howard has attracted many important African-American scholars, researchers, and political leaders to its staff. Many of Howard's alumni have also gone on to achieve excellence in a number of fields.

Number of Students (1999–2000): 10,211

Grade Average of Incoming Freshman: 3.0

Admission Requirements: Four years of English, two years of math, two years of science, two years of a foreign language, two years social studies; SAT or ACT scores; two letters of recommendation from teachers and one from a counselor.

Mailing Address:
Howard University
Office of Admission
2400 Sixth St. NW
Washington, DC 20059

Telephone: (202) 806-2900

E-mail: admission@howard.edu

URL: http://www.howard.edu

Campus: Howard's 89-acre main campus is located in central Washington, D.C. Smaller campuses include the Beltsville campus, West campus, Divinity School campus, and Silver Spring campus. Buildings on the main campus include three art galleries, language labs, a computer lab, Howard University Hospital, which includes the Center for Sickle Cell Disease, and the Moorland-Spingarn Center, one of the nation's most important archives of African-American history and culture. The university library houses over two million documents.

Special Programs: Howard University Center for Urban Progress; Ralph J. Bunche International Affairs Center.

Extracurricular Activities: Student government, student newspaper, the *Hilltop*; radio station; television station; four fraternities and four sororities; organizations, including Baptist Student Union, the African Cultural Ensemble, a gospel choir, and drama clubs; athletics (men's baseball, basketball, cross-country, diving, football, soccer, swimming, tennis, track-and-field, wrestling; women's basketball, bowling, cross-country, diving, lacrosse, soccer, swimming, tennis, track-and-field, volleyball).

Howard Alumni: Thurgood Marshall (1908–1993), former U.S. Supreme Court justice; actress and choreographer **Debbie Allen** (1950–); **Andrew Young** (1932–), former mayor of Atlanta, Georgia; writer and Pulitzer Prize-winner **Toni Morrison** (1931–).

Howlin' Wolf

BLUES SINGER
June 10, 1910–January 10, 1976

Howlin' Chester Arthur Burnett was born in West Point, Mississippi. He began playing guitar as a teenager under the main influence of bluesman Charley Patton, who lived on a plantation in the Mississippi Delta. Burnett began performing in the late 1920s, traveling to various southern plantations. The moans and high-pitched wails that defined his vocal style earned him the nickname "Howlin' Wolf." After serving in the U.S. Army during World War II (1939–45), Howlin' Wolf moved to West Memphis, Arkansas, where he formed his first band and began recording in 1951. Following the success of "Moanin' at Midnight," he signed with Chess Records and moved to Chicago, Illinois, where he remained for the rest of his life. He continued to perform and record, touring the United States and Europe, and to define the postwar Chicago **blues** style. He died in Hines, Illinois.

Hudson, Hosea

UNION LEADER, COMMUNIST ACTIVIST
1898–1988

Hosea Hudson of Birmingham, Alabama, was a union leader who believed in communist ideas (communism is a political system in which the government owns all industry and is ruled by one political party.) As a working-class black, he lacked a focus for his discontent until he joined the Communist Party of the U.S.A. (CPUSA) in 1931. Within a year he had lost his job because of his communist beliefs. Although he was able to earn irregular wages through odd jobs, his wife never forgave him for putting the welfare of the CPUSA before that of his wife and child.

During the **Great Depression,** Hudson was active with a series of organizations in and around the CPUSA. He helped the Unemployed Councils secure relief payments and fight evictions on behalf of the poor. In his first trip outside the South, he spent ten weeks in New York State at the CPUSA Party National Training School in 1934, during which time he

learned to read and write. Returning to Birmingham in 1937, he founded the Right to Vote Club (which would earn him a key to the city of Birmingham in 1980 as a pioneer in the struggle for black civil rights).

After the creation of the Congress of Industrial Organizations (CIO), a union group that supported workers, Hudson joined the campaign to organize nonunion workers. As the demand for labor during World War II increased, Hudson went to work in a steel factory and became recording secretary of Steel Local 1489, a workers' union; he then organized United Steel Workers Local 2815. He remained president of that union from 1942 to 1947, when he was stripped of leadership for being a Communist. With a justified sense of the historical importance of his life, Hudson initiated two books on his experiences: *Black Worker in the Deep South* (1972) and *The Narrative of Hosea Hudson* (1979). Active in the Coalition of Black Trades Unionists until his health failed in the mid-1980s, Hudson died in Gainesville, Florida, in 1988.

Hughes, Langston

WRITER
February 1, 1902–May 22, 1967

James Langston Hughes was born in Joplin, Missouri, grew up in Lawrence, Kansas, and attended high school in Cleveland, Ohio. In June 1921 he published a poem in **The Crisis** magazine and enrolled at Columbia University (New York). He withdrew from college after a year, eventually traveling through parts of Africa, Europe, and the Mediterranean before returning to spend a year in Washington, D.C.

Before long, Hughes was recognized as perhaps the most striking new voice in African-American verse. His poems revealed his deep admiration for blacks, especially the poor. He was inventive in blending the rhythms of **jazz** and **blues,** as well as black speech, with traditional forms of poetry. In 1926 he published his first book of verse, *The Weary Blues,* and in that year he also enrolled at Lincoln University (Chicago, Illinois). He graduated in 1929 and published his first novel, *Not Without Laughter,* in 1930. Over the next few years, Hughes traveled extensively, visiting the Soviet Union (at the time he was a socialist—a person who believes that the community as a whole should own and control the economy), California, and Mexico. After his father's death, Hughes moved to Ohio.

Throughout the 1930s Hughes wrote several plays that were produced both on Broadway and in Cleveland, and in 1938 he founded the Harlem Suitcase Theater in New York. In 1940 he published an **autobiography,** *The Big Sea.* In 1942 he began a weekly column that ran for more than twenty years; the column's most popular feature was a character named Jesse B. Semple, or Simple. His work writing song lyrics on Broadway enabled Hughes to buy a home and settle in Harlem in 1947. Hughes, who never married, lived there with a pair of family friends.

As a writer, Hughes worked in virtually all forms, although he saw himself mainly as a poet. In most of the poems he published from 1947 to 1951,

"HARLEM (A DREAM DEFERRED)"

What happens to a dream deferred?
Does it dry up like a raisin in the sun?
Or fester like a sore—
and then run?
Does it stink like rotten meat?
Or crust and sugar over—
like a syrupy sweet?
Maybe it just sags
like a heavy load.
Or does it explode?

(Source: "Harlem (A Dream Deferred)," by Langston Hughes. *The Norton Introduction of Poetry.* 4th ed. New York: W. W. Norton, 1991, p. 321.)

he used the newly emerging jazz rhythm of bebop to capture the mood of an increasingly troubled Harlem. In the 1950s he also translated several works by Caribbean or South American authors, published a collection of short stories, and wrote the lyrics for several operas.

Anti-Communist groups, remembering Hughes's earlier visit to the Soviet Union, steadily attacked Hughes in the early 1950s for his alleged membership in the Communist Party—even though Hughes denied ever being a party member. In 1953, forced to appear before an investigating committee led by Senator Joseph McCarthy, Hughes professed that some of his earlier political writing had been mistaken. He later published about a dozen books for children, and with the photographer **Roy DeCarava** he published an acclaimed book of pictures, *The Sweet Flypaper of Life* (1955). His second volume of autobiography, *I Wonder as I Wander,* came in 1956.

Perhaps the most inventive works of Hughes's later career were his plays, especially gospel plays such as *Black Nativity* (1961). He was also an editor who helped collect and publish several volumes of African-American poetry, fiction, and humor. In 1961 he was admitted to the National Institute of Arts and Letters. He died in New York City.

Hunt, Henry Alexander

EDUCATOR
October 10, 1866–October 1, 1938

Southern educator Henry Hunt was born near Sparta, Georgia, the son of a white father and an African-American mother. He traveled to **Atlanta University** when he was sixteen, and completed a technical course in 1876. He later returned to receive his bachelor's degree in 1890.

After working at Biddle University (Charlotte, North Carolina; now Johnson C. Smith University) for more than ten years, Hunt became prin-

cipal of Fort Valley High and Industrial School (near Macon, Georgia). When he arrived in 1904, Fort Valley had only four wooden buildings and little community support. Hunt proceeded to offer many new programs and services, found outside financial support, and increased the numbers of students. When Hunt died in 1938, Fort Valley had a modernized campus and more than one thousand students. Only a year later, the school became part of Georgia's higher education system, becoming Fort Valley State College.

Hunt believed that ending racial discrimination and increasing economic opportunities were the only ways to improve the position of African Americans in the United States. Because of his work helping blacks in rural Georgia, he was awarded the Spingarn Medal in 1930 by the **National Association for the Advancement of Colored People (NAACP).** In 1933 Hunt was named assistant to the governor of the federal Farm Credit Administration (FCA).

Hunt, Richard

SCULPTOR, GRAPHIC ARTIST, EDUCATOR
September 12, 1935–

Richard Hunt developed his talent for sculpture early in life at children's classes at the Art Institute of Chicago. There, in 1953, he saw the work of Julio Gonzalez, a Spanish sculptor of welded metal whose technique differed radically from traditional western methods. Hunt, still a high school student, built a studio in the basement of his father's barbershop. He taught himself to weld in two years. Hunt also encountered the work of Richmond Barthé (1901–1989), an African-American sculptor. Although their styles differed, Hunt found the older artist inspiring.

In 1953 Hunt enrolled in the Art Institute with a scholarship. He taught himself welding by talking to professional metalworkers and by taking metalcraft classes where he made jewelry. He graduated four years later with a degree in art education and was awarded a grant to visit Europe.

From 1951 to 1957 Hunt worked part-time in the zoological experimental laboratory at the University of Chicago. His experiences there later influenced his sculpture. His work suggests tentacles, bones, wings, thoraxes, antennae, and tendons. One of these early works, *Arachne*, was acquired for the permanent collection of the Museum of Modern Art in New York while he was still a student. His first one-person show followed in 1958. Exhibitions and purchases from major museums and universities in the years immediately following his graduation indicate his early artistic maturity.

Hunt's early work used discarded metal parts, which he welded into small-scale human and animal shapes. Other sources for this style were the metal African sculpture he had seen with his mother at the Field Museum of Natural History (Chicago), as well as Greek, Roman, and Renaissance sculpture. By the late 1960s Hunt received more opportunities to create public sculpture. He increased the mass of his forms to give them a stronger visual presence in the out-of-doors. His works are often designed to protrude from their bases as if they are being manipulated by some overwhelming force. This work demonstrates Hunt's interest in natural processes of growth and change.

Hunt has been included in many national and international exhibitions since he began showing his work in 1955. He has received several awards for his work.

Hunter, Alberta

BLUES SINGER
April 1, 1895–October 17, 1984

Alberta Hunter was born in Memphis, Tennessee, and by the time she was twelve had left to seek a career on the stage in Chicago, Illinois. At the age of fifteen she earned a spot as a singer-dancer in a club. Hunter's style of blues singing, a mixture of love song and sexy sophistication, propelled her into the spotlight in Chicago's South Side club circuit. She recorded more than a hundred songs (including some she had written) on several labels, both under her own name and various stage names. Her song "Down Hearted Blues" (1922) is a **blues** classic.

Known for her intelligence, beauty, and fashion sense, Hunter performed in film, on stage, and on radio in the United States and Europe. She abruptly abandoned her singing career after a return from entertaining World War II (1939–45) troops in Europe; she took up nursing for thirty years, and then was persuaded to rejoin the nightclub circuit by a New York club owner. She performed regularly in New York City until her death.

Hurston, Zora Neale

NOVELIST, FOLKLORIST
c. 1891–January 28, 1960

Alberta Hunter (Corbis Corporation. Reproduced by permission)

The exact date of Zora Neale Hurston's birth is unknown (the most likely estimate is 1891), but she was born and grew up in Eatonville, Florida, one of eight children. In Eatonville, the first black incorporated town in the United States, African Americans were not demoralized by poverty and racial hatred, unlike the case in most of the turn-of-the-century South. Hurston grew up surrounded by a lively and creative culture in which she learned the dialect, songs, and folktales that are central to her work.

After the untimely death of her mother in 1904, Hurston left to take a job as a maid. She ended up in Baltimore, Maryland, where she attended high school and graduated in 1918. She took courses at **Howard University** in nearby Washington, D.C., until 1924, and her first story, "John Redding Goes to Sea," appeared in the university's literary magazine in 1921.

Hurston arrived in New York in 1925, at the height of the **Harlem Renaissance,** a period of exciting cultural development in the black community. She studied anthropology at Barnard College and graduated in 1928. Between 1929 and 1930 Hurston returned to the South and began to collect **folklore.** From this extensive research she wrote *Mules and Men* (1935), a collection of black folklore. Hurston was a member of numerous anthropology groups and scientific academies, and her work earned her a pair of fellowships that allowed her to research folk religions in the Caribbean nations of Haiti and Jamaica. *Tell My Horse,* based on this research, was published in 1938.

As an anthropologist, Hurston had a perspective on black culture that was unique among black writers of her time, but she was fully absorbed in the creative life of the Harlem Renaissance as well—with several close friends, she edited and published an issue of a journal for young black writers, *Fire!!* Hurston's first novel, *Jonah's Gourd Vine* (1934), reveals an almost musical quality to her writing and a mastery of black dialect. For its beauty and richness of language, *Their Eyes Were Watching God* (1937) is considered Hurston's finest art and remains her most popular work, considered by scholars to be the first black feminist novel. Other works include *Moses, Man of the Mountain* (1939), *Seraph on the Suwanee* (1948), and a controversial **autobiography,** *Dust Tracks on a Road* (1942).

Reviews of Hurston's books in her time were mixed. Because she was so different from most black writers, she was often misunderstood by both

"I Love Myself When I Am Laughing"

"Someone is always at my elbow reminding me that I am the granddaughter of slaves. It fails to register depression with me. Slavery is sixty years in the past. The operation was successful and the patient is doing well, thank you. The terrible struggle that made me an American out of potential slave said 'On the line!' The Reconstruction said 'Get Set!'; and the generation before said 'Go!' I am off to a flying start and I must not halt in the stretch to look behind and weep. Slavery is the price I paid for civilization, and the choice was not with me. It is a bully adventure and worth all that I have paid through my ancestors for it. No one on earth ever had a greater chance for glory."

(Source: Excerpt from *I Love Myself When I Am Laughing*, by Zora Neale Hurston (edited by by Alice Walker). New York: Feminist Press, 1979.)

black and white critics. None of her books sold well enough while she was alive to relieve her of a lifetime of financial stress, and she and her writings disappeared from public view from the late 1940s until the early 1970s. Interest in Hurston revived, however, after writer **Alice Walker** went to Florida "in search of Zora" in 1973 and reassembled the puzzle of Hurston's later life. Walker discovered that Hurston returned to the Deep South in the 1950s and, still trying to write, supported herself with menial jobs. After suffering a stroke in 1959, she entered a welfare home, where she died in 1960 and was buried in an unmarked grave. On her pilgrimage, Walker marked a site where Hurston might be buried with a headstone that pays tribute to "a genius of the South."

Huston-Tillotson College

Founded: Huston-Tillotson was formed in 1952 when Tillotson College (founded 1877) and Samuel Huston College (founded 1876) merged.

Location: Austin, Texas

Religious Affiliation: United Methodist Church and United Church of Christ

Number of Students (1999–2000): 575

Grade Average of Incoming Freshman: 2.0

Admission Requirements: ACT or SAT scores; four years of English, three years of math, two years of science, including lab science, two years of social studies; personal essay.

Mailing Address:
Huston-Tillotson College
Office of Admission
900 Chicon St.
Austin, TX 78702

Telephone: (512) 505-3027

URL: http://www.htc.edu

Campus: Huston-Tillotson's 23-acre campus is located one mile from downtown Austin, Texas. Buildings include a science center. The Downs-Jones Library contains over eighty thousand documents.

Special Programs: African-American studies; combined engineering program with Prairie View A&M (near Hempstead, Texas).

Extracurricular Activities: Student government; student newspaper; four fraternities and four sororities; over sixteen organizations, including honor societies, Brothers and Sisters in Christ, a pre-law society; athletics (men's baseball, basketball, tennis; women's basketball, tennis, volleyball).

Huston-Tillotson Alumni: Dr. Hubert G. Lovelady, inventor; Azie Taylor Morton, former U.S. treasurer.

Hyers Sisters

SINGERS

Anna Madah Hyers (c. 1853–1920s) and her sister, Emma Louise Hyers (c. 1855–1890s) were born and raised in California. They studied piano and voice, and their father arranged their first public performance in 1867. The girls performed selections from the Italian composer Verdi. Celebrated as extremely talented, they continued to give local recitals. They sang opera pieces in Salt Lake City, Utah, in 1871, and performed with great success in major concert halls in Cleveland, Ohio, New York, and Boston, Massachusetts. They became the first black women to gain national fame on the American concert stage, performing music ranging from opera to minstrel works (shows featuring jokes, songs, and dances). In 1873 Emma married the bandleader of a minstrel group.

In the mid-1870s the Hyers sisters were traveling with their own theater and began to confront issues of race directly in musical dramas and comedies. They toured America in the 1880s. In the 1890s the sisters began to appear separately more often. Emma, for example, appeared in an 1894 production of **Uncle Tom's Cabin.** Emma is believed to have died in Sacramento, California, by 1900. Anna continued to perform in the United States, Canada, and New Zealand. Anna is believed to have died sometime during the 1920s in Sacramento.

Hyers Sisters: Selected Performances

Out of Bondage
(1875)

Urlina, the African Princess in San Francisco
(1879)

The Underground Railway

Princess Orelia of Madagascar

Blackville Twins
(1891)

Colored Aristocracy
(1891)

Hyman, Flora "Flo"

VOLLYBALL PLAYER
July 29, 1954–January 24, 1986

Flora "Flo" Hyman was considered by many to be the best female volleyball player in the world at her time. She combined her height (six feet five inches) with her natural abilities to lead the United States in World Cup and Olympic events.

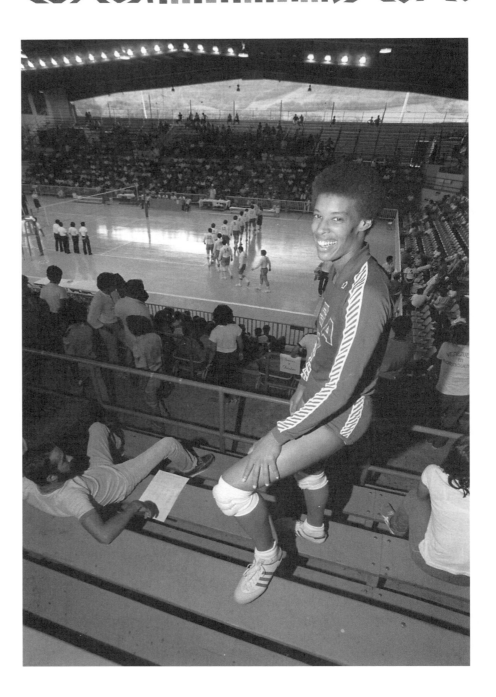

Born in Inglewood, California, Hyman graduated from Morningside High School in 1972. At the University of Houston (Texas) Hyman took up volleyball and became an all-American three times. In 1976 she was named the top college player in the nation. Hyman began rigorous training in Colorado that led to her invitations to play for the United States in the World Cup (1978 and 1982). In 1984 she helped the United States win a silver medal in the 1984 Olympics.

Hyman was at the beginning of her professional volleyball career in Japan when tragedy struck. During a routine substitution of players, she collapsed and died of heart failure. She was recognized for her achievements on the court by being inducted into the Women's Sports Hall of Fame (1986),

and an award was created in her honor. The Flo Hyman Award is given annually to the female athlete who exhibits the same "dignity, spirit, and commitment to excellence" with which Hyman played the game of volleyball.

Idaho

First African-American Settlers: The first blacks to enter the region that would become Idaho were explorers and trappers; York, the servant of Lt. William Clark, crossed the northern region of Idaho during the Lewis and Clark expedition of 1804–06.

Civil War: While the American **Civil War** (1861–65) was being waged, the first black settlers were lured to Idaho by the promise of gold. They were among the 63,000 gold seekers who rushed into the region between 1860 and 1863. The Idaho goldfields also attracted pro-Confederate Missourians who migrated west to avoid military service. These miners used their political power to discourage black migration to the region. By 1863, soon after Idaho became a separate territory, white miners in Boise County passed a law excluding blacks and Chinese from prospecting.

Reconstruction: By 1870, 60 blacks, the vast majority of them miners, had arrived in Idaho. Rhodes Peak in the Bitteroot Mountains was named after William Rhodes, an early African-American prospector. At least three geographical formations in the Sawtooth Mountains are named after another miner, George Washington, a former Missouri slave. Although there were a few black homesteaders, most turn-of-the-century black Idahoans were urbanites, settling in the state's two largest cities, Boise and Pocatello; the majority worked as barbers, waiters, servants, maids, maintenance workers, and laborers. These limited employment opportunities, coupled with an increasingly hostile racial climate, discouraged additional black migration to Idaho. The black population in 1890, the year Idaho became a state, was 201; that population reached 920 in 1920.

The Great Depression: Idaho's black population, which had experienced a decline in the first few decades of the twentieth century, increased with the industry created by **World War II** (1939–45). In 1940 the state's population of blacks was 595; by 1950 it passed 1,000 for the first time.

Current African-American Population: According to U.S. Census Bureau estimates, the total black population in Idaho was 7,158 (approximately 0.6 percent of the state population) as of July 1, 1998.

Key Figures: James Beckwourth (1798–1866), frontiersman and explorer; Mayor T. Les Purce (1947–) of Pocatello, the first black mayor in Idaho's history.

Illinois

First African-American Settlers: In 1717 Philip Francis Renault hauled five hundred enslaved blacks to work in a mining operation in French Louisiana

Territory's "Illinois Country." The mine eventually failed, and in 1744 Renault sold three hundred of his slaves to local whites.

Slave Population: By the time the British took over the area in 1763, there were six hundred slaves, mostly house servants and laborers on small farms. A slave code passed in 1803 deemed that servants could be disciplined, sold, and inherited like slaves. After its 1818 admission to statehood, Illinois passed a constitution that forbade slavery.

Free Black Population: In 1778 **Jean Baptiste DuSable,** a black trader, became Chicago's first settler; other **free blacks** soon settled in the territory. The 1803 slave code required free blacks to post $1,000 bonds and carry passes, and blacks were denied the right to testify against whites in court. A law was passed in 1848 barring freedmen from moving to Illinois, and an 1853 law imposed heavy fines on whites who brought blacks into the state.

Civil War: Illinois blacks, organized into the 29th U.S. Colored Infantry in April 1864, fought bravely in the **Civil War** (1861–65). The pressure generated by the Union (Northern) victory and by black participation in the war effort eventually solidified the power of the Republican Party. The harsh slave codes were subsequently abolished in 1865.

Reconstruction: Illinois became an important destination in the post–Civil War black exodus to Northern cities; most blacks, however, faced low wages and poor living conditions. Growing racial tensions led to urban race riots, which contributed to the establishment of the **National Association for the Advancement of Colored People (NAACP).** During the notorious **Red Summer** of 1919, a lakefront incident in overcrowded Chicago ignited several days of violence by both whites and blacks. By the time order was restored, twenty-three African Americans were dead and hundreds were injured.

The Great Depression: The Great Migration (a massive exodus of blacks from the rural South to find jobs in the industrialized North) established Chicago as the center of the black population in Illinois. Beginning in 1928, when Chicago alderman Oscar DePriest became the first African American in the North to be elected to the House of Representatives, Illinois has had the nation's longest run of black representatives in Congress. The outbreak of **World War II** (1939–45) brought about an economic boom in Illinois industry and sparked a wave of black immigration that continued for at least twenty-five years.

Civil Rights Movement: In 1966 the U.S. Civil Rights Commission held hearings in Cairo, Illinois, and uncovered widespread discrimination. A second set of hearings six years later revealed that African-American residents faced chronic police harassment and unemployment and were often refused medical and dental care. Many blacks felt that the **Civil Rights movement** had completely passed by the region.

Current African-American Population: According to U.S. Census Bureau estimates, the total black population in Illinois was 1,839,744 (15 percent of the state population) as of July 1, 1998.

Key Figures: Jean Baptiste DuSable (c. 1750–1818), founder of Chicago; modern dance pioneer **Katherine Dunham** (1909–); **Carol Moseley-Braun** (1947–), the first African-American woman in the U.S. Senate; television personality **Oprah Winfrey** (1954–).

(SEE ALSO **ABOLITION; UNDERGROUND RAILROAD.**)

Indiana

First African-American Settlers: People of African descent first arrived in the area of Indiana as slaves of French colonists. **Slavery** persisted when the British took over the region in 1763 and lasted until the area's transfer to the new United States.

Slave Population: Indiana achieved statehood in 1816. By 1820, 190 African-American Indianans were officially enslaved under laws permitting the transport of slaves into the state, and several hundred more were indentured servants. Most worked on farms, growing grain or cotton.

Free Black Population: White Indiana settlers wished to rid the state of African Americans, and the state created colonization societies to send blacks to **Africa.** Despite this and other legal obstacles, thousands of African Americans migrated to Indiana before 1850. Most were fugitive or freed slaves who were trying to avoid the restrictive laws of the slaveholding Southern states.

Reconstruction: In the years after the **Civil War** (1861–65), large numbers of blacks from the South moved to Indiana. The state's black population more than doubled from 1860 to 1870, although blacks still represented barely 1 percent of the total population. Racist practices severely limited African Americans in their pursuit of employment and educational opportunity; by the turn of the twentieth century, few black farmers remained, and 80 percent of the state's blacks lived in urban areas by 1910. During the Great Migration during and after **World War I** (1914–18), thousands of blacks from the South entered Indiana and others migrated from the southern part of the state to the northern half.

The Great Depression: During the Depression, as steel and other industries stalled, black workers, stuck in unskilled, low-paying jobs, were laid off in large numbers. Despite local and federal relief, many became destitute. By **World War II** (1939–45), however, many factory and skilled jobs previously closed to blacks opened in response to labor shortages caused by the war.

Civil Rights Movement: During the 1960s the **Civil Rights movement** became a force in Indiana. The **Southern Christian Leadership Conference (SCLC)** organized an Indiana chapter. Activists conducted demonstrations against segregated public facilities and worked to eliminate job discrimination.

Current African-American Population: According to U.S. Census Bureau estimates, the total black population in Indiana was 490,626 (8 percent of the state population) as of July 1, 1998.

Key Figures: Shirley Graham Du Bois (1896–1977), writer and political activist; **Madame C. J. Walker** (1867–1919), the first female African-American millionaire; basketball Hall of Famer **Oscar Robertson** (1938–); entertainer **Michael Jackson** (1954–).

Indian Wars

Before the American **Civil War** (1861–65) African Americans were not allowed to serve in the military. But after the end of the Civil War in 1865, African Americans began to serve in many military campaigns, including the Indian Wars in the American West. The Indian Wars were fought during the last part of the nineteenth century, and they involved the U.S. Army and various Indian tribes who refused to give up their land. Although African Americans did not begin to fight in those wars until 1865, they continued until the Indian Wars ended in 1890.

In 1866 Congress created six regiments of African-American soldiers. In 1869 these regiments were combined into two—the Twenty-fourth and Twenty-fifth Infantry. Organizing and training these new regiments was difficult. Most of the new soldiers had no military experience, and white officers were reluctant to take over command of the all-black regiments. Many white officers treated the black soldiers with little respect. In one case, an officer at Fort Leavenworth, Kansas, ordered black soldiers to camp in an area that was filled with water, and then complained when the men got muddy.

The black regiments were stationed mainly in the Southwest, in places such as Texas, New Mexico, and Arizona. Tension between black soldiers and white settlers (whites who lived in those areas the army was trying to protect) was often high. It was not uncommon for black soldiers to be lynched (hanged) for simply associating with a white woman. The relationship between African-American soldiers and Native Americans wasn't much better. Native Americans viewed African Americans as representatives of the U.S. government, and therefore as enemies. Native Americans nicknamed black soldiers "Buffalo Soldiers," apparently because of the similarities between their hair and that of the buffalo.

The duties of African-American soldiers were similar to those of white soldiers. They spent long days patrolling difficult land to protect settlers from Native Americans and outlaws. In 1877 a group of African-American soldiers under the command of a white officer were ordered to chase a group of Apaches who had attacked several stagecoaches. After a weeklong chase, the soldiers found no Apaches and ran out of water. They suffered four days without water, and four soldiers died before they found a water supply.

Several African-American soldiers received the Congressional Medal of Honor (one of the highest military honors a soldier can receive) for their bravery during battles with Native Americans. In 1879 a group of African-American soldiers from the Ninth Cavalry was called in to rescue another army unit under attack. When they arrived, they were surrounded by three hundred Native Americans. Henry Johnson, an African-American sergeant,

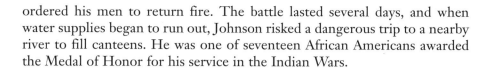

ordered his men to return fire. The battle lasted several days, and when water supplies began to run out, Johnson risked a dangerous trip to a nearby river to fill canteens. He was one of seventeen African Americans awarded the Medal of Honor for his service in the Indian Wars.

Ink Spots, The

POPULAR MUSIC GROUP

The Ink Spots were one of the most popular and influential singing groups of the late 1930s to early 1950s. Their numerous hit records in the 1940s helped create the musical styles known as **rhythm and blues (R&B)** (a type of music that contains elements of **blues** and **jazz**) and doo-wop (a type of rock and roll featuring nonsense syllables).

The Ink Spots were formed in 1934 by four doormen at New York's Paramount Theater: tenors Charles Fuqua and Jerry Daniels (1915-), baritone Ivory Watson (d. 1969), and bass Orville "Hoppy" Jones (1905-1944). Their gentle ballads supported Daniels's soaring lead voice. They first became popular in the mid-1930s when their European concerts were broadcast on the radio in the United States. It wasn't until 1939, however, after Bill Kenny (1915-1978) replaced Daniels as lead singer, that the group achieved wide popularity with their recording of "If I Didn't Care," which sold nineteen million copies.

In the 1940s The Ink Spots had many hugely successful records, including "To Each His Own" (1946). They also made several recordings with famous jazz singer **Ella Fitzgerald** (b. 1918), including "Into Each Life Some Rain Must Fall" (1944). They appeared in two films, *The Great American Radio Broadcast* (1941) and *Pardon My Sarong* (1942).

Over the years, many band members came and went, and eventually three different groups, all calling themselves The Ink Spots, were formed. Since the early 1950s all three groups have continued to perform and record. In 1989 the original Ink Spots were honored at the Rock and Roll Hall of Fame as early influences on rock music.

Innis, Roy

CIVIL RIGHTS ACTIVIST
June 6, 1934–

Roy Innis dedicated his life to public service and has combated racial inequality many different ways, most notably through his activism with the **Congress of Racial Equality (CORE).** (CORE is an interracial civil rights group that is committed to fighting racism without the use of violence.) In addition to his political activism, Innis is known for adopting a conservative Republican political position later in life. This was unusual at the time because the **Civil Rights movement** has been largely associated with political programs of the Democratic Party.

Born in St. Croix in the U.S. Virgin Islands, Innis moved to New York City in 1946. After serving in the army, he attended the City College of New York (1952-56). Innis was working as a chemist when he became involved with CORE in 1963. As chairman of the education committee, Innis promoted the idea that communities, not political bodies, should control public schools. Innis became chairman of CORE's Harlem chapter and founded another organization designed to promote black business owners in Harlem.

In 1968 Innis became the national director of CORE and incorporated the ideas of the **Black Panther Party** into the organization. This was a different approach for CORE, because the Panther Party believed in the use of violence and that the best way for the black community to flourish was to separate from whites. As a result of these changes, membership in CORE declined. Innis then founded the *Manhattan Tribune* and received national attention for a televised debate with a Nobel Prize-winning physicist who claimed that blacks were genetically inferior. Despite the objections of many members, Innis became national chairman of CORE and radically changed his political views. He became a pioneer of black **conservatism,** supporting Republican political figures, the most controversial of whom was Robert Bork (who had opposed the Civil Rights Act of 1965). Roy Innis, with the help of his son Niger, has helped CORE forge a strong relationship with the Republican Party. (In 2000 CORE voted former Republican president Ronald Reagan the man of the century.) In his later years Innis made a few unsuccessful attempts to enter politics.

Inventors and Inventions

Historians are just beginning to discover the contributions of African-American inventors and inventions to American technology. In the seventeenth century, most African Americans were slaves and were not allowed to read or write. Therefore, they left no written records of their discoveries. But many brought skills and knowledge from Africa that they used in their work. African Americans have made particularly important contributions to boatbuilding, cultivating rice, and making musical instruments.

In the eighteenth and nineteenth centuries, black inventors began to gain more recognition. In 1790 Congress passed the first U.S. Patent Act, registering inventors' inventions to ensure that no one else could lay claim to them. The patent law not only allowed inventors—both black and white—to take credit for their inventions but also ensured that they would benefit financially from any commercial uses arising from their inventions. Although many black inventors applied for patents and did not receive them, several did. The first African American who received a patent for his invention was Thomas Jennings, for a dry-cleaning process he invented in 1821. Following him was Henry Blair, who patented a corn seed planter in 1834 and a cottonseed planter in 1836.

Despite these successes, it was difficult for African Americans to patent their inventions. It was harder for them to get work as an apprentice (or assistant) in order to learn a trade. Most black inventors had to rely entirely on themselves. Most African-American inventions were created in occupations that were filled primarily by blacks, such as carpentry, domestic service, and farming.

Although slaves were not allowed to hold patents, many invented new techniques and machinery that improved the businesses of their masters. This led to the difficult legal question of who actually "owned" the invention: the slave who created it, or his master. In the 1850s slave owner J. E. Stuart requested a patent for the invention of his slave, Ned. Ned had invented a cotton scraper. Since slaves were not legally entitled to hold patents, Stuart applied for the patent himself. In 1858 the U.S. attorney general denied Stuart's request, saying that although the patent could not be granted to the rightful inventor because he was a slave, it also could not be granted to Stuart, because he was not the inventor.

After the **Civil War**, no one could be denied a patent because of race or legal status. This resulted in a dramatic increase in the number of patents awarded to blacks. On August 10, 1894, the names and inventions of ninety-two blacks were recorded by Congress. By 1900 blacks had been awarded more than four hundred patents.

Many African Americans made contributions to the new technologies and industries developed in the nineteenth and early twentieth centuries. Elijah McCoy designed an oil lubricator that was adopted by railroad and shipping companies. His standards of quality were so rigorous that the term "the real McCoy" came to be used to describe high-quality products. Granville Woods and Lewis Latimer contributed to the emergence of electricity as an energy replacement for natural gas.

As the twentieth century wore on, however, technology grew more complicated. Solitary, self-motivated inventors were replaced by teams of well-paid, highly educated researchers working for large companies or for the government. Few blacks qualified for those positions. Those who did were often discriminated against. This is one of the reasons that, at the end of the twentieth century, fewer African Americans were involved in patenting and invention than at the beginning of the century.

Iowa

First African-American Settlers: A seeming "promised land," Iowa appeared to African Americans to be a safe haven, a place without the hostile history of the Southern states. The first blacks appeared before 1838 in the company of white explorers.

Slave Population: When Congress approved Iowa's settlement in 1838, the territory was slave-free. Iowa gained statehood on December 28, 1846. The Missouri Compromise (1819–21) legally prohibited **slavery** in any land north of Missouri's border (which included Iowa), yet slaves did exist in pre–**Civil War** Iowa. The 1840 federal census showed that sixteen slaves lived in the state.

Free Black Population: A set of so-called black codes enacted in 1838 and 1851 sought to prevent Iowa from becoming a refuge to **free blacks** and runaway slaves. "Negroes" who entered Iowa after April 1, 1839, were required to have a "certificate of freedom" and to post a $500 bond as "proof that they would not become a public charge."

Civil War: Iowa's men served gallantly in the Civil War (1861–65). Among them was the 1st Regiment Iowa African Infantry, organized in July 1863, which later became the 60th Regiment in 1864. The 60th Regiment fought one battle and was used mostly to man a military post at Helena, Arkansas. It was one of 222 such African-American volunteer Union (Northern) units.

Reconstruction: When the Civil War ended, Iowa's African-American population increased so that by 1870 there were 5,762 blacks. This figure nearly doubled by 1890. The state's African-American population sought employment mostly in railroading, mining, and shipping. The 1900s saw continued progress as the first African-American bar (law) associations, military officers' training facilities, and integrated public schools were established.

The Great Depression: Many prominent African-American Iowans began their postsecondary education as state colleges were opened to blacks. Despite this, although there were no written laws or posted signs outlining segregation, many blacks continued to experience discrimination.

Civil Rights Movement: The Des Moines chapter of the **Congress of Racial Equality (CORE)** was established in 1963. The Iowa Civil Rights Act was passed in 1965 and signed into law by Governor Harold Hughes.

Current African-American Population: According to U.S. Census Bureau estimates, the total black population in Iowa was 56,880 (2 percent of the state population) as of July 1, 1998.

Key Figures: George Washington Carver (c. 1864–1943), the first African American to attend Iowa State University; bass-baritone singer **Simon Estes** (1938–); James Alan McPherson (1943–), short story writer.

(SEE ALSO **UNDERGROUND RAILROAD.**)

Irvin, Monte

BASEBALL PLAYER
February 25, 1919–

Monte Irvin was a power hitter in the Negro Leagues and the major leagues. At the time he played **baseball** (1950s), racism made it difficult for African Americans to play professional baseball. Irvin was such a great player that many expected him to be the first black admitted into the majors. However, Irvin took time off from baseball to serve in the U.S. Army, which set back his baseball career.

In 1949, two years after **Jackie Robinson** broke through baseball's color barrier, Irvin and Hank Thompson became the first blacks to play for the New York Giants. In 1951 Irvin helped the Giants win a championship, averaging .312 at the plate with a league-leading 121 runs batted in (RBIs). Irvin played eight years in the majors with the Giants (1949–55) and the Chicago Cubs (1956). He was voted to the Baseball Hall of Fame in 1973. After retiring from baseball, Irvin worked as an assistant to the commissioner of baseball.

Islam

The religion of Islam began in the seventh century and is based on the visions and life of a prophet named Muhammad. Islam quickly spread throughout Arabia (the Middle East) and northern Africa. Black Africans who converted to Islam were called "Moors." In Europe, the Moors developed a reputation as skilled navigators and sailors. They accompanied Spanish explorers such as Christopher Columbus in their fifteenth- and sixteenth-century travels and introduced Islam to North and South America.

African Muslims who had been captured and sold as slaves were mainly responsible for the rise of Islam in North America. (A Muslim is someone who follows the beliefs of the Islamic religion.) Historians estimate that at least thirty thousand Muslim slaves were imported into the United States, but, despite these numbers, the influence of Islam before the American Civil War (1861–65) was small.

After the Civil War, Christian churches were so dominant in black communities that only those few African-American leaders who had traveled to Africa knew anything about Islam. In 1867 a Christian missionary named Edward Wilmot Blyden wrote a book claiming that Islam was a better choice of religions for African Americans because it had a better record of racial equality than Christianity.

During the first decades of the twentieth century, more than four million African Americans left the countryside to move to cities in the Northeast and Midwest, most looking for jobs and better social conditions. The sudden rise of so many African-American communities in the cities contributed to a new political awareness among African Americans. In 1913 Timothy Drew, a black preacher from North Carolina, founded the first Moorish Holy Temple of Science in Newark, New Jersey. Drew rejected Christianity as "the white man's religion" and established temples throughout the Midwest and the South. The Moorish Science movement grew quickly after World War I (1914–18). Although the movement lost power after Drew's death in 1929, it had laid the groundwork for many other black Islamic groups.

In the 1920s, an African Islamic movement called the Ahmadiyyah began to send missionaries to the United States. Unlike the Moorish Science Temple, the Ahmadiyyah did not limit its membership to blacks. In 1933 an American convert named Wali Akram opened a mosque in Cleveland, Ohio, where he taught Islam to several generations of midwesterners, including many African Americans.

During the same time, another group of Muslims led by Sheik Faisal established a mosque (an Islamic temple) in Brooklyn, New York. Like the Ahmadiyyah, Sheik Faisal practiced a version of Islam that was closer to that being practiced throughout Africa and the Middle East. These groups presented the first opportunity for American Muslims to interact with the international Muslim religion.

During the 1930s a man named **Wallace D. Fard** began to spread word of a new religion, designed for African-American men. He quickly found a following and established Temple No. 1 of the Nation of Islam (NOI). Master Fard (as he came to be known) preached that black people were members of an African tribe called Shabazz and owed no loyalty to the United States, which had enslaved and tormented them. When Fard disappeared in 1934, his chief lieutenant, **Elijah Muhammad,** led followers to Chicago, Illinois, where he established Muhammad's Temple No. 2 as the headquarters for the NOI.

Many of the beliefs of the Nation of Islam contradicted those of the Islamic religion. One example is Elijah Muhammad's belief that white people were "devils." However, the main purpose of the movement was to

PROPHET NOBLE DREW ALI AND THE MOORISH SCIENCE TEMPLE

After World War I, as the Moorish Science movement grew, its founder, Prophet Nobel Drew Ali, recruited members who were better educated—but also less dedicated—than his first followers. Some of these new members began to cheat the less educated by selling them magic charms, potions, and herbs. Ali was voted from power when he attempted to stop these practices. In 1929 Ali was murdered; his killers were never caught. After his death the movement split into several smaller, less effective groups.

Despite its difficult history, the Moorish Science Temple movement still survives, with active temples in Chicago, Detroit, Michigan, and New York. Modern-day worshipers have included both Islamic and Christian traditions in their worship. Like Muslims, they face Mecca (an Islamic holy city) when they pray. But they also pray to Jesus and sing Christian hymns during their services.

spread the message of **black nationalism** and to create a separate black nation. Elijah Muhammad focused on two principles: self-knowledge and economic self-sufficiency. He supported a strict lifestyle that included one meal per day and a ban on tobacco, alcohol, drugs, and pork. From 1934 until his death in 1975, Muhammad and his followers established hundreds of temples, schools, grocery stores, restaurants, bakeries, and other small businesses.

Perhaps the most important convert to Elijah Muhammad's message was **Malcolm X**. Born Malcolm Little, he converted to the NOI while serving time in a Boston, Massachusetts, prison in 1946 for armed robbery. An intelligent and charismatic man, Malcolm X worked tirelessly for the NOI, opening temples throughout the country and establishing a newspaper. He became minister of Temple No. 7 in Harlem and was appointed as the national representative by Elijah Muhammad. Malcolm X was the first person to attack the use of the word "Negro" to describe African Americans. He believed the word contributed to a "slave mentality" among African Americans. His philosophy and beliefs laid the groundwork for some of the most important political movements of the 1960s.

In 1964 Malcolm X left the NOI because of disputes with Elijah Muhammad. He journeyed to the holy city of Mecca (Saudi Arabia) and adopted a more orthodox version of Islam. Malcolm X was assassinated in 1964 while giving a lecture in Harlem for his newly formed Organization for Afro-American Unity. After Malcolm X's death, Minister **Louis Farrakhan** replaced him as the national representative of the NOI

After the death of Elijah Muhammad in 1975, his son Wallace Deen Muhammad was chosen to lead the NOI. He quickly announced an end to the movement's racial doctrines in order to adopt a more orthodox form of Islam. Several leaders then left the movement, including Louis Farrakhan, who established a new Nation of Islam in Chicago.

In its various forms, Islam has had a much longer history in the United States, particularly among African Americans, than most people realize. In the last decade of the twentieth century, about one million African Americans belonged to some sort of Islamic group. It has become the fourth major religious tradition in American society.